ADAPTIVE INTELLI

Adaptive Intelligence is a dramatic reappraisal and reframing of the concept of human intelligence. In a sweeping analysis, Robert J. Sternberg argues that we are using a fatally-flawed, outdated conception of intelligence; one which may promote technological advancement, but which has also accelerated climate change, pollution, the use of weaponry, and inequality. Instead of focusing on the narrow academic skills measured by standardized tests, societies should teach and assess adaptive intelligence, defined as the use of collective talent in service of the common good. This book describes why the outdated notion of intelligence persists, what adaptive intelligence is, and how it could lead humankind on a more positive path.

Robert J. Sternberg is Professor of Human Development at Cornell University and Honorary Professor of Psychology at the University of Heidelberg, Germany. He is a past winner of the Grawemeyer Award in Psychology, and the William James and James McKeen Cattell Awards of the Association for Psychological Science.

ADAPTIVE INTELLIGENCE

Surviving and Thriving in Times of Uncertainty

ROBERT J. STERNBERG

Cornell University

CAMBRIDGE
UNIVERSITY PRESS

University Printing House, Cambridge CB2 8BS, United Kingdom

One Liberty Plaza, 20th Floor, New York, NY 10006, USA

477 Williamstown Road, Port Melbourne, VIC 3207, Australia

314–321, 3rd Floor, Plot 3, Splendor Forum, Jasola District Centre,
New Delhi – 110025, India

79 Anson Road, #06–04/06, Singapore 079906

Cambridge University Press is part of the University of Cambridge.

It furthers the University's mission by disseminating knowledge in the pursuit of
education, learning, and research at the highest international levels of excellence.

www.cambridge.org
Information on this title: www.cambridge.org/9781107154384
DOI: 10.1017/9781316650554

© Cambridge University Press 2021

First published 2021

A catalogue record for this publication is available from the British Library.

ISBN 978-1-107-15438-4 Hardback
ISBN 978-1-316-60797-8 Paperback

This book is dedicated to my wife Karin and my five children – Seth, Sara, Samuel, Brittany, and Melody – all of whom have made and will continue to make my world, and I hope, everyone's world, a much better place.

Contents

Tables

Preface

I started studying intelligence when I was thirteen years old – in seventh grade. I was interested in intelligence and intelligence testing because I had bombed the intelligence tests I was given as a child. My seventh-grade science project was my chance to make sense of it all. The project did not go altogether well. The head school system psychologist found out I was giving IQ tests to my classmates and warned me never to bring the book – *Measuring Intelligence* – into school again.[1] I didn't. Instead, I have spent my career studying intelligence as a researcher.

This book, *Adaptive Intelligence,* is the culmination of the work I started in seventh grade, trying to understand what intelligence is and how it manifests itself in the world. The years have gone by. Psychometricians' understanding of intelligence has evolved a bit since 1937 – the most accepted models are now hierarchical ones that build on the work of Charles Spearman, Alfred Binet, Lewis Terman, David Wechsler, Raymond Cattell, John Horn, John Carroll, and other pioneers in the field of intelligence. My own understanding of intelligence has changed radically from when I was thirteen years old, and even from when I wrote my first book about intelligence in 1977.[2] At that time, I thought the challenge of understanding intelligence was to understand its information-processing components. Today, I think the challenge is to understand how intelligence can help to save the world – or destroy it. That is what this book is about – how we either use our intelligence to adapt to the environment, in a broad sense, or else use it to bring about our own destruction as a species. We – humanity individually and collectively – have a choice.

I am extremely grateful to my wife and children, who have supported me during the writing of this book and also during my many successes and failures in my career and life. I also wish to thank my editors at Cambridge, David Repetto and Stephen Acerra, for their patience in waiting for this book manuscript to be finished. I further am grateful to Emily Watton for her editing assistance and to Angela Valente, the copyeditor. I have had wonderful colleagues in the Department of Psychology at Yale and in the Department of Human Development at Cornell and have been truly blessed to have had many student collaborators over the course of the years, without whom very little of my research ever would have come to fruition. Finally, I wish to thank some special colleagues – my undergraduate advisors, first the late Alexander Wearing and then Endel Tulving at Yale; my graduate advisor, the late Gordon Bower at Stanford; my faculty mentor, the late Wendell Garner, during my faculty years at Yale; and my close friend of many years, Ellen Berscheid, who exemplifies all that is right about the field of psychology. I further would like to thank my collaborators Sareh Karami and Ophelie Desmet (team leaders), and Aakash Chowkase, Mehdi Ghahremani, and Fabio Andres Parra Martinez for their current work in developing a test of adaptive intelligence, and also my students Jenna Landy and Vina Wong at Cornell for their current work to the same end.

As is always the case, some cling to outdated paradigms until the bitter end, and so I also want especially to thank all those colleagues in the field of intelligence who have sought to broaden the concept of intelligence and have been willing to "defy the crowd" in the face of entrenched and sometimes bitter opposition to such ideas. Finally, I want to thank all those many colleagues in the field of intelligence with whom I have had sometimes profound professional disagreements but who have brought the field to its current level of scholarly advancement. Fields are always built on the work of scholars who disagree but who, through their disagreements, carry the field forward.

Notes

1. Terman, L. M., & Merrill, M. A. (1937). *Measuring intelligence*. Boston, MA: Houghton-Mifflin.
2. Sternberg, R. J. (1977). *Intelligence, information processing, and analogical reasoning: The componential analysis of human abilities*. Hillsdale, NJ: Erlbaum.

CHAPTER I

Introduction

We live in an era in which advertisers, politicians, and other people whose desire to persuade exceeds their desire to do the right thing. They often are content to present fiction as fact, lies as truth, moral actions as immoral, and immoral actions as moral. Their goal is to blur or render useless the distinctions between these categories. In some places, George Orwell's 1984 finally has come true. Surveillance is pervasive, as in Xinjiang, China, where many people are constantly watched, and some are placed into so-called "reeducation camps."[1] Many other countries are going the same route, including the United States, where treatment of potential refugees is no better, and possibly worse.[2] The perversion goes right to the top in many countries, with presidents, prime ministers, various politicians, and phony "journalists" shading, and sometimes utterly ignoring, the truth with no compunction. Meanwhile, everywhere there are gullible citizens eager to indulge in groupthink and ready to believe whatever they hear from the sources they foolishly trust.[3]

We are living, as I write this book, in a time of a pandemic (March, 2020). Scientists have made clear what needs to be done to combat the pandemic. Politicians, including the president of my own country, are busily doing what they can to make the pandemic worse.[4] They will not stand trial for the deaths they cause. What hope is there for people who want to see any kind of intelligence at all from their leaders, aside from whatever sliver of practical intelligence they use to calculate how to enhance their prospects of reelection?

This book is not about political beliefs. Politicians of all parties some-times make mistakes and they also sometimes lie; so do advertisers and pretty much everyone around the world. Moreover, people have treated each other badly since as far back as humans go. Recently, a 5,300-year-old mummified body, nicknamed Ötzi, was found and identified as having died as a result of being shot by a bow and arrow.[5] Humans have never treated each other all so kindly, Rousseau's optimistic view of human nature notwithstanding.[6] If, as Rousseau argues, it is society that corrupts human nature, we have to remember that society is merely the association of humans with each other – in other words, that, at best, human nature corrupts human nature. At its best, human nature can be positive and uplifting, rather than negative and corrupting. Human nature is positive and uplifting when it is adaptive rather than maladaptive to the circumstance it confronts, and sometimes creates in the world.

1.1   Intelligence as Adaptive Behavior

This book is about intelligence as adaptive behavior – adaptive intelligence. Political beliefs and actions can, and do, have a cost with respect to adaptively intelligent behavior. That cost has gotten greater because, whereas individuals of the past may have had to worry about a bow and arrow and some wild beasts, today, a single malevolent individual with some like-minded collaborators could, at least in principle, destroy every last person on the planet through the push of a button that launches nuclear weapons. There is a reason, evolutionarily, that humans (or really, any other species) have evolved to distinguish truth from falsehood and good from evil.[7]

Suppose someone tells you that they have a surefire investment and you should put a lot of money into it, perhaps your life savings. They convince you. It turns out they were lying. Moreover, they knew that you would go under financially as a result of their scam. You have now lost a ton of money. This happens all the time.[8] Or perhaps someone tells you that they love you when they are only interested in your money, or in having sex, or in sending compromising photos over the Internet. This too happens all the time too.[9] People lie when they sell used (and sometimes new) cars, jewelry that is not what it is cracked up to be, phony luxury goods, and much more. Each time people lie to you, you are at risk, and it is up to you to figure out the truth.

People think of those who fall for scams as gullible. But scams are no longer the property of just a few hucksters selling swampland in Florida as choice real estate with only "upside potential." Scams are a constant presence in everyday life, whether on TV stations or other media that pretend to be independent but simply mimic the government line or in claims of anti-vaxxers that the measles vaccine is dangerous. In fact, measles is far more dangerous than the measles vaccine and can not only cause serious illness; it can also wipe out the child's built-up immune protections – the child's "immune memory" – against various diseases, resulting in children contracting diseases against which they formerly were immune.[10] What good is IQ or education if people do well on IQ tests and their proxies, go to prestigious colleges, and then allow their children, and possibly themselves, to contract a serious and possibly fatal illness because they are gullible?

Mere "gullibility," I argue here, is no longer sufficient to characterize what is going on in a world in which sophisticated media blitzes by unscrupulous actors lead even generally "intelligent" people down ruinous paths. The Internet and social media have preyed upon everyone's gullibility.[11] What is needed now is the kind of intelligence that will enable us to adapt to an environment that is very different from any in previous human history. High scores on IQ tests or their proxies, such as the SAT or ACT, are little consolation if one loses one's life savings to a scam or if one allows oneself to be taken in by hucksters of any kind, whether in sales, investment, or politics.

We need to redefine what we mean by *intelligence* to enable us to understand adaptation to the modern world (or any other world), regardless of the pedigree people may have through their schooling and test scores. Today, what matters most is not IQ, but rather, adaptive intelligence – the ability to adapt to a rapidly changing environment. Without that real-world adaptive ability, IQ points do not matter. Similarly, emotional and social intelligence do not fully cut it. They too often are used for destructive ends: Someone could be very good at understanding how to use their emotional or social intelligence to prey on people whom we traditionally call "gullible," but who now encompass much of the population of a world enchanted by would-be and actual dictators and purveyors of ideas that are leading humanity down a perilous path.

Some of the greatest lies in modern society concern issues of truly great importance. For example, some politicians and columnists falsely, or at best, ignorantly claim that global climate change is not a threat, or at least not a serious threat.[12] Maybe some of them – probably not many – even believe they are telling the truth. They also may believe or say they believe that coal, ultimately, is a good energy source for current times.[13] People believe all sorts of things. People gained a lot of weight when they were told, falsely, that the main cause of obesity was fats rather than sugars in the diet, a lie that only recently has been corrected.[14] Similarly, you would not want someone to lie about whether there are dangerous snakes in an area, or sharks in the water in which you will swim, or human predators lurking nearby. What good is IQ if one falls for the nutritional or other lies that can kill them and others? People are worried about postponements of standardized tests while society is failing the most important test of all – adaptation to the real environment, not the contrived and trivial ones of standardized tests. What is adaptation if not the survival not only of the individual but of humanity and of other species as well?

1.2 Adaptive Intelligence Perpetuates a Species

I argue in this book that one of the most serious falsehoods permeating our society is the belief that standardized tests of intelligence and related attributes – IQ tests, SATs, ACTs, GREs, most standardized achievement tests, and the like – are good and somehow highly meaningful and comprehensive measures of intelligence and what emanates from it. The relevant argument is simple. On the positive side, we have many conveniences in modern life that have been made possible by the cleverness of inventors of various kinds. On the negative side, evolutionarily, our first responsibility is to care not only for our present generation but also for future generations – we are here to create our successors. Intelligence is not about problem-solving on a contrived standardized test; it is about problem-solving in the real world.

Many psychologists studying intelligence have engaged in a remarkable false turnaround with regard to what predicts what. Intelligence tests were originally designed to predict real-world performance. The test scores were useful only to the extent they predicted such performance. The testers have turned things around to make the IQ, or the score on some other test of general intelligence, the criterion. The IQ has become, to them, more important than whatever it is that the tests are supposed to predict. If you read through my own edited *Cambridge Handbook of Intelligence*, you find, in case after case, investigators who have done very solid scientific work on intelligence validate the work on the basis of the extent to which it is consistent with the notion of intelligence as IQ, rather than the notion of intelligence as indicating what kinds of problems people can solve in their lives. What good was the presumably high IQ of a political leader who is also a medical doctor when he went about his busy social life interacting with other people while waiting for his COVID-19 test result, which came back positive, meaning that he exposed many of his friends to the risk of illness caused by the virus?[15] Is intelligence about the doctor/senator's IQ, or is it about his failure to protect both himself and his colleagues and friends from a potentially deadly disease? Does intelligence have nothing to do with how we care for ourselves and others, including future generations? Is it just about solving tricky but ultimately trivial puzzles on tests?

It is hard to claim we are adequately caring for our successors when 95 percent of baby foods tested in a recent assessment were found to contain toxic metals, such as arsenic, lead, mercury, and cadmium.[16] That scarcely gives babies a just lease on their new lives. Of course, we could blame the baby-food manufacturers, but the problem is not just with baby food. It is with many children's foods, including even ones we have thought to be healthful, such as oats (which contain glyphosate, a possible carcinogen)[17] and rice, used in a variety of cereals but often containing arsenic. In particular, the US Food and Drug Administration found that contamination of baby rice cereals by arsenic has reached what only could be called unacceptable levels: 104 ppb in infants' dry white-rice cereal and 119 ppb in infants' dry brown-rice cereal.[18] Why is society allowing such contamination?

We do not know exactly what is causing worldwide declines in fertility rates. In 2018, the United States, for example, had its lowest fertility rate on record.[19] It is tempting to blame this, and everything else that goes wrong, on the great recession of 2008, except that the recession happened more than a decade ago and the economy in 2019, when the article was written, was thriving. Future generations are in trouble. We are poisoning ourselves and our children and creating a world that is not viable. Right now, as I write, Sydney, Australia, is bathed in smoke from wildfires[20] and the air in Delhi and other cities in India and elsewhere continues to be practically unbreathable.[21]

By 2050, the world will be in serious trouble for climatic reasons as well as food and water challenges. Already, more than 110 million people live in areas that will be below the high-tide line in 2050.[22] The projected population by 2050 is 9.8 billion, compared with less than 2.6 billion in 1950. This is an increase of 7 billion, or roughly 377 percent in just a century. With land disappearing under water and many parts of the world becoming uninhabitable because of rising temperatures, how are we going to feed these people? What will happen when major parts of large countries get submerged under water? How will they handle, despite the flooding, lack of potable water? The world of the future, and in some places the world of the present, faces a serious water crisis.[23] If humans are such an intelligent species, how could they let this happen and what are they going to do about it? What will people do about areas that become too hot to live in? Whatever people's so-called general intelligence, what about their intelligence as the ability to adapt to the environment – their adaptive intelligence? Just to be clear: These issues are not about environmentalism or do-goodism or political movements, such as the "Extinction Rebellion."

This is about survival, of the individuals and societies of today but, more consequentially, of all future generations. Can we really afford the luxury of pretending that IQ tests and SATs and ACTs measure what is important when we are killing ourselves and our future? That is not a matter of political views; that is a matter of adaptive intelligence versus mass suicide. That is a matter of letting go of our mental servitude to standardized tests and becoming real about the intelligence we need to survive and thrive, individually and as a species.

Some might think that the slow-motion suicide of humans, taking many other species with them, much as does a drunken driver who drives his or her family into the sea, has nothing to do with intelligence. This is what I ask readers of this book to consider, or reconsider.

A reader of this book indicated in his review that he did not accept the notion that humans somehow are committing mass suicide. That is, perhaps, because we are used to thinking of suicide as something done individually and quickly. People shoot themselves, or take poison, or jump off a cliff. But suicide does not have to be individual and it does not have to be quick. If people, collectively, destroy the water they drink, the air they breathe, the climate in which they live, they are doing collectively and slowly what a person may do individually and quickly. The ultimate effect is the same. Not every individual will die; but most suicide attempts are not successful either: Fewer than 10 percent of attempts succeed.[24] Humans seem to be much better at seeing short-term consequences for individuals than long-term consequences for either individuals or collectivities. They avoid thinking sufficiently about the long-term future. But that is a flaw in their intelligence: To be adaptively intelligent, one must look not only at the short-term, but also at the long-term, as illustrated by the tragedy of the commons.

1.3   The Relevance of the Tragedy of the Commons

Start with the so-called "tragedy of the commons." The traditional presentation of the tragedy is in terms of cattle grazing on a common, say, in colonial New England (in the northeast of the United States). The common supplies the main source of food for the cattle. If all the farmers who own the cattle share the grass plot equitably, there will be enough grass to go around.

Inevitably, some clever farmer will realize that if he (it typically was a "he") allows his cattle to graze on more than their fair share, then his cattle will be fatter than the cattle of the others and hence will be worth

more at market. So, inevitably, some of the farmers have their cattle
"overgraze." These farmers may feel guilty about what they have done, or
they may not – their cattle will be worth more! But then other farmers
start to notice what is going on. They do not want to be in a situation
where, because of the selfishness of others, they are deprived. So, they
now allow their cattle to overgraze. Eventually, the outcome is certain.
The grass will be depleted, none of the farmers will have grass available
for their cattle to graze, and it will be every man for himself, with many, if
not most, of the cattle dying for lack of food. The tragedy of the
commons is that what is clever at the individual level in the short term
is tragic at the level of the group in the long term – hence the name,
"tragedy of the commons." How intelligent were the farmers, really?
Their individual intelligence resulted in a long-term loss on account of
a short-term gain.

   If the problem of the tragedy of the commons were limited to cattle in
colonial New England, the tragedy of the commons would be an interesting
but quaint problem. But of course, the problem is much broader than that.
Consider the Brazilian rain forest, which under President Jair Bolsonaro, is
being depleted at a greater rate than ever before.[25] The reason for the
depletion is simple. There are, as in the above example, short-term gains –
more farmlands, trees for which the wood can be sold, increased land for
homesteads, and so forth. But the world, including but not limited to Brazil,
depends on the Brazilian rain forest for many different things, most notably,
the absorption of carbon dioxide by the abundant trees and plant life. In
a world where carbon dioxide is increasing at an alarming rate, that is no
small deal. But the tragedy of the commons is playing out as I write, and
carbon levels in the atmosphere are increasing at unprecedented rates.

   Of course, it gets much worse, because the mentality of the Brazilians
under Jair Bolsonaro is not all that different from the mentality of those under
leaders of many other countries, including of the United States (at least in
current times).[26] Now imagine a slightly different situation extending the idea
of the tragedy of the commons.

   Seven-and-a-half billion people are sharing a common planet. They
have used the planet not only for food but also for other resources that
the planet has provided – petroleum, natural gas, diamonds, precious
metals, rare earths, and on and on. If they took care of those resources
and their own population growth, the planet would provide them with
resources for many years, indeed, many decades or even centuries, to come.
But like the clever farmer, some saw ways to advantage themselves over
others. They did not take just a little more of the metaphorical grazing

"grass" but a whole lot more of it. Meanwhile, others took almost none of the metaphorical grass. In a few cases, it may have been through their own lack of cleverness, but in many cases, it was because they happened to be born at the wrong time or in the wrong place, or both, or of the "wrong" parents, at least with respect to having opportunities. So, some – think of the children of the ultra-rich – had to do very little to get a lot of the resources whereas others, no matter how they tried, could get scarcely any at all. This raises the question of what we mean by merit in our society.

1.4   Whose Merit, and What Kind of Merit Anyway?

Eventually, the have-nots came to realize that the system was stacked against them. Some were so downtrodden that they could do nothing. Others, throughout various periods of history, revolted. In the United States and many other countries, we are in a second Gilded Age, and who knows where that will go?[27] What is clear is that something is wrong.

As a university administrator (university dean, then provost, then president), I got to witness a part of this wrongness on almost a daily basis. High school students would apply to the universities in which I held administrative positions. For many of them, admission was solely a merit-based proposition. But whose merit? Theirs? Or their parents'? And what kind of merit? Beyond those admitted for academic merit, there are those who are admitted largely because their parents have donated a lot of money, those who are admitted largely because they have relatives who went to the university, those who are admitted because they took up sports that are limited largely to students from wealthy families (e.g., golf, water polo), those who are admitted largely because their parents were able to afford expensive college counselors or tutors, and on and on. The kids do not have to get extra resources; neither do their parents. It may be enough that the parents inherited money, which itself may have been inherited. For them, their IQ or general intelligence or whatever does not matter much; they are taken care of.

1.5   Diminishing Importance of IQ

So, let us return to the tragedy of the commons as a metaphor for much of what is wrong with the world today and change the circumstances just a bit. Imagine that, instead of cattle sharing a pasture, the commons problem was changed to humans sharing a world. One possibility would be for each human to maximize his or her individual gain, much as do farmers contributing to the tragedy of the commons. The result would be the same as that of the tragedy of the commons. Or, instead, people could try to maximize their joint outcomes. They could, but for the most part, they do not. On November 4, 2019, the United States pulled out of the Paris climate agreement.[28] One day later, more than 11,000 scientists warned that the world faces a catastrophic threat from global climate change, essentially beyond most people's imagining.[29] The crisis will involve not only rising temperatures but a cascade of events that will make the Earth unlivable for many, and only marginally livable for many more. As the article points out, such warnings have been published by scientists for many years and largely have gone unheeded.

Meanwhile, the results of climate change are to be seen in many locations, as those who have been forced to evacuate their homes for various reasons, such as wildfires and hurricanes, know. Really, what difference do IQs make if they do not lead to sufficiently responsible behavior that people will leave a decent world for their children and grandchildren to live in, much less, for them to live in? The effects of climate change, for example, are being and will be experienced by many of today's adults, but the most adverse effects will be upon their children.[30] Are we really that inconsiderate and uncaring of our children and our children's children? Are we that greedy? That stupid? That adaptively unintelligent?

I argue in this book that we have badly misconceived intelligence, to the benefit of the already benefited and to the detriment of practically everyone else. It is not surprising, perhaps, that any group that controls society seeks its own benefit. It may be pathetic, but it is not surprising to find high-IQ individuals grasping at the IQ straw in the same way royalty once grasped at the royalty straw, white people have grasped at the white-people (supposedly advanced-civilization) straw, and rich people historically have grasped at the money straw (as in, "if I'm rich, I must know what I'm doing").

Suppose that, to be admitted to the top universities in a country, one only had to be tall. (We could use any arbitrary criterion in place of height, such as wealth, eye color, or skin color). Now, the top universities choose to admit undergraduates on the basis only of height. They admit graduate and professional students on the same basis, except that the requirements are even more stringent. The universities do not even have to say that they are admitting by height. They only have to believe that height matters, ask applicants and recommenders about height, and advertise in magazines and elsewhere how tall their students are. They could claim to admit "holistically," but everyone would know that it is a weak cover for admitting by height.

After some number of years, tall people absolutely would dominate the student bodies of the most prestigious universities, especially at the graduate and professional levels, where admissions criteria are the most stringent. The top firms in the country, some of which only bother to recruit at the "best" colleges and universities, would now be looking for tall people. It would not matter that height was irrelevant to actual performance. If people believed that height matters greatly, they would give people all sorts of advantages that would multiply the advantages tall people experience anyway throughout their lives. (And in fact, tall people do have an advantage!)

Eventually, tall people would come to dominate positions of power and wealth in society, much as do high-IQ and wealthy people today. Those people never, ever would attribute their success merely to their height, or, for that matter, to the genes they inherited from their parents. They would know that, yes, they were selected for their height, but that height had proven to be a true predictor of success.

In fact, the environment was set up to make this come true. The high correlation between height and success was created by humans, not ordained by nature. Once people believe that tall people, or rich people, or people of a certain religion or ethnicity or caste or skin color are better, humans will reshape the environment to perpetuate their belief and turn it into a self-fulfilling prophecy. Then a corps of behavioral scientists trying to justify their own success, no matter how great or pitiable it might be, will do a slew of mindless correlational studies showing that height (or race, or wealth, or IQ, or whatever) is correlated with success, thereby "proving" that the trait actually mattered to success. In fact, it will have mattered, but in large part because people shaped the world to make that belief come true. They gave the lion's share of the opportunities to tall people, so tall people succeeded and came to believe in their tallness as causal to their success. It was causal, but only because people believed it to be and thus made it to be. In the United States, at least, zip codes separated by a city block or two, or even within a city, can spell the difference between great chances of societal success and hardly any chance at all. But those in the wealthier zip codes probably attribute their success to their herculean efforts, not to the correlates of the zip code in which they live.

This book will examine how our faulty notions about intelligence have shaped the societies we live in, and why a seemingly new, but actually, very old notion of "adaptive intelligence" is a much better way to think about intelligence. This will mean that people who, purposely or by accident, have used IQ-related measures to create and preserve socioeconomic advantages for themselves and their progeny will, in many cases, have to do things to make life better for everyone, not just for themselves and perhaps their family and friends. But if we do not change our notion of intelligence, and if we do not give up on our false "meritocracy," in a small number of generations, we humans will have nothing to worry about. It will be up to the cockroaches, bacteria, and other hardy species that survive human-made devastation to determine the future course the world will take.

This message may sound like a pessimistic one. I would argue that it is anything but. The message is that there can be a bright future for humanity – just not if we go on pretending that IQ-based abilities are what really matter. We see how well those abilities are working today, with some of very high-IQ, whether at Facebook or other social media platforms, creating and maintaining their social media platforms allowing people to lie through their teeth. Repeatedly, they have developed and refined ways of making it increasingly hard to distinguish truth from falsehood.

We do not have to focus exclusively or even mostly on IQ in thinking about intelligence. We need to think more broadly.

1.6 A Choice

We have a choice. If we choose to value deception and malevolence as much as honesty and benevolence, so long as the deception and malevolence have high-IQ manipulativeness behind them, then truly we humans are doomed. If we simply decide to make no choice, then we are doomed. If we decide affirmatively to continue to use criteria that benefit humanity only in the very short term, then we are doomed. The point is – we do have a choice. What do we choose? What do you choose and what will you do about it?

The academic field of intelligence has made its choice, and I believe it is the wrong choice. It has stuck with a paradigm that is over a century old. Science does not advance by retaining paradigms for over a century. Charles Spearman published a paper in 1904 showing that so-called intelligence tests tend to be positively intercorrelated with each other, suggesting that there is some kind of general factor underlying intelligence; researchers have stuck with him, refining his theory and adding details, but basically adhering to the formula.[31]

What, exactly, is general intelligence? Spearman did not know in 1904, and more than a century later, still no one knows. It is a hypothetical construct that basically represents a set of positive intercorrelations among tests. How does one validate a new intelligence test – by comparing it to old intelligence tests, or by comparing it to school grades or professional success. What is wrong with this picture? It preserves what already exists and does not allow change.

I recognized the problem when I started my own research in 1977. How did I know what to measure? I drew on problems that were like those on IQ tests. How did I know whether my model was good? I compared scores to those on IQ tests. I knew then, as I know now, how conceptually weak this procedure was. Essentially, I was just doing a dance variation on a very old dance. Researchers since then have studied psychometric, cognitive, and biological bases of intelligence, but they always have resorted to correlations with so-called general intelligence to validate what they are doing; so they have been basically doing the Spearman Two-Step. (Spearman's theory was called the "two-factor" theory, because Spearman postulated specific factors of intelligence as well as the general factor.) Spearman's work was extremely impressive for 1904, but perhaps it is time to move on? The field keeps doing variations on the same theme.

I am proposing in this book that the field of intelligence needs a new dance, or if you prefer, a Kuhnian revolution.[32] We need to stop using scores on old tests of general intelligence, and their proxies, as the ultimate criteria for any new tests. Instead, we need to use adaptive behavior as the ultimate criteria – is what people are doing adapting to the environment in the biological sense of creating a better world for their heirs? Are they helping to create a better world or are they leaving the world in its current mess, or actually making it worse, as by using their general intelligence to pollute the air, pollute the water, increase global poverty and income disparity, foster bacterial resistance to antibiotics, and so forth? This, I would argue, is the true meaning of biologically based intelligence, not a scattering of correlations of brain waves or aspects of functional magnetic resonance imaging (fMRI) pictures or measures of brain size. Biologically based intelligence allows a species to thrive and to multiply; it does not destroy the environment upon which the species depends, no matter how impressive the fMRI picture of their brains. Scientists in some fields have been truly innovative. Intelligence, in general, is not one of those fields, because we have allowed ourselves to remain with a comfortable model of 1157 years ago. It is time for both science and society to move on.

As a reader, a fair question to ask would be: "Why should I believe you?" Most of the rest of the field accepts and even admires IQ and the theories it has helped to generate. (The theories came after IQ, not before IQ, as would be more typical in science.) So, let me close this chapter by answering this question as best I can.

Imagine life in the ages of the dinosaurs. For 165 million years, dinosaurs roamed the Earth, establishing various kinds of interactions with the world in which they lived and with each other. They had dominance hierarchies – some were more feared, others, less so. Then their luck ran out. A meteor (or other heavenly body) struck the Earth near what is now Chicxulub, Mexico. It set off a chain reaction of events that wiped out the dinosaurs and made the way for future ecosystems. Had it not been for that event, you and I probably would not be here. There is absolutely nothing the dinosaurs could have done to prevent the impact.

About 200,000 or perhaps somewhat more years ago, humans appeared. Their run on Earth has been far shorter than that of the dinosaurs. Someday, a meteor may wipe us out too – probably not much we can do about that, although we might start preparing. But humans have chosen not to wait for the meteor. We have chosen to be human meteors, destroying the Earth, but slowly so that the effects are noticeable but not quite do dramatic. Most likely, we still can do something about it. The odd thing is that, unlike the dinosaurs, we know that we are destroying our own environment but nevertheless are not doing enough to prevent the destruction. Many of us are hastening our own demise.

Scientists are susceptible to the same tribal mentalities as everyone else. Moreover, like everyone else, they tend to focus on extremely short-term outcomes. In the case of abilities research: What grades did a student get in the years after he or she took a college-admissions test? Did the student graduate, and if so, how quickly? How well did some test predict the student's later health or income? In the course of evolutionary time, the time spans the field of intelligence research typically looks at are infinitesimally small. On a planetary timeline, they are not even a blip.

If others in the field of intelligence are not, in their professional work, paying much or any attention to the state of the world in general, why should I? Why should you? If the field does not start caring about humans of the future rather than merely today's socioeconomic and political pecking order, we all will end up like dinosaurs, or like the chickens on a chicken farm who think their life is fine until one day, unpredictably, it not only is not fine, but is not. That is the choice. By not making a choice, we are nevertheless making it. We are choosing to view intelligence in terms of IQ and SAT and ACT scores. And we are choosing extinction because we were, as a species, too stupid to do anything to preserve our own future. If allowing, or even actively choosing, extinction while paying attention to social pecking orders is intelligence, what is stupidity? We have what might seem like a somewhat stupid notion of intelligence – one that serves us poorly in dealing with the world we face today.

1.7 What Exactly Is Wrong with the Traditional Notion of Intelligence?

If one is presenting a new model of intelligence, it behooves us to ask what is wrong with the old one? I have discussed some of the issues earlier but would like to dig a bit deeper to photograph the hole into which we all have dug ourselves. The themes below will be elaborated throughout this book. One of these themes is our focus on the individual.

1.7.1   Individualism

Most European cultural milieus, and certainly the American one, are highly individualistic.[33] It therefore is not shocking that definitions of intelligence have developed in an individualistic way. Not all cultures are as individualistic as ours are; and in some cultures, the very idea of taking a test as an individual seems strange,[34] since many, perhaps most, activities in life are performed in an interpersonal context. Even if one works on one's own, one is doing so in the context of many people in one's environmental milieu.[35]

The individualistic definition of intelligence has served, to some extent, to create a hierarchy in society based in large part upon cognitive ability as we define it through existing standardized tests. That is because these tests are used for so many purposes – for measuring school achievement, for private-school admissions, for college admissions, and for admissions to graduate programs of various kinds (including law, medicine, business, dentistry, etc.). The question this book addresses is whether the particular hierarchy tests create is the right one, or even a particularly good one, or perhaps a notably bad one.

There are several reasons that the individualistic conceptualization of intelligence and intelligence testing may be a rather grand mistake.

First, in any society, even individual actions may have collective outcomes. That is, what an individual does almost inevitably affects others, even if that is not their intention. As a rather prosaic and simple, but personally meaningful example, we have neighbors who love deer. What is there not to love? They feed the deer in the winter so that the deer do not starve. This certainly is a noble cause, at least for them. But their action has consequences for the neighborhood of which they are oblivious. Attracted by the feedings, more and more deer are coming into our neighborhood. This is resulting in potential traffic hazards, as the deer are relatively inattentive to automobile traffic and sometimes simply end up staring at car headlamps as a car approaches. Second, the male deer are rubbing their antlers against young trees, in the process harming the bark and the trees. Third, deer ticks appear to be on the rise. One of my daughters got bitten by a deer tick and had to be treated prophylactically for Lyme disease. Finally, not everyone on the block is actually enchanted with having the deer around.

Of course, deer are a small issue in the grand scheme of things. But the deer incident shows something we all know – that the actions of the individual often have unintended consequences for the group, and the actions of small groups often have unintended consequences for large groups. Ironically, people who are very intelligent and use their intelligence in their own interests or in the interests of those close to them may well be more effective in maximizing self-interest than those who are not so intelligent, but because their self-interest may not correspond to collective interest, maximizing smart people's opportunities to act in self-interested ways potentially may hurt society more than maximizing the opportunities of people who are less able to advance their self-interest at the expense of others.

Fortunately, not all of life is a zero-sum game. Smart people can also work to maximize collective interests. But for many people, maximizing collective interest may not be seen as a way of paying for their house, or getting their kids into college (potentially meaning that other people's kids do not get into those colleges), or supporting various purchases they individually want to make. Moreover, even those who care about others may tend to perceive things more over the short run than over the long run. Even brilliant inventions, such as oil refineries, trucks, and Facebook, have proved to have long-term consequences that were not well foreseen, such as pollution of air, water, and, perhaps, minds.

Second, as noted above, much of the work we actually do in our lives is in collective contexts. We make joint decisions in our personal relationships and at work. The fact that someone is effective individually does not mean that the person is effectively collectively. The result is that, too often, people who are selected for their individual skills fail in group contexts. To some extent, constructs like emotional intelligence,[36] social intelligence,[37] and practical intelligence[38] deal with people's abilities to relate to others. But they differ from adaptive intelligence in that they do not necessarily serve a common good, which is the key to adaptive intelligence. Quite the contrary. Salespeople and consumer psychologists may use emotional, social, and practical intelligence in their work to manipulate people – to buy things they do not need or to buy things that are of less than satisfactory quality, or to believe things that are not true. Adaptive intelligence simultaneously balances individual with collective goods.

Third, through our use of testing, we have sent and reinforced a message that individual accomplishment is what matters – that the common good is not of any great relevance. The tests measure people's ability to solve problems for themselves, not for others. Moreover, the kinds of problems on them have not significantly changed in years, but the world has changed, and hence what constitutes intelligence has changed.

1.7.2   The Changing Nature of Intelligence

What is important to intelligence changes over time.[39] But we measure intelligence as though it is the same thing as when Binet and Simon first created their intelligence tests at the beginning of the twentieth century.

For example, skill in information retrieval is far more important now than it was 120 years ago. One no longer simply goes to a library and looks things up in a card catalog. There is a dizzying array of information available through search engines, but one has to find it. Usually, there is no librarian around to assist in the task.

Furthermore, skill in information evaluation is far more important than before. One used to be able to trust major media, at least, for much of their reporting. Today, anything can be published on the Internet, and no matter what lies people tell, especially people in power, there will be conventional media and social media to support what they say. Citizens need to know how to discriminate the wheat from the chaff. Success in academia does not necessarily predict that ability to discriminate.

1.7.3   The Role of Academic Success

What is considered mentally (and physically and socially) "successful" changes with people's age. At the beginning and end of life, physical health probably matters more than anything. For a newborn baby to be successful, one hopes for a score of ten on the APGAR scale. For a ninety-year-old to be successful, one hopes for reasonably good health and, perhaps most of all, freedom from dementia! But in the middle, mental and social success are more important. Alfred Binet, the originator of the current model of intelligence testing, was given the task of distinguishing children who were slow learners from those who were not, largely so that teachers would not recommend for remedial classes children who were behavioral challenges but who were mentally adept.[40]

Thus, the origin of current intelligence testing was in an academic context. This origin made sense in terms of a major criterion for success in childhood, namely, academic performance. The test largely measured, directly or indirectly, academic types of performances. Had intelligence tests been created in a different context, they might have looked quite different. In a sense, the way intelligence testing was formalized was an historical accident. It was designed validly to predict success in school, but no more.

1.7.4 The Role of Predictive Validity

As it turned out, the academically oriented tests of Binet and others used to measure intelligence predicted many other things – for example, job performance, health, marital success, mortality.[41] This was taken as evidence that the tests measure intelligence. One can certainly see why psychologists and others would draw this conclusion. Of course, in the United States, many other characteristics also predict various kinds of success, such as having white skin, being of upper socioeconomic status (SES), being male, and so forth.[42] These are status variables. There are also a number of performance-related variables that correlate in some measure with various indices of success, such as graduation from college and the prestige of the college from which one was graduated.

These variables may be partly determined by test scores, but variables are so interactive that it is hard to separate them. For example, both standardized test scores and college graduation are correlated with SES. Indeed, most positive outcomes in life are correlated with SES.[43] All these correlations are based on individual differences, but should our notion of intelligence be tied to individual differences?

1.7.5 The Role of Individual Differences

The study of intelligence as introduced by Alfred Binet and by Charles Spearman, his contemporary, was based on the study of individual differences. One approach, the psychometric approach, has emphasized, almost exclusively, understanding intelligence from the standpoint of individual differences – who is more or less intelligent than someone else?[44] From the very beginning of my career, I have believed this almost exclusive emphasis on individual differences to be a major mistake.[45]

Studying individual differences obviously puts an emphasis on ways in which people are different, to the exclusion of looking at ways in which they are alike. Perhaps this is the reason that the field of intelligence, and so-called differential psychology more generally, has been somewhat alienated from psychology as a whole, or at least experimental psychology, which tends to emphasize how people are similar.[46]

People are much more alike than they are different. Genetically, people are 99.9 percent alike.[47] One can, of course, focus on 0.1 percent of the genome, but if a field wishes to represent biological reality, it would seem that the field would also want to focus on what about intelligence is common among individuals.

The biological approach to intelligence – focusing, in part, on areas of the brain that are responsible for intelligent thinking and behavior – does look for ways people are similar and not just different. But validation studies often then end up focusing on whether activation of those areas of the brain predicts the same kinds of individual differences in scores on intelligence tests that the psychometric approach focuses on.[48]

The risk is that the *raison d'être* of intelligence research, and indeed, for the concept of intelligence, becomes individual differences. From the standpoint of adaptive intelligence, this is potentially tragic, literally, because the problems facing humankind today that require their serious intelligence to solve are not individual-difference problems but rather species-common problems. Solving a problem such as how to tackle new illnesses, for example novel coronavirus (COVID-19) or, just a few years ago, SARS (severe acute respiratory syndrome), is not about who is smarter than whom. Major contemporary problems include whether we, humanity, can outsmart viruses (or other parasitic organisms) that threaten to wreak havoc on humankind. Efforts to find cures inevitably are collective efforts, not merely efforts of each individual competing with all of the others.

There is nothing intrinsically wrong with an individual-differences mentality. Of course, there are individual differences in intelligence, as there are individual differences in many other things. But we can focus on individual differences, as there are in height, without realizing that what gives us an advantage as a species is often that we are similar, as we are in height, compared, say, to ants. We can do many things that are adaptive for us that ants could never do because of our many common features with other humans. Of course, ants also can do many things we cannot do that are adaptive for them because of their common small size and strength for their size.

The crucial problem with any exclusively differential approach is that it leads us to focus on the wrong things, or at best, a very limited subset of things. It focuses our attention on those relatively less important aspects of intelligence in which people differ. Indeed, if people do not differ substantially in them, they never will show up in the kinds of statistical analysis psychometricians perform to identify the factors that are alleged to comprise intelligence. What makes us, as a species, intelligent is totally neglected because it is not necessarily a major source of individual differences. Rather, it is based on Darwinian theory. Evolutionarily, our goal needs to be to create the next generation so that they can create the generation after them, and so on. This has nothing to do with individual differences. It is what preserves a species – or allows it to die off. It is hard to see, in the long run what difference it makes if some members of a species are smarter than others, if the whole species allows itself to die off. One is reminded of *Ozymandias*, a poem by Percy Shelley, that might apply to species as well as it applies to any one individual:

> I met a traveller from an antique land,
> Who said – "Two vast and trunkless legs of stone
> Stand in the desert. . . .. Near them, on the sand,
> Half sunk a shattered visage lies, whose frown,
> And wrinkled lip, and sneer of cold command,
> Tell that its sculptor well those passions read
> Which yet survive, stamped on these lifeless things,
> The hand that mocked them, and the heart that fed;
> And on the pedestal, these words appear:
> My name is Ozymandias, King of Kings;
> Look on my Works, ye Mighty, and despair!"
> Nothing beside remains. Round the decay
> Of that colossal Wreck, boundless and bare
> The lone and level sands stretch far away.[49]

Adaptive intelligence is about not letting happen to us, as a species, what happened to Ozymandias, where nothing remains except the memory. But the extinction of humanity would be worse, because there would be no one even to remember.

Scientists, at least in some fields, no longer think much about "humanity." When I started studying psychology, they did. Psychologists, especially in the humanistic tradition, thought a lot about what psychology could tell us to help the future of humanity. Notable exemplars were like Carl Rogers, Erich Fromm, Erik Eriksen, and Abraham Maslow.[50] But today, many social scientists think much more about physics than about humanity, not for its content, but rather, for its methods.

1.7.6   The Role of Physics Envy

Psychology, like many other socially oriented sciences, has long had a tendency to envy the hard, natural sciences, and to be granted by society the kind of respect that the hard sciences, like physics, command. But how does a science gain this kind of respect?

One way to gain it is to quantify everything one can and show, or at least, hope that the measurements one takes will be as solid as the measurements taken in physics. The study of individual differences in intelligence, by quantifying differences from the start, has sought to gain this kind of credibility.

The problem is that no social, economic, or educational policy has ever been formed around gravity or the weak force, and, to my knowledge, no one's life has ever been wrecked because of the existence of atoms or quarks. Unfortunately, the same cannot be said of psychometric, individual-difference-based approaches to intelligence. Not only have people's educational aspirations been thwarted, but whole groups have been discriminated against because they were not believed to be as "intelligent" as other groups.[51] The worship of physics came at a cost. Mid-level correlations of 0.3 to 0.7 between intelligence tests and various educational and other criteria may be impressive at the collective level, but they mean that if tests are used to make individual predictions, many people will be misclassified. Such correlations represent a range of 9 percent to 49 percent of variance accounted for in criterion performance. When individual-level prediction is the goal, those numbers are not all so impressive. Moreover, they represent the imperialistic view of a small number of cultures, worldwide, as to what matters for prediction.

1.7.7   The Role of Cultural Imperialism

Intelligence tests were based entirely on particular certain (although certainly not all) Western cultural values, at least in early twentieth-century France. The tests were and still are a fair representation of a portion of the skills that principals and teachers in elementary and secondary schools believe to be important for academic success. But a fair question would be just how universal those values are. As you will see in Chapter 2, different cultures have different conceptions of what intelligence is and also different adaptive requirements for what constitutes intelligent behavior.[52] Sometimes, those cultures have been laudatory of their own values and deprecating of the values of other cultures.

1.7.8 The Role of Xenophobia and So-Called "Scientific" Racism

Many countries have a history of xenophobia and the so-called "scientific" racism that goes with it. The racism is so-called "scientific" because it is racist ideology masking as science. Of course, when we think of so-called scientific racism, we tend to think of Nazi ideology regarding a phony Aryan race. Many of the early intelligence researchers, and some of the present ones, believed that some races are superior to others intellectually.[53] The actual evidence in favor of racial differences always has been questionable and based on fraught assumptions.[54]

In particular, an assumption has been that a particular test measures the same thing for everyone. After all, the items are the same, unless they are translated from one language to another, as sometimes happens when an attempt is made to tailor the tests to people in different nations with different languages. One problem is that, in any given country, there are likely to be a variety of languages. For example, English is not the native language of everyone in the United States, any more than French is the native language of everyone in Belgium.

A second issue is that the same apparent item does not necessarily measure the same thing from one culture or subculture to another. Consider children who grow up with English as a first language and with a lot of books in the house. If the parents interact at a sophisticated linguistic level with their children, those children, regardless of race, will have an edge on almost any IQ test over those children who were brought up under more IQ-challenging situations.

Race has been a red herring for intelligence research almost from the start. It has distracted people from studying more important issues, such as what we mean by intelligence in the first place and whether it even means the same thing from one group to the next. Often, it seems that researchers go into their research expecting to find something and then find what they want to find.

Another red herring has been a misunderstanding of the significance of evolution for understanding intelligence.

1.7.9   The Mistaken Role of Evolutionary Differences

Evolution has played an important role in the development of intelligence over secular time.[55] And of course, evolutionary considerations are important, in that intelligence, like all other human traits, is an evolved construct.

A problem with some evolutionary interpretations of intelligence is that the basic question they have asked is how we got to be so much more intelligent than other species. This is actually an assumption rather than a fact. We are more intelligent by our own standards. If the standard is constructing complex inventions, humans certainly have done well. If the standard is preservation of the species, humans are not doing so well, with various forms of human-originated pollution and other environmental catastrophes killing people on a steady basis. Worst, perhaps, is humans' hubris with respect to what even constitutes intelligence. Viruses, which are invisible to the naked eye, have no brain, and are not even "alive" in the sense of being able to maintain their lives in the absence of a host, might be seen as being about as stupid as any organism can get. Yet, in the fight against novel coronavirus, as of late August 2020, it is not clear which species will get the best of things, the humans or the viruses. So far, the viruses are winning. If we are so smart, why have more than 18 million people around the world been infected by the virus and why have many thousands of people – more than 700,000 as of August 5, 2020 – died?[56] To some extent, our battle against the virus is being hurt by commercialization.

1.7.10   The Role of Commercialization

Finally, the study of intelligence has been hurt by commercialization. Commercialization, of course, always can help research by providing funding. But as any academic knows, the rub with commercial research is that organizations like ideas and research findings that support their products. I am just one of many researchers who, upon obtaining research findings that did not support the product of a funding organization, found my funding cut off. As researchers get trained, funding, consultation jobs, and other perquisites from organizations that produce products related to standard conceptions of intelligence, it becomes harder to get away from these products. Just ask any doctor who has prescribed drugs (namely, virtually all doctors) and finds him or herself beseeched by drug companies to prescribe their product. And in the fight against COVID-19, there have been innumerable fake cures that have been commercialized with the sole purpose of making money for their producers, not of saving lives.

The Kool-Aid of the IQ testing establishment has been, and is, being presented by some to the world as fact. Everything else is alleged to be myth.[57] Meanwhile, the world gets hotter, the forests burn, catastrophic weather events become more powerful, many governments become more destructive of human lives, people eat food that leads to life-shortening illnesses such as diabetes and cancer, people drink foul water, people breathe in polluted air, people lose their jobs, and people die in pandemics because of human stupidity and greed. When there are no people left, there will be no one to write self-congratulatory works on the wonders of IQ testing. There will be no one left to read the books, only microorganisms to feed on their pages flapping in the wind. And the microorganisms will care not a whit about the IQs of the people who read the works, nor of those who wrote them.

With that introduction, let us move to a consideration of intelligence and its manifestations.

Notes

1. Buckley, C., & Mozur, P. (2019). "How China uses high-tech surveillance to subdue minorities." *New York Times*, May 22. https://nyti.ms/2Xkjgww
2. Sacchetti, M. (2019). "'Kids in cages': House hearing examines immigration detention as Democrats push for more information." *Washington Post*, July 10. https://wapo.st/3i5UsR9
3. Miller, M. B. (2019). "America's dangerous gullibility." *The Bay State Banner*, May 15. https://bit.ly/3k7Hhks
4. Schake, K. (2020). "The damage that 'America first' has done." *The Atlantic*, March 20. https://bit.ly/3k3xmw9
5. Scully, R. P. (2019). Ötzi's attempt to flee his pursuers charted. *New Scientist*, November 9–15, p. 16.
6. Rousseau, J.-J., & Scott, J. T. (2014). *The major political writings of Jean-Jacques Rousseau: The two "discourses" and the social contract*. Chicago, IL: University of Chicago Press.
7. Kagan, J. (2013). *The human spark: The science of human development*. New York: Basic Books.
8. Australian Competition and Consumer Commission. (N.D.). Investment scams. https://bit.ly/3g09lOj
9. Federal Trade Commission.(2019). What you need to know about romance scams. https://bit.ly/2DoRgkp
10. Guglielmi, G. (2019). "Measles erases immune 'memory' for other diseases." *Nature*, October 31. www.nature.com/articles/d41586-019–03324-7
11. Haidt, J., & Rose-Stockwell, T. (2019). "The dark psychology of social networks." *The Atlantic*, December. https://bit.ly/2PfZFtc

12. Roberts, E. (2019). Socialism, not climate change, is the real threat. *RealClear Politics*, September 24. https://bit.ly/33mDn1e

13. Kentucky Coal and Energy Education Project. (2007). "10 reasons coal is a good energy source." www.coaleducation.org/q&a/10_reasons_why_coal.htm

14. Leslie, I. (2016). The sugar conspiracy. *The Guardian*, April 7. https://bit.ly/31bwPjb

15. Basu, Z. (2020). Sen. Rand Paul tests positive for coronavirus. *Axios*, March 23. https://bit.ly/330p10e

16. Jackson, S. (2019). 95 percent of baby foods tested contain toxic metals, new report says. *NBC News,* October 17. https://nbcnews.to/2Xq9NnI

17. Goodman, B. (2018). Roundup chemical in your cereal: What to know. *Web MD*, August 15. https://wb.md/2Ddd2b6

18. Dennis, S., & Fitzpatrick, S. (2016). Arsenic in rice and rice products: Risk assessment report. *US Food and Drug Administration (FDA)*, March. https://bit.ly/3gn2JzG

19. Stack, L. (2019). U.S. birthrate drops 4th year in a row, possibly echoing the great recession. *New York Times,* May 17. www.nytimes.com/2019/05/17/us/us-birthrate-decrease.html

20. "Sydney shrouded in bushfire smoke as Melbourne swelters (2019)." *The Guardian,* October 31. https://bit.ly/2XhiXmn

21. "Delhi air quality: Last day of odd-even but not relief yet, AQI hovers around 500-mark." (2019). *India Today,* November 15. https://bit.ly/33mvBnJ

22. Lu, D., & Flavelle, C. (2019). Rising seas will erase more cities by 2050, new research shows. *New York Times,* October 29. https://nyti.ms/3fsImQ1

23. "The power of water." Water.org. https://water.org/our-impact/water-crisis/

24. Centers for Disease Control and Prevention, National Center for Injury Prevention and Control. Web-based Injury Statistics Query and Reporting System (WISQARS). https://www.cdc.gov/ncipc/wisqars

25. Woodward, A. (2019). The "lungs of the planet" are burning at a record rate. If too much of the Amazon disappears, that "dieback" could turn the land into a savanna. *Business Insider*, August 22. https://bit.ly/2ELP72X

26. Friedman, L. (2020). Trump's move against landmark environmental law caps a relentless agenda. *New York Times,* January 9. https://nyti.ms/300We9T

27. O'Donnell, E. T. (2019). Are we living in the Gilded Age 2.0? History.com, January 31. www.history.com/news/second-gilded-age-income-inequality

28. Beitsch, R. (2019). Trump pulls out of landmark Paris climate agreement. *The Hill,* November 4. https://bit.ly/3hVInOa

29. Ripple, W. J., Wolf, C., Newsome, T. M., Barnard, P., & Moomaw, P. R. (2019). World scientists' warning of a climate emergency. *BioScience*, November 5. https://bit.ly/2EOf7Lf

30. Pierre-Louis, K. (2019). Climate change poses threats to children's health worldwide. *New York Times,* November 13. https://nyti.ms/31cLFG7

31. Spearman, C. (1904). "General intelligence," objectively determined and measured. *American Journal of Psychology*, 15, 201–92.

32. Kuhn, T. S. (2012). *The structure of scientific revolutions* (50th anniversary ed.). Chicago, IL: University of Chicago Press.

33. Nisbett, R. E. (2004). *The geography of thought: How Asians and Westerners think differently . . . and why.* New York: Free Press; Markus, H. R., & Conner, A. (2014). *Clash: How to thrive in a multicultural world.* New York: Plume.

34. Greenfield, P. M. (1997). You can't take it with you: Why ability assessments don't cross cultures. *American Psychologist,* 52(10), 1115–24. https://doi.org/10 .1037/0003-066X.52.10.1115

35. Flynn, J. R. (2007). *What is intelligence? Beyond the Flynn effect.* New York: Cambridge University Press; Aristotle. (2009). *The Nicomachean ethics.* New York: Oxford University Press.

36. Rivers, S. E., Handley-Miner, I. J., Mayer, J. D., & Caruso, D. R. (2020). Emotional intelligence. In R. J. Sternberg (Ed.), *Cambridge handbook of intelligence.* (2nd ed., pp. 709–35). New York: Cambridge University Press.

37. Kihlstrom, J. F., & Cantor, N. (2020). Social intelligence. In R. J. Sternberg (Ed.), *Cambridge handbook of intelligence (2nd ed., 756–79).* New York: Cambridge University Press.

38. Hedlund, J. (2020). Practical intelligence. In R. J. Sternberg (Ed.), *Cambridge handbook of intelligence (2nd ed., pp. 736–55).* New York: Cambridge University Press.

39. Greenfield, P. M. (2020). Historical evolution of intelligence. In R. J. Sternberg (Ed.), *Cambridge handbook of intelligence (2nd* ed., pp. 916–39). New York: Cambridge University Press.

40. Sternberg, R. J. (2020). Early history of theory and research on intelligence. In R. J. Sternberg (Ed.), *Human intelligence: An introduction* (pp. 47–64). New York: Cambridge University Press.

41. Deary, I. J., Whalley, L. J., & Starr, J. M. (2009). *A lifetime of intelligence: Follow-up studies of the Scottish Mental Surveys of 1932 and 1947.* Washington, DC: American Psychological Association.

42. Sternberg, R. J. (1997). *Successful intelligence.* New York: Plume.

43. American Psychological Association. (N.D.). *Education and socioeconomic status.* www.apa.org/pi/ses/resources/publications/education

44. Kaufman, A. S., Schneider, W. J., & Kaufman, J. C. (2020). Psychometric approaches to intelligence. In R. J. Sternberg (Ed.), *Human intelligence: An introduction* (pp. 67–103). New York: Cambridge University Press.

45. Sternberg, R. J. (1977). *Intelligence, information processing, and analogical reasoning: The componential analysis of human abilities.* Hillsdale, NJ: Erlbaum.

46. Cronbach, L. J. (1957). The two disciplines of scientific psychology. *American Psychologist,* 12(11), 671–84.

47. Genome News Network. (2003). *Genome variations.* GNN, January 15. http s://bit.ly/2PjkfJ5

48. Haier, R. J. (2020). Biological approaches to intelligence. In R. J. Sternberg (Ed.), *Human intelligence: An introduction* (pp. 139–73). New York:

Cambridge University Press; Tan, M., & Grigorenko, E. L. (2020). Genetics/ genomics and intelligence. In R. J. Sternberg (Ed.), *Human intelligence: An introduction* (pp. 227–52). New York: Cambridge University Press.

49. Shelley, P. B. (1818). Ozymandias. *Poetry Foundation*. www.poetryfoundation.o rg/poems/46565/ozymandias

50. House, R., Kalisch, D., & Maidman, J. (Eds.) (2017). *Humanistic psychology: Current trends and future prospects*. New York: Routledge.

51. Castles, E. E. (2012). *Inventing intelligence: How America came to worship IQ.* Westport, CT: Praeger.

52. Sternberg, R. J. (2004). Culture and intelligence. *American Psychologist*, 59(5), 325–38.

53. Bruner, F. G. (1912). The primitive races in America. *Psychological Bulletin*, 9 (10), 380–90. doi:10.1037/h0072417; Rushton, J. P. (2000). *Race, evolution, and behavior: A life history perspective* (abridged ed.). London, Ontario, Canada: Charles Darwin Research Institute; Lynn, R. (2016). *Race differences in intelligence: An evolutionary analysis*. Augusta, GA: Washington Summit Publishers.

54. Loehlin, J. C., Lindzey, G., & Spuhler, J. N. (1975). *Race differences in intelligence*. New York: W. H. Freeman; Neisser, U., Boodoo, G., Bouchard T. J. et al. (1996). Intelligence: Knowns and unknowns. *American Psychologist*, 51(2), 77–101; Daley, C. E., & Onwuegbuzie, A. J. (2020). Race and intelligence: It's not a black and white issue. In R. J. Sternberg (Ed.), *Cambridge handbook of intelligence* (2nd ed., pp. 373–94). New York: Cambridge University Press; Suzuki, L. A., Larson-Konar, D., Short, E. L., & Lee, C. S. (2020). Racial and ethnic group differences in intelligence in the United States: Multicultural perspectives. In R. J. Sternberg (Ed.), *Cambridge handbook of intelligence* (2nd ed., pp. 346–72). New York: Cambridge University Press.

55. Stenhouse, D. (1973). *The evolution of intelligence*. Sydney, Australia: Allen & Unwin; Itzkoff, S. W. (1983). *The form of man: The evolutionary origins of human intelligence*. New York: Paideia Publishing; Sternberg, R. J., & Kaufman, J. C. (Eds.) (2001). *The evolution of intelligence*. Mahwah, NJ: Lawrence Erlbaum Associates; Bates, L. A., & Byrne, R. W. (2020). The evolution of intelligence: Reconstructing the pathway to the human mind. In R. J. Sternberg (Ed.), *Cambridge handbook of intelligence* (2nd ed., pp. 428–50). New York: Cambridge University Press.

56. Gayle, D., & Murray, J. (2020). Coronavirus live: Global death toll passes 15,000 as WHO warns spread of virus is accelerating. *The Guardian*, March 23. https://bit.ly/3laib55

57. Warne, R. (2020). *In the know: Debunking 35 myths about human intelligence*. New York: Cambridge University Press.

CHAPTER 2

What Is Intelligence? A Panoply of Views

As discussed in Chapter 1, a lot of accounts of intelligence, including in textbooks, assume that intelligence is basically whatever it is that intelligence tests and their proxies – SAT, ACT, GRE, etc. – measure.[1] Other accounts talk about intelligence without even defining it. So, let us start with how intelligence is defined and see if it is really that simple. It certainly might seem like a simple issue – IQ tests as we know them have been around for more than a century. But really, what is intelligence? Is it nothing more than what IQ tests test?

When you meet some people, your reaction may well be that they are truly intelligent. Other people you meet may seem to be very dull and perhaps, at best, flickering bulbs. What exactly is the difference between people in the first group and those in the second group?

2.1 Expert Definitions by Psychologists

Although the difference between intelligent and not so intelligent people might seem straightforward, scholars of intelligence have tried for many years, with less than complete success, to pin down the difference. They simply have not reached any complete or even almost complete consensus as to just what the difference is. Rather, scholars have differed in their definitions of intelligence, and thus of what makes a person more or less intelligent.

One modern definition of intelligence attracted fifty-two scholars,[2] only some of them experts on intelligence, to sign onto it:

> A very general mental capability that, among other things, involves the ability to reason, plan, solve problems, think abstractly, comprehend complex ideas, learn quickly and learn from experience. It is not merely book learning, a narrow academic skill, or test-taking smarts. Rather, it reflects a broader and deeper capability for comprehending our surroundings – "catching on," "making sense" of things, or "figuring out" what to do.

27

That would seem to be a lot of signatories and a lot of agreement. And indeed, there are a number of aspects of the definition with which I believe most modern-day theorists would agree. For example, most theorists would agree that intelligence involves reasoning, problem-solving, abstract thinking, comprehension of complex or otherwise difficult ideas, and the ability to learn from experience, quickly when necessary. However, the article in which the definition appeared was rather controversial.

The statement was sent to 131 scholars in all, meaning that fewer than half signed on. The failure of other scholars to sign it may have pertained to other statements beyond the definition of intelligence in the full *Wall Street Journal* article. For example, one further claim in the article was that genetics plays a larger role in intelligence than does environment; another was that intelligence tests are not culturally biased. Statements such as these may have turned off some potential signers (including the author of this book), although it is hard to know exactly why most scholars requested to sign on ultimately did not sign. Another issue was that not all the scholars who signed actually studied human intelligence: All were experts, but in a variety of fields. Sometimes, experts have firm opinions beyond their own field, but those opinions are not "expert opinions" when the experts go outside their own field.

There have been many other definitions of intelligence over time and place. Alfred Binet and Theodore Simon, turn of the twentieth century French scholars, emphasized judgment, or good sense.[3] They also included in their definition one's ability to criticize oneself and to learn from one's mistakes. David Wechsler emphasized the ability to act purposefully, to think rationally, and to adapt to the environment.[4] Howard Gardner has spoken of the need to find, solve, and create problems, and one's ability to create effective products as required.[5] Linda Gottfredson, who led the group of fifty-two scholars that proposed the definition of intelligence given above, highlighted the ability to deal with complexity.

Attempts by psychologists to define intelligence go back to the early years of the twentieth century. In 1921, the *Journal of Educational Psychology* published a symposium, "Intelligence and Its Measurement," in which the authors, experts on intelligence, grappled with the question of what intelligence is.[6] They came up with diverse definitions. One was that intelligence is the power of good responses from the point of view of truth or facts (Edward L. Thorndike). A second definition was that intelligence is the ability to carry out abstract thinking (Lewis M. Terman). A third definition was that intelligence is the ability to learn and adjust oneself to the environment (S. S. Colvin). There were many more definitions.

Sixty-five years later, Robert Sternberg and Douglas Detterman asked two dozen experts to define intelligence.[7] They came up with definitions rather similar to the earlier ones. But in the more recent symposium, there was more emphasis on what sometimes is called "metacognition." This is one's understanding and control of one's cognition (e.g., memory, reasoning, problem-solving, etc.).

One of the most famous definitions of intelligence is that of Edwin G. Boring.[8] Boring argued that intelligence is what intelligence tests test. Such a definition is sometimes referred to as an "operational definition," because intelligence is defined in terms of an operation. The advantage of such a definition is that one gets a rather clear-cut basis for defining intelligence. It is what is measured as intelligence. The downside of such a definition, obviously, is that it is circular.[9] Intelligence tests are created to measure this thing called "intelligence." Then intelligence is in turn defined in terms of the tests that were created to measure the thing the tests were created to measure. Figure that one out!

There are other potential downsides to the operational definition of intelligence. Consider three.

First, the definition enshrines the intelligence test as the ultimate arbiter of what intelligence is. But different intelligence tests available at a given time do not all measure precisely the same thing. So, they do not definitively define intelligence, even as an operational definition.

Second, the nature of items on at least some of the tests has changed over the years. For example, arithmetic computation used to appear on some tests based on the work of Louis Thurstone and Thelma Gwinn Thurstone.[10] But in the age of electronic calculators and computers, arithmetic computation seems less important to some test constructors than it once did. So, it is less likely to appear on current tests. Indeed, the nature of intelligence itself seems to change over time.[11] Patricia Greenfield has suggested that what people have meant by intelligence, and what people need to be intelligent, both have changed over the course of time. In earlier times, and today still, in some societies, intelligence has been viewed as involving social responsibility, wise thinking, and possibly some kind of spirituality or connection to the natural and sometimes supernatural world.[12] In such a society, people might view an intelligent person as understanding the social norms and conventions of his or her society and contributing to that society in a way that benefits the society as a whole.[13] In more economically developed societies, the emphasis instead is on advanced cognitive skills, often involving thinking about complex and abstract matters outside their natural contexts, as the definition of the fifty-two scholars suggested. On this view, an intelligent person is one who can solve complex mathematical problems or who knows the meanings of a lot of abstract and possibly abstruse words.

Third, if, as some theorists believe, intelligence needs to be measured in different ways in different cultures, then necessarily intelligence is defined as being, at least in part, culturally specific.[14] This issue is discussed further below but consider a simple example that is relevant to current times. Consider the ability to spot predatory animals that are naturally camouflaged, such as certain kinds of snakes. This ability is essential in some environmental settings but not others. The ability is related to others that Howard Gardner might call "naturalist" intelligence.[15] In natural environments, naturalist abilities (or "naturalist intelligence," as Gardner would call it) are very important, whether for predator evasion or for hunting and gathering. But for someone living in New York City, Hong Kong, or Tokyo, such abilities matter much less. These people may encounter little of natural environments. People in these environments have their own challenges with predators, of course, but the challenges generally are different. Some of the contemporary predators may be more likely to go after people's bank accounts than to go after the people physically. Modern predators are likely to take different forms from naturally camouflaged snakes lying in the brush; and if these people hunt, it likely will be on a recreational trip, not on a trip necessary for daily sustenance.

It might seem that a definition as old and potentially as empty and even as boring as Boring's would go out of date fast. Yet the operational definition remains popular, as noted at the beginning of this chapter. One author of a book on intelligence pretty much opens his book with a detailed description of the most recent edition (fourth) of the Wechsler Adult Intelligence Scale (WAIS-IV).[16] An issue with this opening is that it can be seen as defining intelligence in terms of a test, instead of specifying what a test should measure in terms of a definition. Ancient philosophers did precisely that – they were concerned with what intelligence is in the real world, not with a test score.

2.2   Ancient Philosophical Conceptions of Intelligence

Of course, attempts to define intelligence did not start in the twentieth century. Homer, in the *Odyssey*, distinguished between good looks, on the one hand, and good thinking, on the other. He noted that one person may make a poor physical impression because he is unattractive. Yet he or she may nevertheless speak in an articulate and persuasive way. Another person may be good-looking and well-groomed. But at the same time, that person may lack the ability to communicate well with others.

Plato also reflected on the nature of intelligence and associated mental abilities. In the Platonic dialogue *Theaetetus*, the Greek philosopher Socrates asks Theaetetus, an interlocutor, to imagine something about the mind. In particular, imagine that there exists in the mind of each person a block of wax. The block is of different sizes in different people. The block of wax also can differ in various properties. These properties include hardness, moistness, and purity. Socrates, citing Homer, suggests that one possibility is that the wax is pure, clear, and deep. In this case, the mind easily will learn and retain information. It will not be subject to confusion. It only will think things that are true. And because the impressions in the wax are clear, these impressions will be distributed (by means not really specified) quickly into their proper places on the block of wax. But suppose instead that the wax is muddy or impure or very soft or very hard. Then there will be defects of the intellect. People whose wax is soft will be good at learning. But they will be apt to forget things. Then there will be people whose balls of wax are shaggy and rugged or gritty, or whose wax has an admixture of earth or dung. These people's balls of wax will have only indistinct impressions. Those with hard wax will have the same problem because there will be no depth to their thoughts. But things are not much better if the wax is too soft. Then the impressions will be indistinct. That is because those impressions easily can be confused or remolded.

Aristotle also had some fairly well-formed views about the nature of intelligence. In the *Posterior Analytics Book 1*, he conceived of intelligence in terms of "quick wit." For example, suppose an intelligent person sees someone in conversation with a man of wealth. That intelligent person might conclude quickly that the "someone" is seeking to borrow money from the man of wealth. An interesting feature of this conception is that Aristotle is implicitly recognizing that intelligence is not just cognitive (or mental), but also social in nature.

2.3 Lay (Popular) Definitions

Of course, one does not have to ask experts what they believe intelligence to be. One also can ask laypeople. Why should one ask laypeople? After all, when all is said and done, they have no expertise at all in the field of intelligence. The answer is simple: The overwhelming majority of judgments about people's intelligence are not made by experts but rather by laypeople. These laypeople have never formally studied intelligence at all.

Nevertheless, laypeople make judgments all the time. They do so when they hire people for jobs and later, perhaps, when they fire people from those same jobs. They also make judgments about intelligence when they go out on dates, or consider going out on dates, or perhaps getting married. In each of these instances, they may seek a partner who is as intelligent as they are. Or they may want to be more intelligent than their partner – or less intelligent! Parents make judgments about their children, just as the children make judgments about their parents. Adults make judgments about intelligence when they decide whom to hire to work on their house, their car, or their health. In short, most judgments in the world about intelligence are not the result of scores on standardized tests but rather the result of informal judgments laypeople make in their daily lives.

My colleagues and I studied people's conceptions of intelligence.[17] (These studies looked at particular groups of Westerners; conceptions of people in other cultures are considered later in this chapter.) The findings boiled down to three factors in people's conceptions of intelligence: practical problem-solving, verbal ability, and social competence. These lay conceptions, then, have more of a real-world, everyday slant than at least some of the expert definitions. Laypeople in the United States (and, as it turns out, in other cultures) place more emphasis than do experts on intelligence as it manifests itself in everyday use. How do experts see intelligence?

2.4   What Is the History of Ideas About What Intelligence Is?

Psychologists have a long history of trying to understand what intelligence is. Consider some of the more classical approaches.

2.4.1   A Psychophysical Approach

Psychological ideas about the nature of intelligence date back to the work of Sir Francis Galton (1822–1911), a British scientist. Galton believed that intelligence is a function of psychophysical abilities. These abilities include attributes such as strength, hand-eye coordination, pitch sensitivity, and the like. For several years, Galton maintained an at-the-time modern, well-equipped anthropometric laboratory (a laboratory that measures various aspects of the human body) at the Kensington Museum in London. At the lab, visitors could subject themselves to being measured for their level of skill on a variety of psychophysical tests. These tests allowed the visitors to assess themselves for a broad range of psychophysical skills and sensitivities. One example of a test was weight discrimination. This test measured the ability to notice small differences in the weights of various objects. Another example of a test was pitch sensitivity. This test measured the ability to hear small differences between musical notes. A third example of one of Galton's tests was an assessment of physical strength.[18]

An ardent follower of Galton was a professor at Columbia University, James McKeen Cattell. Cattell brought many of Galton's ideas over from England to the United States. Unfortunately for Cattell, a student of his, Clark Wissler, decided to test Cattell's tests. Wissler attempted to detect relations between the various psychophysical tests. He also looked at the relations of the psychophysical tests to academic performance at Columbia University.[19] He hoped that the discovery of such relations would show some kind of unity in the various dimensions of psychophysically based intelligence. But Wissler detected no unity. The various psychophysical tests were barely correlated with each other. Moreover, the psychophysical tests used by Cattell failed accurately to predict college grades. Thus, Galton's psychophysical approach to assessing intelligence soon faded almost into oblivion. From time to time, there have been attempts to bring back the approach, but with little success.

There is an irony in the work of Wissler: His results appear to have been correct. But his methodology was seriously flawed. First, correlations tend to be low when there is a restriction of range in a variable. For example, height is, in general, a good predictor of basketball skill. But it is not a good predictor among professional basketball players, who almost all are quite tall to begin with. There just is not that much variation in heights among professional basketball players, at least relative to the general population. Wissler tested only Columbia University students. Columbia students could be expected to be within a restricted range of intelligence, much like the pro basketball players who typically are within a restricted range of height. Second, the measures Wissler used were of doubtful reliability. That is, if you took the test on one day, your score might be quite different from what it would be on another day. So, it is not clear that the tests could have had high correlations with anything. Whatever the case may be, investigators in France had other ideas about the nature of intelligence.

2.4.2 A Judgment-Based Approach

Contemporary measurements of intelligence had their start with Albert Binet and his associate Theodore Simon in France, mentioned above. They believed that higher level, judgmental abilities, not lower level psychophysical ones, provide the keys to understanding intelligence. These abilities include thinking, reasoning, and problem-solving.[20] Thus, Binet and Simon started an intellectual tradition distinct from that of Galton and Cattell.[21] Binet and Simon emphasized complex rather than simple information processing as a basis for understanding intelligence.

The Ministry of Public Education in Paris, France, asked Binet to devise a procedure for distinguishing normal learners from slow learners. As a result, Binet and Simon set out to measure intelligence as a function of the ability to learn and think within an academic setting. They devised a test based on an individual's ability to learn, reason, and show good judgment. Thus, they measured skills like vocabulary, arithmetic problem-solving, and spatial visualization, among many others. Lewis Terman of Stanford University in the United States built on Binet and Simon's work in Europe. He constructed the earliest version of what is today known as the Stanford–Binet Intelligence Scale.[22]

Galton and Binet started with distinct conceptions of intelligence, either as psychophysically or judgmentally based, respectively. After them, many later researchers turned to a specific methodology to derive theories of intelligence – factor analysis. Instead of starting with a theory and contriving tests, therefore, they started with tests and then contrived theories. In some ways, their approach harked back to that of Boring in that, rather than starting with a conception of intelligence, many of them started with tests of intelligence.

2.5   Metaphors of Mind

There are different ways to conceive of intelligence. These different ways can, in a sense, be viewed as "metaphors of mind." What a scholar or anyone else "means by" intelligence depends in large part upon the metaphor of mind to which he or she adheres, perhaps without even thinking much about it.[23] These metaphors are briefly described here and will be elaborated upon throughout the book. The first of the metaphors to be considered is a geographic one.

2.5.1   *The Geographic Metaphor: Intelligence as a Map of the Mind*

The most widely known metaphor is what I have called a *geographic* one. This metaphor is also called a *psychometric* or *test-based* one.[24] The idea underlying this metaphor is that the mind can be viewed much as can be a map. It has different regions. Each region tends to understand and produce different kinds of things. One region might handle verbal tasks, another, mathematical tasks, and still another, spatial-orientation tasks. Of course, these regions may work together on many tasks, just as different regions of a country do. But the goal is to understand the geography and topography of the mind. Then one can use that information to determine how abilities are organized. One further can understand how people use abilities to greater or lesser effect. This is the metaphor that has been used by IQ testers ever since the beginning of the twentieth century.

2.5.1.1 The Theory of General Intelligence

Charles Spearman (1863–1945), an English psychologist, invented a statistical technique mentioned briefly above called *factor analysis*. This technique analyzes correlations (relations) among tests. It purports to identify the psychological sources of individual differences underlying the tests. Spearman discovered that a single general factor seemed to pervade performance on all tests of mental ability.[25] To Spearman, the general factor, which he labeled "*g*," provides the key to understanding intelligence. Spearman believed "*g*" to be a direct consequence of "mental energy," a belief that has been highly influential.[26] Spearman asserted that each psychometric test loaded on (was related to) the general factor. Each test also loaded on a factor specific to that test. He called each of the specific factors "*s*." Thus, his theory is sometimes referred to as a "two-factor theory," although in fact it refers not to two factors but rather to two types of factors.

2.5.1.2 The Theory of Bonds

Godfrey Thomson had a different idea about why all psychometric tests seem to intercorrelate positively with each other.[27] This generally positive relationship about which Thomson theorized is sometimes called a *positive manifold*. He proposed that, in fact, there is no psychological meaningful single general factor (one underlying ability) that encompasses all of the tests. The single factor that appeared in Spearman's work is essentially a chimera. Rather, according to Thomson, there are very large numbers of "bonds," or independent elements. Together, these elements are sampled by many of the psychometric tests. The bonds give the appearance of a single entity when in fact there are many diverse entities that just happen to be sampled at the same time. Edward Lee Thorndike had a similar idea.[28] He believed that shared associations that are formed in associative learning could explain much of intelligence. In this case, an example of associative learning would be to associate the word "cow" with "milk." So,

Thomson, like Spearman, believed in the existence of a general statistical factor, but not of a general psychological ability (g). In his view, the general statistical factor obscured the many independent elements that contributed to it.

2.5.1.3 Primary Mental Abilities

Louis Thurstone came to believe that intelligence comprises seven primary mental abilities.[29] A first ability is verbal comprehension, that is, understanding meanings of words and texts. A second, related ability is verbal fluency, or producing words as rapidly as needed, such as in speaking or writing. A third ability is number, or arithmetic computation and problem-solving. A fourth ability is spatial relations, involved, for example, in rotating figures in one's mind. A fifth ability is perceptual speed, as in discerning rapidly the letters or words before one. A sixth ability is memory, or remembering symbols, words, numbers, and so forth. And a seventh ability is inductive reasoning, or predicting the future from the past, as in a number-series problem. These abilities tend to be related to or correlated with each other. Thus, if one "factors the factors" – that is, does a factor analysis on the factors – one ends up with a general factor.

Spearman eventually convinced Thurstone of the existence of some kind of general factor. But Thurstone believed it to be secondary to understanding the nature of intelligence. There was no way, at least at the time, of truly saying whether Spearman's general factor or Thurstone's primary mental abilities truly were more "basic" in any meaningful sense.

2.5.1.4 Structure of Intellect

The field of intelligence learned an important lesson as a result of a so-called "structure of intellect" model proposed by J. P. Guilford.[30] Guilford suggested that there are 120 (later, 150, and still later, 180!) independent factors of intelligence. He argued that the factors array themselves in a cube, according to processes, contents, and products. For example, one ability would be cognition (process) of verbal (content) relations (product). John Horn and John Knapp later showed Guilford's factor-analytical methods to be artifactual. That is, they were statistically invalid.[31] Guilford, for most theorists, then went from being considered a major theorist of intelligence to becoming a scientifically misguided historical curiosity. Today, Guilford is more well-known for his impetus to research in the field of creativity than he is for his work on intelligence.[32]

2.5.1.5 Radex Model

Louis Guttman proposed quite a different model of intelligence, which he referred to as a "radex."[33] The radex model uses polar rather than Cartesian coordinates to understand intelligence. Imagine a circle. Nearer the center (focus) of the circle are those abilities that are more central to intelligence, such as general intelligence, which is right at the center. As one moves away from the center of the circle, one finds the abilities that are less central. Different conventional abilities, such as verbal, numerical, and spatial abilities, then are arrayed along the periphery of the radex (the circle). In terms of polar coordinates, the coordinate corresponding to closeness to general intelligence is the distance from the center of the circle, and the coordinate corresponding to the kind of ability is the angular coordinate.

2.5.1.6 Hierarchical Models

Today, psychologists who specialize in tests of intelligence believe there is more to intelligence than just *g*. These psychologists have created an economical and statistically defensible way of dealing with a number of factors of the mind. This way is through hierarchical models of intelligence.

One hierarchical model, proposed by Raymond Cattell, suggests that there are two particularly important abilities. They are *fluid ability* and *crystallized ability*.[34] Fluid ability is measured as a person's speed and accuracy of abstract reasoning, especially when dealing with novel problems. Crystallized ability is assessed by measuring accumulated knowledge and vocabulary. A similar model proposed by Philip E. Vernon argued instead for two different factors.[35] The first is what Vernon called verbal: educational ability, which roughly comprises the kinds of verbal, mathematical, and reasoning skills valued by schools. The second ability is kinesthetic: mechanical, roughly the kinds of skills used in mental rotation, mental visualization of three-dimensional structures, and so forth.

A more recent model proposed by John B. Carroll is a hierarchy comprising three strata.[36] Stratum I involves many narrow, specific abilities. These include, for example, spelling ability and speed of reasoning. Stratum II involves various broad abilities. They include, for example, fluid intelligence and crystallized intelligence. (Recall that fluid intelligence is a person's ability to cope with novel situations and to reason abstractly. Crystallized intelligence refers to a person's knowledge base, such as for vocabulary and general information.) And Stratum III comprises just a single general intelligence. This general intelligence is essentially Spearman's *g*. Of these strata, the most interesting is the middle stratum, which is neither too narrow nor too all-encompassing.

In addition to fluid intelligence and crystallized intelligence, Carroll included in the middle stratum several other abilities. They are:

g_f = fluid intelligence (ability to think flexibly and handle novel stimuli)
g_c = crystallized intelligence (knowledge base)
g_v = broad visual perception
g_a = broad auditory perception
g_y = general memory and learning
g_r = broad retrieval ability (recalling information from memory)
g_s = broad cognitive speediness
g_t = reaction time and decision speed (making rapid selections of simple information)

Carroll's model is rather widely accepted today. A more recent version, sometimes called CHC theory (an acronym for Cattell-Horn-Carroll), is perhaps even more widely accepted, and integrates Cattell's earlier theory with Carroll's later one.[37]

Not all psychometrically oriented theorists accept the Carroll model or the CHC model. Wendy Johnson and Thomas J. Bouchard proposed an alternative hierarchical model, the VPR model. They proposed that below general intelligence there are three factors in the second level of the hierarchy, verbal, perceptual, and image rotation (hence, VPR).[38]

There are four aspects of factor-analytic models worth considering. They show the kinds of assumptions inherent in factorially derived theories of intelligence.

First, as mentioned earlier, one starts with test data and then derives a theory based on the data, rather than vice versa. So, the theory starts not with some conception of the mind, in general, or of intelligence, in particular, but with test scores.

Second, the theory can be only as good as those test scores. The theory assumes that the test is measuring intelligence, and presumably, pretty much only intelligence and not a bunch of irrelevant factors. This book will question that assumption from multiple points of view and sources of evidence.

Third, factor analysis analyzes statistical regularities in data. Interesting as statistical regularities are, they do not automatically produce psychological interpretations. For example, there are many possible interpretations of the so-called general factor of intelligence – as mental energy, mental power, speed of neuronal conduction, accuracy, or neuronal conduction, and so on. One has to be very careful about reifying what is, at its base, a statistical phenomenon.

Fourth, identifying factors depends on the existence of individual differences. If there are no individual differences in an ability, or at least no discernible ones, then factor analysis will not identify the ability. If one had only a set of identical twins in the world, one would have great difficulty identifying their abilities by factor analysis, or if there was only one person left on a desert island, one would be totally unable to identify the abilities of the person on the island.[39]

Fifth, and finally, factor analysis of mental tests is, in a certain way, an extremely conservative procedure. It may be that it is time to rethink what intelligence is for the early twenty-first century as opposed to the early twentieth century. Today, some skills matter less than before. Arithmetic computation and spelling are obvious examples because of the advent of computers that can do very fast computations and can correct spelling errors. Other skills matter more, such as finding information in far-flung data bases and analyzing the validity of information that has not been vetted (such as by schools, libraries, newspaper or magazine editors). Someone might be quite good at twentieth-century skills and yet fail miserably at twenty-first-century ones. Indeed, arguably, many people are that way, good at understanding vetted information but unable to distinguish false and worthless information on the Internet from valid and useful information. They might thus perform well on an IQ test but not in their daily lives.

2.5.1.7 What Is IQ?

In practice, the psychometric approach of the geographic metaphor manifests itself through the use of IQ. IQ is an abbreviation for "intelligence quotient." IQ is referred to as a quotient because it originally was computed in that way – as:

IQ = (mental age/chronological age) × 100

Chronological age (also called "CA") is simply one's physical age, usually expressed in physical years and months, for example 6 years, 0 months (or "6–0"). Mental age (also called "MA") refers to level of mental functioning. If someone has a chronological age of 6 and a mental age of 6, that someone's IQ is 100. But suppose the individual's level of mental functioning is comparable to that of an eight-year-old. Then his or her IQ would be 133 (8/6 × 100).

Intelligence testing as we know it and the concept of mental age were introduced by Alfred Binet and Theodore Simon in 1905 but the concept of *intelligence quotient* was introduced later by German psychologist William Stern in 1912.

Why even have an intelligence quotient? Well, the idea was that Binet's concept of mental age was useful for telling educators or others at what mental level an individual was functioning. But it was not so useful for telling anyone how intelligent a child of a certain age was in comparison with other children of the same age. In the above example, the child of six was performing at the level of an average eight-year-old, which is clearly above average. But how much above average? The IQ of 133 suggests that the child is *a lot above average*. But again, by how much?

Tables were constructed to tell educators and others how to interpret IQs. For example, an IQ of 100 would represent the 50th percentile. The 50th percentile represents an average (or, to be precise, a median) score. It means that half the individuals who take the test score above an IQ of 100; half score below. A score of 133 is very high – between the 98th and 99th percentiles. This percentile range means that in a sample of 100 individuals, between 1 percent and 2 percent would achieve a score this high. At the other side of the distribution, a score of 67 (gotten by subtracting 33 points from an IQ of 100) would be very low. That level of IQ is achieved by fewer than 2 percent of people at the bottom of the IQ distribution. Table 2.1 shows a breakdown of how IQs sort themselves out. The table is based in

Table 2.1 *Verbal descriptions of IQ ranges*

145–160. **Highly advanced or highly gifted**. The individual is way above average in intellectual level and is capable of very highly advanced work.

130–144. **Gifted or very advanced**. The individual is well beyond the average in intellectual level and is capable of very advanced work.

120–129. **Superior**. The individual is substantially above average in intellectual level and is capable of advanced work.

110–119. **High average**. The individual is slightly above average in intellectual level and is capable of doing age-appropriate work at a slightly above-average level.

90–109. **Average**. The individual is roughly average in intellectual level and is capable of doing age-appropriate work at a typical level.

80–89. **Low average**. The individual is slightly below average in intellectual level and is capable of doing age-appropriate work at a slightly below-average level.

70–79. **Borderline intellectually disabled**. The individual is capable of functioning toward the bottom of the normal level and may need remedial work.

55–69. **Mildly intellectually challenged**. The individual is functioning below the normal level and likely will need remedial work, which nevertheless may not or may not bring her up to a normal level of functioning.

40–54. **Moderately intellectually challenged**. The individual is functioning well below the normal level and likely will need intensive remediation to reach a minimal standard of performance.

Below 40. **Severely intellectually challenged**. The individual is functioning at a level that will make intellectually normal performance nearly impossible. The individual probably will require assistance to do many intellectual tasks.

part according to the manual of the Stanford–Binet Intelligence Scales (5th ed.).[40]

The idea of a so-called "ratio IQ" (the ratio between mental age and chronological age multiplied by 100) once was very attractive because it was so simple. One could compare two children and directly infer how intelligent each is in comparison with the other. IQ scores, it was thought, could be used for many things. For example, educators believed they could be used for identification of an individual as gifted, or as having a general intellectual disability (formerly called "mental retardation"). Or suppose a specific achievement score was relatively much lower, such as in reading, than the IQ. Then a child might be diagnosed as having a specific learning disability.

As is so often the case in psychology and, really, in life, things that seem to be simple prove, in the end, to be more complex than they initially seemed to be. So it was with IQ.

The first difficulty the concept of mental-age-based IQ encountered is that, although mental ages increase in childhood, after a certain point (as mentioned earlier), the increase slows down and even stops. So, it became apparent rather quickly that the mental-age concept required for the computation of a ratio IQ was in some sense defective. It just did not work at higher ages. The exact age at which development slows down is not clear. Usually, intelligence tests placed them somewhere between fifteen years six months and eighteen years. That is, after about age sixteen, chronological ages were fixed at sixteen (or fifteen years six months or whatever).

The second difficulty with the concept of IQ is that mental ages not only decrease in their rate of increase, but usually start to decrease in older age. The exact age, again, is a matter of dispute – actually, great dispute. Some kinds of intelligence seem to start showing gradual declines in the thirties, others not until the sixties, seventies, or even eighties. Moreover, the point at which the decline starts differs for different people. As individuals grow older, the differences in their rates of decrease in mental functioning differ profoundly. And if one of the individuals stays intellectually active and mentally challenges him or herself on a regular basis, some abilities may continue to increase even into old age.

The third difficulty is that it is not clear that mental ages show a *continuous* increasing trend. The assumption of IQ measurement is that differences in mental age are continuous – that an increase of six months means the same thing at any age level. On this view, an increase of six months at age five means the same thing in terms of intellectual growth as an increase of six months at age ten. But stage theories call this view into question. Many such theories view intellectual growth as discontinuous, meaning that intellectual growth moves along in fits and starts. Hence, increases at different ages may mean quite different things in terms of intellectual growth. Although one can question Jean Piaget's theory of intellectual development or any other stage theory of intellectual development as well, there is at least some reason to believe that intellectual development is not fully continuous, and hence, that the idea of a smooth increase in mental age is flawed. For example, children do not show continuity in language development, but rather show bursts as they develop. For a few months they may seem to show little development and then, all of a sudden, they seem to spurt upward in their language skills.

The fourth difficulty with the mental-age concept is that the use of mental ages led some people to draw incorrect conclusions about the nature of the IQ scale. Age is expressed on what is called a "ratio scale." A physical age of zero actually means something tangible. One is counted as age zero the moment one comes into the world. Of course, one could start counting earlier, say, to the moment of conception. But there is still a moment at which conception occurs and at which age post-conception starts being meaningful. This is not the case with IQ, however. A zero IQ does not mean that a person has "no intelligence." Rather, if someone scores 0 on an IQ test, it probably means that the test did not adequately measure his or her intelligence.

IQ is, at best, on what is called an "interval scale." The additive differences between scores are probably meaningful (a difference of ten points is, in theory, twice as great as a difference of five points). But the multiplicative differences are *not* meaningful – an IQ of 120 is not meaningfully twice as high as an IQ of 60. This is because there is no meaningful zero reference point. It is not even clear what "twice as smart" means. In contrast, a person who is twice as old or twice as tall as another really is double the other in some meaningful way. For example, someone who is six feet tall is meaningfully double the height of someone three feet tall.

As a result of these challenges for the ratio IQ measure, test publishers long ago generally stopped using mental ages and ratio IQs. Rather, they started to use a so-called "normal distribution" to calculate IQs. The normal distribution is a distribution that occurs often in nature.

The large majority of IQs are near the center of the IQ distribution, and then IQs tail off as one goes higher or lower in the distribution. In a normal distribution, the average IQ is at the 50th percentile (half of the scores are

Table 2.2 *Percentile
equivalents of some
IQ scores*

IQ	Percentile
60	<01
65	01
70	02
75	05
80	09
85	16
90	25
95	37
100	50
105	63
110	75
115	84
120	91
125	95
130	98
135	99
140	>99

higher, half are lower), so that average IQ is set to 100. Table 2.2 shows some approximate percentile equivalents for various IQs.

But what exactly does IQ measure? Edwin Boring, as noted earlier in this chapter, believed that intelligence is whatever it is that IQ tests measure. Some contemporary theorists, however, consider IQ to be a limited measure of intelligence.

When I was a student in elementary school during the late 1950s, many schools did group IQ testing of all their students on a fairly regular basis. Today, such testing is gone. What happened?

First, the concept of IQ came to appear to some to be fairly rigid. Binet likely would not have been interested in a concept of IQ. Mental ages are flexible. Binet believed in the malleability of intelligence. So, he might have found the idea of IQ too limiting.[41]

Second, there were a number of legal challenges to the use of IQ testing, especially for children of under-represented minority status.[42] For example, it became unclear whether a given score meant the same thing for a child that lived in a household where parents were relatively uneducated versus a household where parents were highly educated.

Third, for some educators, the idea of an IQ became rather toxic. Schools sometimes had been using IQs as though they set some kind of absolute upper limit on what a child could accomplish. And such an upper limit could be discouraging to a school or a teacher seeking to bring out the best in each student.

Fourth, schools discovered that they could accomplish much the same thing that they had accomplished with IQ simply by using tests with other names. At the same time that reliance on IQ tests decreased, reliance on standardized tests increased. But the tests were called achievement tests, or mastery tests, or college-admissions tests, or whatever. It was possible to accomplish the same, often not so positive goals, with tests that had societally more acceptable labels. Essentially, these newer tests are proxies for IQ tests. In a sense, they launder IQ scores, giving roughly the same information but presenting it in a more socially acceptable way.

Eventually, many schools moved on and began using IQ tests, mostly individually administered, only for special purposes, such as for special-education placements. And that is where things are today. But as we shall see later, even some of those uses are questionable. They raise as many questions as they answer.

Not everyone has accepted the geographic metaphor. Indeed, Jean Piaget originally was trained by Alfred Binet but was disillusioned by Binet's focusing on right answers rather than wrong answers. Piaget felt that one learned much more about the development of intelligence from children's errors than from their correct responses.

2.5.2   The Developmental Metaphor: The Piagetian Approach

Jean Piaget believed that the function of cognitive development, in general, and of intelligence, in particular, is to aid in adaptation to the environment. Piaget thought in terms of a continuum of increasingly complex responses to the environment.[43] Piaget further proposed that both intelligence and its manifestations in behavior become increasingly differentiated with age.

Most theorists of intelligence were part of some kind of movement. Jean Piaget, in contrast, was pretty much a force unto himself. He called his approach *genetic epistemology*. The approach, which emphasized cognitive development, was based on a notion of equilibration.

Piaget believed that development occurs in stages that evolve through equilibration. Equilibration is a process of cognitive development in which children seek a balance (equilibrium) between what the environment offers in an encounter and what the child brings to the encounter.

In some situations, a given child's existing ways of thinking, or what Piaget called "schemas," are adequate for confronting and adapting to the challenges of the environment. The child is thereby in a state of equilibrium. At other times, however, information does not fit with the child's existing schemas. Rather, the information creates cognitive disequilibrium. This disequilibrium derives from shortcomings in thinking as the child encounters new challenges. Thus, disequilibrium is more likely to occur during transitions between stages of development.

According to Piaget, equilibration involves two processes: assimilation and accommodation. *Assimilation* is a process of regaining cognitive equilibrium by incorporating new information into existing schemas. For example, a very young child, seeing a cat for the first time, might call it a "doggie," thinking that all pets are "doggies." Piaget suggested that the child would modify existing schemas through *accommodation*. This is the process of responding to cognitive disequilibrium by modifying relevant schemas. The old schemas thus are adapted to fit the new information and reestablish equilibrium. An older child might recognize that the cat does not fit the schema for dogs. That child therefore might create a modified conceptual schema in which cats and dogs are viewed as distinct kinds of pets. Together, the processes of assimilation and accommodation produce a more sophisticated level of thought than was previously possible. In addition, these processes reestablish equilibrium. They offer the individual higher levels of adaptability. The cognitive perspective that follows was in part a reaction to the psychometric approach, which was viewed as too structural and without a clear elucidation of processes. But it was also in part a reaction to Piaget. Piaget was viewed as too oriented toward idealized competencies and not enough toward actual real-world performance.

Piaget also suggested that there are four major stages of intellectual development. The first, the sensorimotor stage, begins at birth and extends until roughly two years of age. During this stage, the child learns how to modify reflexes – inborn responses to stimuli – to make them more adaptive. The child also learns to coordinate actions, to retrieve objects that are hidden (including, deliberately), and, eventually, to begin representing information mentally. During the second, or preoperational stage, from about age two to age seven years, the child experiences development of language and also of mental imagery. The child further learns how to focus on a single perceptual dimension, such as shape or color. The third, concrete-operational stage lasts from about seven to twelve years of age. During this stage, a child develops so-called "conservation skills." That is, the child will recognize that amounts of substances stay the same, regardless of their form. If you reshape a ball of clay, the ball still has the same amount of clay, regardless of its shape. Finally, children emerge into the fourth, formal-operational stage, which begins at roughly age twelve and continues, in theory, throughout the individual's life. The formal-operational child learns to think and, especially, to reason with abstract concepts. For example, the child can understand analogies or what member of a group of numbers does not belong with the others.

There have been many challenges to Piaget's theory. I mention only a few of the major ones here.

One challenge to Piaget's theory is methodological. The data for the theory were largely clinical observations of Piaget's own children. For most scientists, observational data are a perfectly good starting point, but they need to be followed up by detailed experimentation or other controlled research. Piaget never did the research that would give people confidence that the results held up to tight experimentation. Successors, however, did engage in such research.

A second challenge to Piaget is the set of results of such follow-up research. When investigators sought to confirm or disconfirm Piaget's theory, they discovered that it was at least somewhat problematical. In general, the consistent finding was that children were able to perform cognitive operations at ages earlier than Piaget indicated they should be able to.[44]

A third to challenge to Piaget is the whole idea of stages.[45] Does development really occur in discrete stages or is development more or less continuous? Although the development of some behavior seems stage-like – for example, conservation of volume – other kinds of behavioral development, such as of vocabulary or of arithmetic-processing skills, seem to be largely continuous. At best, Piaget seems to oversimplify the complexity of development, which may admit to both stage-like and continuous aspects in different domains.

A fourth challenge to Piaget, even among those who accept stages, is whether the stages Piaget had proposed are the correct ones. These objections have taken two forms. One is that the stages are a good start but not an accurate representation of cognitive development.[46] A second objection is that the stages end too early – that there are one or more stages of cognitive development beyond formal operations. For example, it has suggested that a fifth stage might be problem finding, that is, not just solving problems, but figuring out which problems are worth solving.[47] Another interpretation is that a fifth stage might involve seeing higher-order relations beyond the second, that is, third-order relations such as the relation between two analogies.[48]

A fifth challenge concerns the utility of the theory, given that it is a maturational theory. Piaget believed that development is a result of maturation, that is, of a genetic program unfolding over time. This view means, first, that environment matters little in development, and second and as a consequence, that one can do little to advance a child's development beyond what he or she is "ready for." Such a view has as an advantage the same thing that is a disadvantage. One is prone to realize that there are some cognitive tasks that children just are not ready for; but at the same time, one may fail adequately to challenge children, believing they just are not "ready for the challenge."

The sixth and final challenge, for our purposes, is a cultural one. The data have been mixed on whether Piaget's theory generalizes across cultures. But there are enough data suggesting failure of generalization that some researchers became skeptical, early on, regarding just how generalizable the theory is.[49]

It might sound, from this rather extensive critique, as though Piaget's theory was yet another flash-in-the-pan theory that was so flawed that one can hardly, in retrospect, figure out why the theory generated so much attention. But that would be reaching for too quick a conclusion. Although not entirely original,[50] Piaget's theory was one of the most influential psychological theories of the twentieth century, and with good reason. It introduced a new way of perceiving intellect and its development. Contemporary psychological theories are works in process – they are not final depictions of the psychological functioning of humans or other organisms. Anyone in science who believes he or she has final answers misunderstands the scientific method. The value of Piaget's theory is shown not so much in whether it was finally correct, but rather in its influence on the field. Piaget is one of the most highly cited authors in the field of psychology, exceeded perhaps only by Sigmund Freud (who was not a psychologist, but then, neither was Piaget!). Thus, the theory has been tremendously influential even if it has not proved to be anything close to a final word on how intelligence develops. No theory provides a final word. Piaget's theory, in many ways, served as a precursor for the computational theories that were to follow.

2.5.3   *The Computational Metaphor: Intelligence as Information Processing*

A third metaphor is a computational one.[51] The idea here is that intelligence can best be understood when the mind is viewed as a sophisticated computer. Intelligence, on this view, is largely computational. More intelligent people are either faster computers or have better algorithms and heuristics (convenient, but not necessarily foolproof, methods) for solving problems. The computer metaphor allows for both serial processing (one thing considered after another) and for parallel processing (many things considered at once).

The computational metaphor, at least in the field of intelligence, dates back to the work of Charles Spearman, a British psychologist.[52] Spearman proposed what he offered as three fundamental "qualitative" principles of cognition:

1 *Apprehension of experience.* This principle is essentially the same as what we would call perceptual processing today. It is seeing or hearing something and then encoding it in the mind in a way that makes it recognizable and understandable. For example, if you see a bear, you encode it as a large, probably brown, and possibly dangerous animal that is known to hibernate in the winter.
2 *Eduction of relations.* This is the process of inferring the relations between two things. For example, if you see the words "bear" and "animal," you might think of the relation that a bear is an animal. If you see "bear" and "hibernate," you might think that a bear hibernates in the winter.
3 *Eduction of correlates.* This is the process of applying a relation, perhaps one you just inferred, to a new situation. For example, if you think about a bear being an animal, you might think of groundhogs as also being animals that hibernate.

Spearman thought that the analogy offered the perfect model for understanding the processes of intelligence. An analogy takes the form, A is to B as C is to D, or as it is sometimes written, A : B :: C : D. Analogies have been used since the times of Spearman to measure intelligence, and they are often found on group tests of intelligence. An example of an analogy that might be found on such a test is MAPLE : DECIDUOUS :: PINE : (a) TREE, (b) NEEDLES, (c) EVERGREEN, (d) NORTHERN.

Spearman also proposed some "quantitative" principles of cognition. The most important, from the standpoint of the history of the field of intelligence, was *mental energy*. He believed mental energy to be the mind's "total simultaneous cognitive output constant in quantity, however varying in quality" (p. 131). Mental energy became the basis for his view that intelligence can be understood primarily in terms of a single general factor of intelligence (g), which he believed represented individual differences among people in mental energy.

Spearman argued that these processes best can be understood in terms of the solution of an analogy, such as FLY : INSECT :: FROG : AMPHIBIAN. In this instance, one apprehends experience when one encodes the meaning of each word in the analogy. One educes relations when one figures out how FLY is related to INSECT. One educes correlates when one applies the relation of FLY to INSECT (class membership) from FROG to AMPHIBIAN.

A well-known contemporary and rival of Spearman, Louis Thurstone, a professor at the University of Chicago mentioned earlier in this chapter, also suggested a computational basis for intelligence even before he proposed his notion of primary mental abilities.[53] His suggestion was that intelligence involves the ability to inhibit an instinctive response. This suggestion later formed the basis for an evolutionary theory of intelligence.[54] The idea was that all organisms have instincts that have evolved over eons of time. These instincts operate automatically. Most of the time they are adaptive but some of the time they get us in trouble (whether we are humans or other animals). For example, all of us have instinctively said or done things that, upon reflection, we view as incredibly stupid. "How could we have done such a stupid thing?," we wonder. On this view, the more intelligent individuals are able to inhibit these instinctive responses before they cause trouble.

What is important about the early work on the computational metaphor, as illustrated by the theorizing of Spearman and Thurstone, is that it might have formed the basis for much of the theory, research, and testing that was immediately to follow, but it did not. It more or less died on the vine, only to be rediscovered much later. Instead, work based on the geographic metaphor came to dominate much of theory and research on intelligence. One only can speculate on how the field of intelligence might have evolved had researchers and practitioners paid more attention to processing and less attention to the hypothetical mental geography of the mind.

In so-called "cognitive-correlates" research,[55] intelligence theorists have emphasized processes at relatively low levels of information processing.[56] In so-called "cognitive-components" research,[57] theorists emphasize components at relatively high levels of information processing.[58] Thus, Hunt (as a cognitive-correlates researcher) studied how quickly one could retrieve from long-term memory the names of letters. I (as a cognitive-components researcher) studied how quickly and accurately a subject could solve verbal or pictorial analogies. The nature of human information processing is highly interactive. Therefore, there is no single right or wrong level of analysis. Rather, all levels of information processing contribute to producing intelligent performance. The most useful level of analysis for intelligence depends on one's purpose in studying or measuring intelligence.

An alternative approach to intelligence emphasizes working memory. This kind of memory is often viewed as the activated part of long-term memory. It is what one is thinking about at a given time. Working memory is a critical and very useful component of intelligence.[59] In one experiment, participants read sets of brief passages. After they had read the passages, they were required to recall the last word of each passage.[60] Level of recall was highly correlated with psychometrically measured verbal ability. In another study, participants performed a variety of working-memory tasks. In one task, for example, the participants viewed a set of simple arithmetic problems. Following each arithmetic problem was a word or a digit. An example would be "Is $(3 \times 5) - 6 = 7$?"[61] The participants viewed sets of from two to six such problems. They were asked to solve each one. After solving the problems in the set, the participants tried to recall the words or digits that followed the problems. The number of words or digits recalled was highly correlated with psychometrically measured intelligence.

Working-memory measurements also predict quite well scores on tests of general ability.[62] Thus, an individual's ability to store and manipulate information in working memory is almost certainly an important aspect of human intelligence.

Recent thinking has suggested that working memory in itself might not be synonymous with intelligence but rather might be one of two forces that, in tandem, contribute to intelligence, or at least, fluid intelligence. In particular, one current view is that working memory actually consists of two distinct and oppositional processes: the *maintenance* of information in working memory in the face of distraction or decay of that information, and, at the same time, *disengagement* from old, potentially interfering information in memory in order to allow attention to be devoted to new and potentially relevant and useful information. That is, on the one hand, we need to hold on to some information for the tasks we need to complete; on the other hand, we have to let go of some information to make room for new and potentially more relevant information.[63] Thus, on this view, what matters for fluid intelligence is not working memory as a fleeting storage capacity for information while it is being processed, but rather the interplay between maintenance and disengagement.

The computational metaphor provides something important missing from other metaphors, namely, a detailed account of the processes involved in human intelligence. And yet it, like other metaphors, has limitations.

First, the computational approach can isolate mental processes but there is no real way of saying that the processes thus isolated are in any sense "basic." It is not even clear, at a computational level, what a basic process is. Any process, such as inference, might be further decomposable, into other subprocesses.

Second, computational research has revealed fairly strong content effects. That is, a person's ability to make inferences in the verbal domain might be rather different from the person's ability to make inferences in the mathematical or figural domain.[64] Thus, there are sources of individual differences that remain untapped simply by specifying processes devoid of content.

Third, it has not always been clear at what level to define cognitive theories. For example, in early work, some major theorists suggested that when there is a computer program that simulates human behavior, the program is the theory.[65] Others have suggested higher levels of analysis.[66]

Fourth, computational theories, like the psychometric and developmental theories considered earlier, have relatively little to say about the effects of culture on cognition, even though we know that cognition is very much affected by its cultural context.[67] People in different cultures understand and perform the same tasks in different ways, for example, in their relative emphases on abstract thinking.[68] Thus, simply identifying components of thought tells us relatively little about how those components function in one cultural context versus another.

Finally, the theories have a tendency to oversimplify things. For example, a number of theories have identified intelligence with speed of information processing.[69] Carroll's psychometric model, described earlier, also describes speed factors. Yet, sometimes more intelligent people are actually slower to respond to stimuli.[70] That is, they make an effort, as needed, to think things through carefully. They seem to adjust their speed to the circumstances. At the very least, one does not want to rush to the conclusion that intelligence and mental speed go hand in hand.

Today, computational theories still excite a lot of interest among psychologists studying intelligence. But biologically-based theories seem even more to have come to the fore.

2.5.4   *The Biological Metaphor*

A fourth metaphor is a biological one – that the seat of intelligence is in the brain.[71] On this view, understanding intelligence means understanding the brain and its interconnections. Some of these interconnections are internal within the brain. Others are internal to other parts of the central nervous system. Scientists who adhere to this metaphor often try to figure out what part, or parts, of the brain are responsible for which particular behavior. Or they might measure the volume of the brain itself, for example, looking at brain size and its correlation with intelligence. Scientists studying the brain and its interactions with the central nervous system use diverse methods of analysis. Some scientists utilize brain scans of various types, including positron emission tomography (PET scans) and functional magnetic resonance imaging (fMRI scans). Other scientists compare and contrast the intellectual performance of normal people whose brains are intact with the performance of individuals suffering from brain damage.

Over time, there have been a number of biologically based theories of intelligence. Ward Halstead proposed that there are four biologically based abilities: (a) an integrative field factor, (b) an abstraction factor, (c) a power factor, and (d) a directional factor.[72] Halstead viewed all four of these abilities as emanating from the functioning of the cortex of the frontal lobes.

More influential in the field of intelligence than Halstead has been Donald Hebb, one of the most distinguished and influential psychologists in the history of the field. Hebb suggested a distinction between two types of intelligence, which he called *Intelligence A* and *Intelligence B*.[73] Intelligence A refers to biological intellectual potential; Intelligence B refers instead to the functioning of the brain as a result of the actual cognitive development that has occurred within the individual. Hebb further suggested an Intelligence C, or intelligence as measured by conventional psychometric tests of intelligence. Note, then, that Hebb distinguished the IQ of intelligence tests from intelligence as it is either in the brain or in action as developed over time. Hebb further proposed that learning, which is key to intelligence, is built up through what he called cell assemblies. These are successively more and more complex interconnections among neurons that are built up as learning actually takes place.

A third biological based theory is that of Alexander Luria, another giant in the field of psychology.[74] This theory has had a serious impact on at least some proposed earlier tests of intelligence.[75] Luria suggested that the brain comprises three main units with respect to intelligence: (a) a unit of arousal in the brain stem and midbrain structures; (b) a senior sensory input unit in the temporal, parietal, and occipital lobes; and (c) an organization and planning unit in the frontal cortex.

The more modern form of Luria's theory is called PASS theory, which is an acronym for planning, attention-arousal, simultaneous processing, successive processing.[76] Simultaneous and successive processing – which are similar to parallel and serial processing of information – are related to the sensory-input abilities referred to by Luria. One processes simultaneously when one handles a lot of input at once, as in viewing a picture. One processes successively when one handles pieces of input, one after another, as in solving a problem requiring you to specify the next number in a series, such as 2, 4, 6, 8, . . .?

A next phase of biological theorizing sought to account for more specifically targeted aspects of brain or neuronal functioning. One theory was based on alleged speed of neuronal conduction in the brain. For example, it was proposed that individual differences in nerve-conduction velocity might be a major source of individual differences in intelligence.[77] How, exactly, does one measure speed of neuronal conduction? Two procedures, both of them scientifically speculative, were used to measure neuronal-conduction velocity, whether in the central nervous system (in the brain) or in the peripheral nervous system (e.g., in the arm).

One procedure tested brain-nerve-conduction velocities via two medium-latency potentials, N70 and P100 (the N and the P stand for "positive" and "negative," respectively; the numbers following the letters refer to the number of milliseconds at which the potential was evoked after presentation of a stimulus). In particular, participants viewed a checkerboard pattern presented in black-and-white. The black squares would change to white and the white squares, to black. Over the course of a large number of trials, participants' responses to these changes in shading between black and white were detected by electrodes that were attached in four places to the respondent's scalp.

Correlations of derived latency (reaction time) measures with IQ were rather small (generally in the 0.1 to 0.2 range of absolute value). In some cases, the correlations were statistically significant, suggesting at least a modest relationship between IQ and the latency measures. The problem is that, in this field, correlations in the range of 0.1 to 0.2 are a dime a dozen. Even if they are statistically significant, it is not clear what, if any, practical significance they have. The correlations do not make a compelling case for individual differences in speed of neuronal conduction being in any way causal of differences in IQ.

Two studies, using different methodology, looked at the relation between nerve-conduction IQ and velocity in the arm.[78] In these studies, nerve-conduction velocity was measured in the median nerve of the arm by the investigators' attaching electrodes to the arm. In one of the two studies, the investigators measured nerve-conduction velocity for conduction extending from the wrist to the tip of the finger. The resulting correlations with IQ were in the 0.4 (moderate) range. There also were somewhat smaller correlations with reaction-time latencies (around 0.2). These results suggested a relationship between IQ and speed of information transmission in the peripheral nerves. But the results did not replicate in a later study.[79]

Other research has explored a measure called P300 (positive latency at 300 msec) as a measure of intelligence. Higher amplitudes of P300 waves are sometimes viewed as suggestive of higher levels of extraction of information from stimuli.[80] Higher P300 amplitudes also have been taken to suggest greater attention in adjustment to novelty.

Using PET, Richard Haier found that people with higher IQs typically show lesser activation in relevant parts of the brain than do those people with lower IQs.[81] These results suggest that the higher-IQ people find the tasks to be easier. As a result, they put in less effort than do the poorer performers and hence the brain signals are weaker. P-FIT (parietal-frontal integration) theory, which was proposed by Rex Jung and Richard Haier, argues that general intelligence stems, at least in part, from the efficiency of the communication between particular regions of the brain, in particular, parts of the parietal, frontal, temporal, and cingulate cortices.[82] Today, much of the research on human intelligence based on a biological approach uses fMRI in order to pinpoint intelligent processing in the brain.

None of this research takes into account the cultural factors that affect what people mean by intelligence and that affect what constitutes adaptive behavior in a given cultural milieu.

2.5.5   A Cultural Metaphor

A fifth metaphor is a cultural or anthropological one. This metaphor is based on the view that intelligence is a cultural invention.[83] Scientists who adhere to this metaphor view intelligence as a cultural construct. It is a construct cultures invent to explain why some people do certainly culturally valued tasks better than do others. But the tasks that cultures value differ across cultures. So, what intelligence "is" will be perceived as different from one culture to another. It is for this reason that at least some people were likely unwilling to sign the so-called (by the authors) "Mainstream Science" definition of intelligence described earlier. They did not believe that merely administering intelligence tests measuring skills valued in parts of the West provided a fair measure of the intelligence of people from culturally diverse environments. They may have believed that people in parts of the West might, in many cases, do poorly on tests measuring skills valued in other cultures, such as hunting big game, gathering, ice fishing, building appropriate homes, self-treating parasitic illnesses, and so forth.

Let us consider some of the cultural views on intelligence and how radically they differ from more conventional views. Intelligence may be conceived and thought about in different ways in different cultural settings[84] (see reviews in Berry, 1991; and Sternberg & Kaufman, 1998). For example, the Confucian perspective on intelligence emphasizes benevolence and doing what is viewed as right and proper.[85] As in certain Western notions of intelligence, the intelligent person puts a great deal of effort into learning. He or she enjoys learning and persists with enthusiasm in lifelong learning. Learning, in this view, never stops. In the Taoist tradition, the emphasis is different. In this tradition, the emphasis is on the importance of humility and of freedom from adherence to conventional norms and societal standards of judgment. Also of importance is comprehensive knowledge of oneself as well as of the circumstances in the world in which one lives.

The difference between certain Eastern and Western conceptions of intelligence has persisted over many years.[86] Contemporary Taiwanese Chinese conceptions of intelligence involve five factors. The first is a general cognitive factor. This factor appears to be much like the general (or *g*) factor emerging from factor analysis of scores on conventional Western intelligence tests. The second factor was what might be called "interpersonal intelligence." It included social competence, such as is used in understanding other people and then acting upon that understanding. The third factor was intrapersonal intelligence, or understanding oneself. Interpersonal and intrapersonal intelligence are much as in Gardner's theory of multiple intelligences. The fourth factor was intellectual self-assertion, which is essentially one's willingness and ability to communicate one's views clearly and, if necessary, forcefully to others. And the fourth factor was intellectual self-effacement. This factor involves understanding both of what one knows and also, and perhaps more importantly, of what one does not know.

A different study yielded somewhat different results. It yielded three factors underlying Chinese folk theories of intelligence. The first was nonverbal reasoning ability, or the ability to, reason with abstract symbols such as geometric shapes or numbers. The second factor was verbal reasoning ability, as would be used, for example, in verbal analogies. The third factor was rote memory. This involves remembering precisely what one has read or has been told orally.[87]

The conceptions of intelligence revealed in Taiwan differ quite a bit from those identified in people's conceptions of intelligence in the United States – (a) practical problem-solving, (b) verbal ability, and (c) social competence.[88] But both in Taiwan and in the United States, people's conceptions, or "implicit theories," of intelligence go quite far beyond the kinds of skills that conventional intelligence tests measure. One might be inclined quickly to dismiss the conceptions of the laypeople – after all, what do laypersons know compared with experts? But from a different point of view, experts are entrenched – as a result of their training and general professional socialization, they are used to thinking in a certain way. They often are the last to change their views in response to what is going on in the world.[89]

In Africa, conceptions of intelligence center especially on skills that help to facilitate, maintain, and further develop harmonious and stable relations among members of a group.[90] For example, Chewa adults in Zambia place emphasis on social responsibilities, cooperation, and obedience to authorities as important to intelligence; in particular, intelligent children are expected to be respectful of and obedient to adults.[91] Parents of children in Kenya also emphasize the importance of responsible and socially appropriate participation in family and larger-group social life as important aspects of children's intelligence.[92] In Zimbabwe, the word for intelligence, *ngware*, signifies a trait of someone who is both prudent and cautious, particularly in interpersonal relationships. Among the Baoulé tribe, service to the family and surrounding community as well as politeness toward, and respect for elders, are seen as crucial aspects of intelligence.[93]

The emphasis on the social, interpersonal aspects of intelligence is not limited to African cultural groups. Views of intelligence in many Asian cultures also emphasize the social and other-oriented aspects of intelligence more than does the conventional and highly individualistic Western, or IQ-based, notion of intelligence.[94]

Neither African nor Asian cultural groups emphasize exclusively social aspects of intelligence. They simply emphasize social skills more than do conventional US conceptions of intelligence. But as we saw, people in the United States also view "social competence" as part of intelligence. At the same time, African and Asian cultures recognize the importance of cognitive skills as part of intelligence. In rural Kenya, investigators found that there are four distinct terms constituting conceptions of intelligence – *rieko* (consisting of knowledge and skills), *luoro* (which roughly translates to "respect"), *winjo* (which involves comprehension of how to handle real-life problems), and *paro* (initiative or drive)[95] – with only *rieko* clearly referring to knowledge-based cognitive skills (including but not limited to academic skills).

It is important to realize that, in a given country, there is no one single conception of intelligence that pervades all cultures or subcultures. For example, different ethnic groups in San Jose, California, have rather different conceptions of what it means for children to be intelligent. Latino-American parents of schoolchildren tend to highlight the importance of social-competence, interpersonal skills in their conceptions of intelligence. In contrast, Asian-American parents tend to emphasize the importance of more conventional cognitive skills. Anglo-American parents, like the Asian-American parents, also emphasize more the importance of cognitive skills. Teachers, representing the dominant culture of the country's educational establishment, also emphasize more cognitive- than social-competence skills. The rank order of performance of children in the various ethnic groups (including subgroups within the Latino-American and Asian-American groups) could be predicted perfectly by the extent to which their parents shared the teachers' conventional conception of intelligence.[96] In other words, teachers had a tendency to reward those children who were socialized into a folk theory of intelligence that happened to correspond to the teachers' own folk theory.

Cultural views of intelligence are part of what even broader theories, systems theories, try to take into account in understanding intelligence.

2.5.6 A Systems Metaphor

A further metaphor is a systems metaphor.[97] The idea of a systems metaphor is that intelligence can be understood only in terms of a complex system that integrates mental representations, processes, and other systems of thought. The systems metaphor, in a sense, incorporates many of the other metaphors.

In the intelligence business, the systems metaphor is new, at least, relatively speaking. It inevitably expands our view of intelligence because it views intelligence as involving much more of thinking and acting than just a narrow set of cognitive structures of processes.

The first modern theorist to introduce a systems theory was probably Howard Gardner.

Although intelligence is usually thought of as unitary, Howard Gardner proposed a theory of multiple intelligences.[98] According to this theory, intelligence, broadly speaking, comprises multiple independent constructs. It is not just a single, unitary construct. However, instead of speaking of multiple abilities that together constitute intelligence, as did Thurstone in his theory of primary mental abilities (described earlier in this chapter), this theory distinguishes eight distinct intelligences. The intelligences are alleged to be relatively independent of each other. Each is a separate system of functioning. However, these systems can interact to produce what we see as intelligent performance.

Linguistic Intelligence. This intelligence is used in reading a book, writing a poem, speaking to someone, or understanding a lecture. It is heavily involved in verbal sections of traditional tests of intelligence and of scholastic achievement. Most intelligence tests directly measure linguistic intelligence.

Logical-Mathematical Intelligence. This intelligence is used in solving a mathematics problem, such as a time-rate-distance problem, or adding numbers, or proving a logical theorem. Pretty much all intelligence tests measure logical-mathematical intelligence in some degree. Scholastic achievement tests all measure logical-mathematical intelligence.

Visual-Spatial Intelligence. This intelligence is used to do mental rotations of objects (i.e., imagining objects rotating in space). It also is used to figure out how many suitcases can fit in the trunk of a car, to determine how sharply to steer to make a turn in a car, and in other related tasks. Visual-spatial intelligence is measured by many, but not all, tests of intelligence. It is not measured, for example, by tests that are wholly verbal.

Naturalist Intelligence. This intelligence is used in observing patterns in nature, such as in the classification of trees, flowers, clouds, stars, or other natural patterns. This intelligence is important for people who work in fields such as botany, horticulture, astronomy, and physics. It also is important for people in the arts who draw or write about nature. This purported intelligence is not measured by conventional tests of intelligence.

Bodily-Kinesthetic Intelligence. This intelligence is indispensable to athletic pursuits, such as tennis, basketball, or soccer. But it is also important for everyday activities that require coordination and various motor skills. This purported intelligence also is not measured by conventional tests of intelligence.

Musical Intelligence. This intelligence is used to sing, dance, write music, play music, and listen intelligently to music. The intelligence is important to all musical activity, including even clapping one's hands to rhythm. This purported intelligence, like naturalist and bodily-kinesthetic intelligence, is not measured by conventional tests of intelligence.

Interpersonal Intelligence. This intelligence is used to relate to other people, as in relations with one's significant other, with one's children, or with friends or colleagues at work. It is very similar to what is sometimes called "social intelligence." This intelligence is also not measured by typical psychometric intelligence tests.

Intrapersonal Intelligence. This intelligence is used to understand and have insights into oneself. For example, it would be used to recognize when one needs to make changes in one's life. This intelligence, like most of those in Gardner's theory, is not measured by intelligence tests.

In some respects, Gardner's theory is similar to test-based, factorial theories, such as those of Thurstone or Vernon. It specifies several abilities that are construed to reflect intelligence of some sort. However, Gardner views each ability as a separate and distinct intelligence. He does not see the various abilities as parts of a single whole and unified intelligence. Moreover, there is a crucial difference between Gardner's theory and factorial theories. Factorial theories are based on factor analysis of ability tests. Gardner, in contrast, used converging operations, gathering evidence from multiple sources and types of data.

In particular, the theory uses eight "signs" as criteria for detecting the existence of a discrete kind of intelligence (taken from Gardner, 1983, pp. 63–7):

1 *Potential isolation of a particular intelligence by brain damage.* The destruction or the sparing of a distinct, discrete area of the brain may destroy or else it may spare a particular kind of intelligent behavior. For example, particular areas of the brain can be linked to verbal aphasia—impairment of language functioning.

2 *The existence of exceptional and highly distinctive individuals.* Examples of exceptional individuals would be mathematical or musical prodigies. These individuals demonstrate an extraordinary ability in a particular kind of intelligent behavior. Otherwise, they may have notable deficits in their intelligent behavior.

3 *An identifiable core operation or set of core operations.* An example would be the detection of relationships among a set of musical tones. The core operation or operations are essential to the performance of a particular kind of intelligent behavior, such as behaviors emanating from musical intelligence.

4 *A distinctive developmental history leading an individual from the level of novice to the level of master.* This history is accompanied by varied levels of expert performance. That is, there are many levels of expertise in the expression of the intelligence.

5 *A distinctive evolutionary history of the intelligence.* Each intelligence somehow serves a different adaptive function in the evolutionary history of the organism.

6 *Supportive evidence from cognitive-experimental investigations.* An example of such evidence would be task-specific performance differences across different intelligences. For example, cognitive-experimental research might reveal that visuospatial tasks involve different mental processes from those involved in verbal tasks. These differences would need to be complemented by cross-task performance similarities within particular intelligences. For example, mental rotation of visuospatial imagery and recall memory of visuospatial images should show overlapping cognitive processes as they emanate from the same intelligence.

7 *Supportive evidence from psychometric tests pointing to differentiable and discrete intelligences.* For example, one would expect to find performances on tests of visuospatial abilities loading on different psychometric factors from performances on tests of linguistic abilities.

8 *Susceptibility to encoding of information in a symbol system.* For example, language, mathematics, and music all have their own distinctive symbol systems and notations.

Gardner does not entirely dismiss the use of psychometric tests for measuring intelligence. But the base of evidence used by Gardner goes well beyond the factor analysis of various psychometric tests. Moreover, Gardner believes the psychometric tests are extremely limited in the range of intelligences they test. Primarily, they measure linguistic and logical-mathematical intelligences. Sometimes they also measure visual-spatial intelligence. They are not targeted at measuring the other intelligences.

Gardner views the mind as modular, a view first introduced in a different context by Jerry Fodor.[99] Theorists who believe in the modularity of mind believe that different skills – such as, but not limited to, Gardner's multiple intelligences – can be isolated in performance as deriving from distinct, identifiable, and separate modules, or areas of the brain. On this view, a major task of research on intelligence is to isolate the portions of the brain responsible for each of the multiple intelligences. Gardner has speculated as to where at least some of these locales may be. But hard scientific evidence for the existence of such independent intelligences is still lacking. Furthermore, it is not even clear just how modular the mind is.

Consider, for example, performance of autistic savants. Savants are individuals with severe cognitive and social deficits but nevertheless with corresponding high levels of ability in a relatively narrow domain. Is the existence of such savants really evidence for modular intelligences? Perhaps and perhaps not. The narrow long-term memory skills and highly specific aptitudes of savants may not really be intelligent in the sense that the word "intelligent" usually is used. Contemporary evidence may suggest the opposite of Gardner's claim. It appears that rather than being modular, intelligent functioning, even of a given kind, is widely distributed throughout the brain.

Gardner's theory has several notable strengths. First, it expands the way we think about intelligence. It encourages us all to think of skills as intelligences that previously would have been conceived of merely as talents. Second, it suggests ways in which teachers can teach to children with multiple patterns of abilities. Third, it draws upon diverse sources of information for the delineation of the intelligences.

Gardner's theory also has notable weaknesses. The first is that thirty-five years after the theory was first proposed, there is a lack of hard empirical evidence validating the theory. One attempt failed.[100] Of course, theories are sometimes proposed before predictive empirical data are collected. But one nevertheless would hope that after three and a half decades, there would be adequate hard empirical evidence supporting the predictive power of the theory.

Second, and following from the first point, it is not clear that one can identify eight entirely independent skill sets, or intelligences. There have been literally thousands of studies of the factorial structure of intelligence and abilities such as linguistic, logical-mathematical, and visual-spatial. These studies generally have shown the various abilities to be correlated – that is, people who are better at one tend to be better at the others.[101] It also seems dubious that interpersonal and intrapersonal skills would be entirely independent. They might be, but then one would need predictive empirical evidence to show that to be the case.

Third, some of the intelligences may not be unitary. For example, some people are good readers but not particularly good writers (linguistic intelligence). Others are very good at algebra but could not adequately formulate a complex logical proof. A good singer is not necessarily a good composer. And a good composer may or may not be virtuoso on an instrument. It simply is not clear that the intelligences represent single sources of brain power or variation among people.

Fourth, it is not clear what is to be gained by calling some of the skills sets "intelligences." Perhaps it serves a desirable social function to do so. (For example, one can now say that a star athlete is intelligent in his or her own way.) But social functions are different from scientific ones. Moreover, the different intelligences, at least in today's world, do not have equal or nearly equal adaptive value. People who have a "tin ear" to music generally can get along quite well in their lives. People with severely deficient linguistic or logical skills often find their lives present severe challenges. One could imagine a society in which musical skills were the key to success. They certainly are key to success among musicians. But musicians are a small percentage of the population. There are small percentages of the population where other skills, such as fire-eating, also may be essential for success.

It may sound like I am putting too much emphasis on the predictive value of a theory. But there is a reason for doing so. When scholars review past literature, as Gardner has in his books, they can be selective as to what they choose to review, potentially placing more emphasis on results that suit their theories. All scholars are susceptible to confirmation bias. The problem is that other scholars can review similar literatures, for example, the literature on intelligence, and come to exactly the opposite conclusion. In their reviews (cited earlier in this chapter), for example, John Carroll and Arthur Jensen came to opposite conclusions from Gardner's. Predictive studies enable one to discover which theories can hold up not only to potentially selective reviews of literature, but also to predicting what should happen in the future. What empirical results can we predict in advance that will test the validity of a given theory?

On the one hand, Gardner's theory scientifically has not (at least to date) proved to be entirely viable. But it has served the useful scientific function of broadening our thinking about intelligence. And it has served a very useful societal function of pointing out that schools and society as a whole should not be locked into narrow conceptions of what makes a person capable. Whether the multiple intelligences are truly distinct systems of individual intelligences or perhaps better described as a range of talents, they provide diverse paths for life success. And in today's world, people need to be aware that there are multiple paths to succeeding in life besides having a high IQ. There is more to adaptation than IQ, and Gardner was among the first to point this out in an elegant and educationally compelling way.

A second systems theory is my own, the augmented theory of successful intelligence. Because I will describe it in detail in the rest of this book I will not describe it in detail here as well. Basically, the theory states that intelligence inheres in one's finding a personally and socially meaningful set of goals in life, figuring out how to reach those goals, and then doing one's best to achieve them, given the limitations imposed by one's socio-cultural context. Intelligence, in this view, is not a "thing" that can be fully measured by a single intelligence test because it is not even quite the same thing for one person versus another. A musician who wants to become a composer or a performer needs to find a life path and, particularly, a career path that is different from that of a lawyer or a surgeon. Each individual needs a different set of skills and attitudes, and even within a given profession, there are different ways of achieving success. Intelligence in this view is largely "idiographic" – differing from one person to the next. We all have to find, construct, and continually evaluate our own path.

2.5.7 Beyond Metaphors

Although the theory of adaptive intelligence presented in this book draws upon a systems theory – the theory of successful intelligence – it is, in a sense, beyond metaphors. On this theory, it really does not matter what metaphor one uses – all of them can be useful. One can study adaptation biologically – indeed, adaptation is a biological imperative. One can study adaptation psychometrically by measuring it. One can study the systems underlying adaptation. Regardless of the metaphor under which intelligence is understood, intelligence must serve an adaptive purpose. It must serve to create a fit not only for one individual, but also for individuals collectively, with the world they inhabit. Stephen Ceci recognized the importance of such adaptation in his bioecological view of intelligence.[102] If there is a misfit between individuals or groups and the environment, problems inevitably result. If the individuals who fail to achieve fit become sufficiently powerful and at the same time destructive, the metaphor of mind does not matter. That is, it does not matter whether one views intelligence geographically, biologically, culturally, or in some other way. The powerful individuals collectively may well end up destroying their own habitat and the world as they know it. Those who believe themselves to be "masters of the universe" misunderstand their ultimate role in the universe. They ultimately become victims of the universe they thought they had mastered.

The world is at a crossroads. If, because of global climate change, air pollution, water pollution, poisoned food, or whatever, people eventually kill themselves off, their scores on the clever little tests will be a testament to their own ultimate stupidity. Perhaps no one recognized this better than poet Percy Shelley in Ozymandias, presented in Chapter 1.[103]

Shelley's poem, of course, was about hubris. And hubris is what is taking down humanity and many other species with it. It also has taken down intelligence research, and the views of those who believe they have found definitive answers about intelligence and that everyone who disagrees with them is wrong. Hubris did not work well for the Greek mythological characters like Ajax; it also does not work well for behavioral scientists who believe that only they and their followers have found the ultimate "truth." Their hubris locks them into a single paradigm and prevents them from seeing outside the small, cramped mental black box they have created for themselves. For them, those who disagree with them are believers in myths. But they are the mythmakers. Even physicists have not found ultimate truths; why would behavioral scientists then have had such fantastic success?

Someday some other species will look back and, if it is able, will wonder what happened. What were the forces that destroyed humanity? The dinosaurs, were their descendants still around today, could blame their demise on a heavenly body that, to their bad fortune, landed on Earth. We will have only ourselves to blame. Ozymandias thought he was pretty smart, too. He ended up where we and our descendants will if we do not change course.

2.6   Conclusion

All of the different views on intelligence may suggest that researchers on intelligence have little or no common basis for understanding or studying the phenomenon. But in the end, they actually do have quite a bit of common basis. Most researchers agree that intelligence involves, at minimum, the ability to learn, the ability to reason abstractly, the ability to adapt to the environment and solve the problems life presents, and the ability to understand, and at some level control, one's cognitive processing. The concept of *adaptation to the environment* is key in any definition of intelligence – intelligence is an evolved trait. To the extent that more intelligent rather than less intelligent humans (or any other organisms) have survived, it must be in part because they adapted more effectively to their environments and flexibly when those environments changed. So, despite the differences, you cannot go too far wrong, if in trying to understand intelligence, you focus on learning, reasoning, problem-solving, and most of all, adaptation. Those are keys to understanding what intelligence is, almost without regard to the differences one might find among scholarly definitions. But no one today, including me, has any final answers in this field. We only seek closer and closer approximations to some as yet unknown and possibly unknowable truth.

Intelligence, then, is one of the most important traits that have allowed humans and other organisms to succeed in their environments. But there is one thing always to keep in mind. As the ability to adapt to the environment increases, so can the ability to change the environment. And the changes humans have wrought have not all been positive. They have included global climate change, air pollution, and wars. So, intelligence is an important ability, but like any ability, it can be used toward better or worse ends. One of our responsibilities as citizens of our country and of the world is to use intelligence for ends that will create a better world, not that will destroy the world.

Notes

1. Hunt, E. B. (2010). *Human intelligence.* New York: Cambridge University Press; Mackintosh, N. J. (2011). *IQ and human intelligence* (2nd ed.). New York: Oxford University Press.
2. "Mainstream science on intelligence" (1994). *Wall Street Journal,* December 13, p. A18.
3. Binet, A., & Simon, T. (1916) [1905 for the original French version]. *The development of intelligence in children: The Binet-Simon Scale.* E. S. Kite (translator). Baltimore, MD: Williams & Wilkins.
4. Wechsler, D. (1944). *The measurement of adult intelligence.* Baltimore, MD: Williams & Wilkins.
5. Gardner, H. (2011). *Frames of mind: The theory of multiple intelligences.* New York: Basic.
6. "Intelligence and its measurement: A symposium" (1921). *Journal of Educational Psychology,* 12, 123–47, 195–216, 271–5.
7. Sternberg, R. J., & Detterman, D. K. (Eds.) (1986). *What is intelligence?* Norwood, NJ: Ablex.
8. Boring, E. G. (1923). "Intelligence as the tests test it." *New Republic,* June 6, 35–7.
9. Sternberg, R. J. (1990). *Metaphors of mind: Conceptions of the nature of intelligence.* New York: Cambridge University Press.
10. Thurstone, L. L., & Thurstone, T. G. (1941). *Factorial studies of intelligence.* Chicago, IL: University of Chicago Press.
11. Greenfield, P. M. (2020). Historical evolution of intelligence. In R. J. Sternberg (Ed.), *Cambridge handbook of intelligence* (2nd ed., pp. 916–39). New York: Cambridge University Press.
12. Grigorenko, E. L., Geissler, P. W., Prince, R. et al. (2001). The organization of Luo conceptions of intelligence: A study of implicit theories in

a Kenyan village. *International Journal of Behavioral Development*, 25(4), 367–78.

13. Berry, J. W. (1974). Radical cultural relativism and the concept of intelligence. In J. W. Berry, & P. R. Dasen (Eds.), *Culture and cognition: Readings in cross-cultural psychology* (pp. 225–9). London: Methuen; Serpell, R. (1974). Aspects of intelligence in a developing country. *African Social Research*, 17, 576–96; Azuma, H., & Kashiwagi, K. (1987). Descriptions for an intelligent person: A Japanese study. *Japanese Psychological Research*, 29, 17–26.

14. Sternberg, R. J. (2004). Culture and intelligence. *American Psychologist*, 59(5), 325–38.

15. Davis, K., Christodoulou, J., Seider, S., & Gardner, H. (2011). The theory of multiple intelligences. In R. J. Sternberg, & S. B. Kaufman (Eds.), *Cambridge handbook of intelligence* (pp. 485–503). New York: Cambridge University Press.

16. Deary, I. J. (in press). *Intelligence: A very short introduction* (2nd ed.). Oxford: Oxford University Press.

17. Sternberg, R. J., Conway, B. E., Ketron, J. L., & Bernstein, M. (1981). People's conceptions of intelligence. *Journal of Personality and Social Psychology*, 41, 37–55; Sternberg, R. J. (1985). Implicit theories of intelligence, creativity, and wisdom. *Journal of Personality and Social Psychology*, 49(3), 607–27.

18. Galton, F. (1883). *Inquiries into human faculty and its development*. London: Macmillan.

19. Wissler, C. D. (1901). The correlation of mental and physical tests. *Psychological Review, Monograph Supplements*.

20. Newell, A., & Simon, H. A. (1972). *Human problem solving*. Englewood Cliffs, NJ: Prentice-Hall; Pellegrino, J. W., & Glaser, R. (1979). Cognitive correlates and components in the analysis of individual differences. *Intelligence*, 3(3), 187–215; Nečka, E., & Orzechowski, J. (2005). Higher-order cognition and intelligence. In R. J. Sternberg, & J. E. Pretz (Eds.), *Cognition and intelligence* (pp. 122–41). New York: Cambridge University Press; Lohman, D. F., & Lakin, J. M. (2011). Intelligence and reasoning. In R. J. Sternberg, & S. B. Kaufman (Eds.), *Cambridge handbook of intelligence* (pp. 419–41). New York: Cambridge University Press; Lakin, J. M., Kell, H. J., & Lohman, D. F. (2020). Intelligence and reasoning. In R. J. Sternberg (Ed.), *Cambridge handbook of intelligence* (2nd ed., pp. 528–52). New York: Cambridge University Press.

21. Sternberg, R. J. & Jarvin, L. (2001). Binet, Alfred (1857–1911). In N. J. Smelser, & P. B. Baltes (Eds.), *International encyclopedia of the social and behavioral sciences* (pp. 1180–4). Oxford: Elsevier Science Ltd.

22. Roid, G. (2003). *Stanford–Binet Intelligence Scales*, 5th ed. Boston, MA: Houghton Mifflin Harcourt.

23. Sternberg, R. J. (1985). Human intelligence: The model is the message. *Science*, 230, 1111–18.

24. Spearman, C. (1927). *The abilities of man*. New York: Macmillan; Carroll, J. B. (1993). *Human cognitive abilities: A survey of factor-analytic*

studies. New York: Cambridge University Press; Kaufman, A. S., Schneider, W. J., & Kaufman, J. C. (2020). Psychometric approaches to intelligence. In R. J. Sternberg (Ed.), *Human intelligence: An introduction* (pp. 67–103). New York: Cambridge University Press; Sackett, P. R., Shewach, O. R., & Dahlke, J. A. (2020). The predictive value of general intelligence. In R. J. Sternberg (Ed.), *Human intelligence: An introduction* (pp. 381–414). New York: Cambridge University Press; Walrath, R., Willis, J. O., Dumont, R., & Kaufman, A. S. (2020). Factor-analytic models of intelligence. In R. J. Sternberg (Ed.), *Cambridge handbook of intelligence* (2nd ed., pp. 75–98). New York: Cambridge University Press.

25. Spearman, C. (1904). "General intelligence," objectively determined and measured. *The American Journal of Psychology*, 15(2), 201–93.

26. Gottfredson, L. S. (1998). The general intelligence factor. *Scientific American Presents*, 9(4), 24–9; Sternberg, R. J., & Grigorenko, E. L. (Eds.) (2002). *The general factor of intelligence: How general is it?* New York: Psychology Press.

27. Thomson, G. H. (1916). A hierarchy without a general factor. *British Journal of Psychology, 1904–1920*, 8(3), 271–81.

28. Thorndike, E. L. (1911). *Animal intelligence: Experimental studies*. New York: Macmillan.

29. Thurstone, L. L. (1938). *Primary mental abilities*. Chicago, IL: University of Chicago Press.

30. Guilford, J. P. (1967). *The nature of human intelligence*. New York: McGraw-Hill; Guilford, J. P., & Hoepfner, R. (1971). *The analysis of intelligence*. New York: McGraw-Hill.

31. Horn, J. L., & Knapp, J. R. (1973). On the subjective character of Guilford's structure-of-intellect model. *Psychological Bulletin*, 80, 33–43.

32. Guilford, J. P. (1950). Creativity. *American Psychologist*, 5, 444–54.

33. Guttman, L. (1954). A new approach to factor analysis: The radex. In P. F. Lazarsfeld (Ed.), *Mathematical thinking in the social sciences* (pp. 258–348). New York: Free Press; Guttman, L. (1965a). The structure of interrelations among intelligence tests. *Proceedings of the 1964 invitational conference on testing problems* (pp. 25–36). Princeton, NJ: Educational Testing Service; Guttman, L. (1965b). A faceted definition of intelligence. In R. Eifererman (Ed.), *Studies in Psychology, Scripta Hierosolymitana*, 14, 166–81; Marshalek, B., Lohman, D. F., & Snow, R. E. (1983). The complexity continuum in the radex and hierarchical models of intelligence. *Intelligence*, 7(2), 107–27.

34. Cattell, R. B. (1971). *Abilities: Their structure, growth, and action*. Boston, MA: Houghton Mifflin.

35. Vernon, P. E. (1950). *The structure of human abilities*. London: Methuen.

36. Carroll, J. B. (1993). *Human cognitive abilities: A survey of factor-analytic studies*. New York: Cambridge University Press.

37. McGrew, K. S. (2005). The Cattell-Horn–Carroll theory of cognitive abilities. In D. P. Flanagan, & P. L. Harrison (Eds.), *Contemporary intellectual*

assessment: Theories, tests, and issues (2nd ed., pp. 136–81). New York: Guilford Press; McGrew, K. S. (2009). CHC theory and the human cognitive abilities project: Standing on the shoulders of the giants of psychometric intelligence research. *Intelligence*, 37, 1–10.

38. Johnson, W., & Bouchard, T. J., Jr. (2005). The structure of human intelligence: It is verbal, perceptual, and image rotation (VPR), not fluid and crystallized. *Intelligence*, 33, 393–416.

39. McNemar, Q. (1964). Lost: Our intelligence? Why? *American Psychologist*, 19, 871–82.

40. Roid, G., & Barram, R. (2004). *Essentials of Stanford–Binet Intelligence Scales (SB5) Assessment*. Hoboken, NJ: John Wiley & Sons, Inc.

41. Sternberg, R. J. (1985). *Beyond IQ: A triarchic theory of human intelligence*. New York: Cambridge University Press.

42. Leman, N. (2000). *The big test: The secret history of the American meritocracy*. New York: Farrar, Straus, & Giroux.

43. Piaget, J. (1972). *The psychology of intelligence*. Totowa, NJ: Littlefield, Adams, & Co.

44. Bower, T. G. R. (1967). The development of object-permanence: Some studies of existence constancy. *Perception and Psychophysics*, 2, 411–18; Bower, T. G. R. (1974). *Development in infancy*. New York: Freeman; Brainerd, C. J. (1977). Response criteria in concept development research. *Child Development*, 48, 360–66; Baillargeon, R. (1987). Object permanence in 3½- and 4½ -month-old infants. *Developmental Psychology*, 23, 655–64; Gelman, S. A., & DeJesus, J. (2020). Intelligence in childhood. In R. J. Sternberg (Ed.), *Cambridge handbook of intelligence* (2nd ed., pp. 155–80). New York: Cambridge University Press.

45. Brainerd, C. J. (1978). The stage question in cognitive-developmental theory. *Behavioral and Brain Sciences*, 1(2), 173–213; Sternberg, R. J., & Powell, J. S. (1983). The development of intelligence. In P. H. Mussen Series Ed.), J. Flavell, & E. Markman (Volume Eds.), *Handbook of child psychology* (Vol. 3, 3rd ed., pp. 341–419). New York: Wiley.

46. Rose, L. T., & Fischer, K. W. (2011). Intelligence in childhood. In R. J. Sternberg, & S. B. Kaufman (Eds.), *Cambridge handbook of intelligence* (pp. 144–73). New York: Cambridge University Press.

47. Arlin, P. K. (1990). Wisdom: The art of problem finding. In R. J. Sternberg (Ed.), *Wisdom: Its nature, origins, and development* (pp. 230–43). New York: Cambridge University Press.

48. Case, R. (1978). Intellectual development from birth to adolescence: A neo-Piagetian interpretation. In R. Siegler (Ed.), *Children's thinking: What develops? (pp. 37–72)*. Hillsdale, NJ: Erlbaum.

49. Laboratory of Comparative Human Cognition. (1982). Culture and intelligence. In R. J. Sternberg (Ed.), *Handbook of human intelligence* (pp. 642–719). New York: Cambridge University Press.

50. Baldwin, J. M. (2012). *Mental development in the child and the race: Methods and processes*. London: Forgotten Books.

51. Newell, A., & Simon, H. A. (1972). *Human problem solving*. Englewood Cliffs, NJ: Prentice-Hall; Sternberg, R. J. (1977). *Intelligence, information processing, and analogical reasoning: The componential analysis of human abilities*. Hillsdale, NJ: Lawrence Erlbaum Associates; Hunt, E. B. (1978). Mechanics of verbal ability. *Psychological Review*, 85, 109–30; Sternberg, R. J. (1983). Components of human intelligence. *Cognition*, 15, 1–48; Conway, A. R. A., & Kovacs, K. (2020). Working memory and intelligence. In R. J. Sternberg (Ed.), *Cambridge handbook of intelligence* (2nd ed., pp. 504–27). New York: Cambridge University Press; Ellingsen, V. J., & Engle, R. W. (2020). Cognitive approaches to intelligence. In R. J. Sternberg (Ed.), *Human intelligence: An introduction* (pp. 104–38). New York: Cambridge University Press.

52. Spearman, C. (1923). *The nature of "intelligence" and the principles of cognition*. London: Macmillan.

53. Thurstone, L. L. (1924). *The nature of intelligence*. Chicago, IL: University of Chicago Press.

54. Stenhouse, D. (1974). *The evolution of intelligence: A general theory and some of its implications*. New York: Barnes & Noble Books.

55. Pellegrino, J. W., & Glaser, R. (1979). Cognitive correlates and components in the analysis of individual differences. *Intelligence*, 3(3), 187–215.

56. Hunt, E. B. (1978). Mechanics of verbal ability. *Psychological Review*, 85, 109–30; Hunt, E. B. (1980). Intelligence as an information-processing concept. *British Journal of Psychology*, 71, 449–74; Jensen, A. R. (1982). The chronometry of intelligence. In R. J. Sternberg (Ed.), *Advances in the psychology of human intelligence* (Vol. I, pp. 255–310). Hillsdale, NJ: Erlbaum.

57. Sternberg, R. J. (1977). *Intelligence, information processing, and analogical reasoning: The componential analysis of human abilities*. Hillsdale, NJ: Erlbaum.

58. Mulholland, T. M., Pellegrino, J. W., & Glaser, R. (1980). Components of geometric analogy solution. *Cognitive Psychology*, 12, 252–84; Sternberg, R. J. (1983). Components of human intelligence. *Cognition*, 15, 1–48.

59. Conway, A. R. A., Getz, S. J., Macnamara, B., & Engel de Abreu, P. M. J. (2011). Working memory and intelligence. In R. J. Sternberg, & S. B. Kaufman (Eds.), *Cambridge handbook of intelligence* (pp. 394–418). New York: Cambridge University Press.

60. Daneman, M., & Carpenter, P. A. (1983). Individual differences in integrating information between and within sentences. *Journal of Experimental Psychology: Learning, Memory, and Cognition*, 9, 561–83.

61. Turner, M. L., & Engle, R. W. (1989). Is working-memory capacity task dependent? *Journal of Memory and Language*, 28, 127–54; Hambrick D. Z., Kane, M. J., & Engle, R. W. (2005). The role of working memory in higher-level cognition. In R. J. Sternberg, & J. E. Pretz (Eds.), *Cognition and intelligence* (pp. 104–21). New York: Cambridge University Press; Shipstead, Z., & Engle, R. W. (2018). Mechanisms of working memory capacity and fluid intelligence and their common dependence on executive

attention. In R. J. Sternberg (Ed.), *The nature of human intelligence* (pp. 287–307). New York: Cambridge University Press.

62. Colom, R., Rebollo, I., Palacios, A., Juan-Espinosa, M., & Kyllonen, P. C. (2004). Working memory is (almost) perfectly predicted by *g. Intelligence*, 32 (3), 277–96.

63. Shipstead, Z., Harrison, T. L., & Engle, R. W. (2016). Working memory capacity and fluid intelligence: Maintenance and disengagement. *Perspectives on Psychological Science*, 11(6), 771–99. https://doi.org/10.1177/1745691616650647

64. Sternberg, R. J. (1981). Toward a unified componential theory of human intelligence: I. Fluid abilities. In M. Friedman, J. Das, & N. O'Conner (Eds.), *Intelligence and learning* (pp. 327–44). New York: Plenum.

65. Newell, A., & Simon, H. A. (1972). *Human problem solving*. Englewood Cliffs, NJ: Prentice-Hall.

66. Anderson, J. R. (1983). *The architecture of cognition*. Cambridge, MA: Harvard University Press; Husain, A. (2017). *The sentient machine: The coming age of artificial intelligence*. New York: Scribner; Goel, A. K. (2020). Artificial intelligence. In R. J. Sternberg (Ed.), *Cambridge handbook of intelligence* (2nd ed., pp. 602–25). New York: Cambridge University Press.

67. Nisbett, R. E. (2019). Culture and intelligence. In D. Cohen, & S. Kitayama (Eds.), *Handbook of cultural psychology* (2nd ed., pp. 207–21). New York: Guilford Press.

68. Luria, A. R. (1976). *Cognitive development: Its cultural and social foundations*. Cambridge, MA: Harvard University Press.

69. Nettelbeck, T., Zwalf, O., & Stough, C. (2020). Basic processes of intelligence. In R. J. Sternberg (Ed.), *Cambridge handbook of intelligence* (2nd ed., 471–503). New York: Cambridge University Press.

70. Sternberg, R. J., & Rifkin, B. (1979). The development of analogical reasoning processes. *Journal of Experimental Child Psychology*, 27, 195–232; Sternberg, R. J. (1981). Intelligence and nonentrenchment. *Journal of Educational Psychology*, 73, 1–16.

71. Gazzaniga, M. S. (1970). *The bisected brain*. New York: Appleton-Century-Crofts; Luria, A. R. (1973). *The working brain*. London: Penguin; Barrett, P. T., & Eysenck, H. J. (1992). Brain evoked potentials and intelligence: The Hendrickson paradigm. *Intelligence*, 16(3–4), 361–81; Haier, R. J. (2016). *The neuroscience of intelligence*. New York: Cambridge University Press; Haier, R. (2018). A view from the brain. In R. J. Sternberg (Ed.), *The nature of human intelligence* (pp. 167–82). New York: Cambridge University Press; Haier, R. J. (2020a). Biological approaches to intelligence. In R. J. Sternberg (Ed.), *Human intelligence: An introduction* (pp. 139–73). New York: Cambridge University Press; Haier, R. J. 2020b). The biological basis of intelligence. In R. J. Sternberg (Ed.), *Cambridge handbook of intelligence* (2nd ed., pp. 451–68). New York: Cambridge University Press.

72. Halstead, W. C. (1949). *Brain and intelligence: A quantitative study of the frontal lobes*. Chicago, IL: University of Chicago Press; Halstead, W. C. (1951). Biological intelligence. *Journal of Personality*, 20, 118–30.

73. Hebb, D. O. (1949). *The organization of behavior: A neuropsychological theory.* New York: Wiley.

74. Luria, A. R. (1973). *The working brain.* New York: Basic Books; Luria, A. R. (1980). *Higher cortical functions in man* (2nd ed., rev. & expanded). New York: Basic.

75. Kaufman, A. S., & Kaufman, N. L. (1983). *Kaufman assessment battery for children: Interpretive manual.* Circle Pines, MN: American Guidance Service; Naglieri, J. A., & Das, J. P. (1997). *Cognitive Assessment System.* Itasca, IL: Riverside Publishing.

76. Das, J. P., Kirby, J. R., & Jarman, R. F. (1979). *Simultaneous and successive cognitive processes.* New York: Academic Press; Naglieri, J. A., & Das, J. P. (1990). Planning, attention, simultaneous, and successive cognitive processes as a model for intelligence. *Journal of Psychoeducational Assessment,* 8, 303–37; Naglieri, J. A., & Das, J. P. (1997). *Cognitive Assessment System.* Itasca, IL: Riverside Publishing; Naglieri, J. A., & Das, J. P. (2002). Practical implications of general intelligence and PASS cognitive processes. In R. J. Sternberg, & E. L. Grigorenko (Eds.), *The general factor of intelligence: Fact or fiction* (pp. 55–86). Mahwah, NJ: Erlbaum.

77. Reed, T. E., & Jensen, A. R. (1992). Conduction velocity in a brain nerve pathway of normal adults correlates with intelligence level. *Intelligence,* 16, 259–72.

78. Vernon, P. A., & Mori, M. (1992). Intelligence, reaction times, and peripheral nerve conduction velocity. *Intelligence,* 8, 273–88.

79. Wickett, J. C., & Vernon, P. A. (1994). Peripheral nerve conduction velocity, reaction time, and intelligence: An attempt to replicate Vernon and Mori. *Intelligence,* 18, 127–32.

80. Johnson, R. Jr. (1986). A triarchic model of P300 amplitude. *Psychophysiology,* 23, 367–84; Johnson, R. Jr. (1988). The amplitude of the P300 component of the vent-related potential: Review and synthesis. In P. K. Ackles, J. R. Jennings, & M. G. H. Coles (Eds.), *Advances in psychophysiology: A research manual* (Vol. 3, pp. 69–138). Greenwich, CT: CAI Press.

81. Haier, R. J., Siegel, B., Tang, C., Abel, L., & Buchsbaum, M. S. (1992). Intelligence and changes in regional cerebral glucose metabolic rate following learning. *Intelligence,* 16, 415–26.

82. Jung, R. E., & Haier, R. J. (2007). The parietal-frontal integration theory (P-FIT) of intelligence: converging neuroimaging evidence. *Behavioral and Brain Sciences,* 30(2), 135–54.

83. Berry, J. W. (1984). Towards a universal psychology of cognitive competence. In P. S. Fry (Ed.), *Changing conceptions of intelligence and intellectual functioning* (pp. 36–61). Amsterdam: North-Holland; Cole, M. (1996). *Cultural psychology: A once and future discipline.* Cambridge, MA: Harvard University Press; Greenfield, P. M. (1997). You can't take it with you: Why abilities assessments don't cross cultures. *American Psychologist,* 52, 1115–24; Sternberg, R. J. (2017). Creativity, intelligence, and culture. In V. P. Glaveanu (Ed.), *Palgrave handbook of creativity and culture* (pp. 77–99). London: Palgrave.

84. Berry, J. W. (1974). Radical cultural relativism and the concept of intelligence. In J. W. Berry, & P. R. Dasen (Eds.), *Culture and cognition: Readings in cross-cultural psychology* (pp. 225–9). London: Methuen; Sternberg, R. J., & Kaufman J. C. (1998). Human abilities. *Annual Review of Psychology*, 49, 479–502.

85. Yang, S., & Sternberg, R. J. (1997). Conceptions of intelligence in ancient Chinese philosophy. *Journal of Theoretical and Philosophical Psychology*, 17, 101–19.

86. Yang, S., & Sternberg, R. J. (1997). Taiwanese Chinese people's conceptions of intelligence. *Intelligence*, 25, 21–36.

87. Chen, M. J. (1994). Chinese and Australian concepts of intelligence. *Psychology and Developing Societies*, 6, 101–17.

88. Sternberg, R. J., Conway, B. E., Ketron, J. L., & Bernstein, M. (1981). People's conceptions of intelligence. *Journal of Personality and Social Psychology*, 41, 37–55.

89. Frensch, P. A., & Sternberg, R. J. (1989). Expertise and intelligent thinking: When is it worse to know better? In R. J. Sternberg (Ed.), *Advances in the psychology of human intelligence* (Vol. 5, pp. 157–88). Hillsdale, NJ: Lawrence Erlbaum Associates.

90. Ruzgis, P. M, & Grigorenko, E. L. (1994). Cultural meaning systems, intelligence and personality. In R. J. Sternberg, & P. Ruzgis (Eds.), *Personality and intelligence* (pp. 248–70). New York: Cambridge.

91. Serpell, R. (1974). Aspects of intelligence in a developing country. *African Social Research*, 17, 576–96; Serpell, R. (1996). Cultural models of childhood in indigenous socialization and formal schooling in Zambia. In Hwang, C. P., & Lamb, M. E. (Eds.), *Images of childhood*. (pp. 129–42). Mahwah, NJ: Lawrence Erlbaum; Serpell, R. (2002). The embeddedness of human development within sociocultural context: Pedagogical, and political implications. *Social Development*, 11(2), 290–5.

92. Super C. M., & Harkness, S. (1982). The development of affect in infancy and early childhood. In D. Wagnet, & H. Stevenson (Eds.), *Cultural perspectives on child development* (pp. 1–19). San Francisco, CA: W.H. Freeman; Super, C. M., & Harkness, S. (1986). The developmental niche: A conceptualization at the interface of child and culture. *International Journal of Behavioral Development*, 9, 545–69; Super, C. M., & Harkness, S. (1993). The developmental niche: A conceptualization at the interface of child and culture. In R. A. Pierce, & M. A. Black, (Eds.), *Life-span development: A diversity reader*. (pp. 61–77). Dubuque, IA: Kendall/Hunt Publishing Co.

93. Dasen, P. (1984). The cross-cultural study of intelligence: Piaget and the Baoulé. *International Journal of Psychology*, 19, 407–34.

94. Lutz, C. (1985). Ethnopsychology compared to what? Explaining behaviour and consciousness among the Ifaluk. In G. M. White, & J. Kirkpatrick (Eds.), *Person, self, and experience: Exploring Pacific ethnopsycholgoies* (pp. 35–79). Berkeley, CA: University of California Press; Poole, F. J. P. (1985). Coming into social being: Cultural images of infants in Bimin-Kuskusmin folk

psychology. In G. M. White, & J. Kirkpatrick (Eds.), *Person, self, and experience: Exploring Pacific ethnopsychologies* (pp. 183–244). Berkeley, CA: University of California Press; White, G. M. (1985). Premises and purposes in a Solomon Islands ethnopsychology. In G. M. White, & J. Kirkpatrick (Eds.), *Person, self, and experience: Exploring Pacific ethnopsychologies* (pp. 328–66). Berkeley, CA: University of California Press; Azuma, H., & Kashiwagi, K. (1987). Descriptions for an intelligent person: A Japanese study. *Japanese Psychological Research*, 29, 17–26.

95. Grigorenko, E. L., Geissler, P. W., Prince, R. et al. (2001). The organization of Luo conceptions of intelligence: A study of implicit theories in a Kenyan village. *International Journal of Behavior Development*, 25, 367–78.

96. Okagaki, L., & Sternberg, R. J. (1993). Parental beliefs and children's school performance. *Child Development*, 64(1), 36–56.

97. Gardner, H. (1983). *Frames of mind: The theory of multiple intelligences*. New York: Basic; Gardner, H. (1993). *Multiple intelligences: The theory in practice*. New York: Basic; Sternberg, R. J. (2003). *Wisdom, intelligence, and creativity, synthesized*. New York: Cambridge University Press; Gardner, H., Kornhaber, M, & Chen, J.-Q. (2018). The theory of multiple intelligences: Psychological and educational perspectives. In R. J. Sternberg (Ed.), *The nature of human intelligence* (pp. 116–29). New York: Cambridge University Press; Sternberg, R. J. (2020). The augmented theory of successful intelligence. In R. J. Sternberg (Ed.), *Cambridge handbook of intelligence* (2nd ed., pp. 679–708). New York: Cambridge University Press.

98. Kornhaber, M. (2020). The theory of multiple intelligences. In R. J. Sternberg (Ed.), *Cambridge handbook of intelligence* (2nd ed., pp. 659–78). New York: Cambridge University Press.

99. Fodor, J. (1983). *The modularity of mind*. Cambridge, MA: Bradford Books.

100. Visser, B. A., Ashton, M. C., & Vernon, P. A. (2006). Beyond *g*: Putting multiple intelligences theory to the test. *Intelligence*, 34, 487–502.

101. Jensen, A. R. (1998). *The g factor*. Westport, CT: Greenwood-Praeger.

102. Ceci, S. J. (1996). *On intelligence . . . more or less* (expanded ed.). Cambridge, MA: Harvard University Press.

103. Shelley, P. B., Freistat, N. (Ed.), & Reiman, D. H. (Ed.) (2002). *Shelley's poetry and prose* (Norton Critical Edition) (2nd ed.). New York: W. W. Norton.

CHAPTER 3

Intelligence as the Broad Ability to Adapt to the Environment

In Chapter 2, I reviewed various notions of intelligence. The thesis of this chapter, and indeed, of this book, is that our Western notion of intelligence – in terms of IQ, general intelligence (g), and scores on proxy tests such as the SAT and ACT – is seriously incorrect. It is so incorrect, I will argue, that it is taking down humanity as we know it.

In large part, as a result of our Western conception of intelligence, we have to worry about whether there will be a viable world left for our children, our grandchildren, and their children and grandchildren. We justifiably may come close to panic if we think about the world we are leaving for our children, grandchildren, great-grandchildren, and beyond. Many people already are panicking. And with good reason. I am writing these pages while teaching at the University of Heidelberg in Germany. Germany, like much of the rest of Europe and many other locations as well, is currently experiencing an unprecedented heat wave with temperatures almost never before found in this part of the world.[1] Parts of India right now are so hot that they are becoming uninhabitable.[2]

I will argue that the relationship between intelligence and the destruction of the world as we have known it is *causal* – that is, that by misconceiving of intelligence, we are doing great damage to the world of the present and much more damage to the world of the future. This damage that we are doing to the world flies in the face of any notion of intelligence that is true to its fundamental definition as consisting of adaptation to the environment.[3]

Where does one even start with a discussion of intelligence as adaptation to the environment? There are lots of places in which one might start, but how about, for today, starting out with a discussion of golf?

---

* Parts of this chapter draw ideas presented in Sternberg, R. J. (2019). A theory of adaptive intelligence and its relation to general intelligence. *Journal of Intelligence.* https://doi.org/10.3390/jintelligence7040023

3.1 Let's Talk About Golf

Golf is no doubt a great sport. It is fun to watch and, for many, fun to play (I would not know; I do not play it). But to play it, you have to have access to a golf course and that, in most instances, will cost money, often, quite a bit of money, and in some golf courses, a real heck of a lot of money.

Many high schools do not have golf teams. In the end, private schools and wealthy public schools are more likely to have golf teams because they are also more likely to be able to gain access to a golf course for their interested students. There are, of course, other kinds of athletic teams that are also more likely to be found in wealthier high schools or preparatory schools, including water polo and lacrosse. Poorer schools simply do not have access to the funds to support teams that would, by some standards, be considered to exotic.

If one looks at the members of, say, the Harvard University undergraduate golf team or water polo team, one finds about what one would expect. The large majority of the students who play varsity golf (or water polo) come from privileged schools – either elite private schools or public high schools in upper-income neighborhoods. Those students who gain an edge for college admissions, at Harvard or elsewhere, by virtue of their playing golf, water polo, or whatever, are trading on their socioeconomic status SES) to gain this edge in admission by virtue of their parents' SES. Once they are admitted, it will not matter that the athletic skills that got them admitted are in a sport primarily for privileged children. The fact that they got a Harvard degree will do much of the rest in setting them up for life, unless they totally blow it. And with a Harvard degree, they really would have to blow it badly to end up failing in life. People usually think of those with a Harvard degree as "intelligent." This so-called 'intelligence" may have consisted in their being born into a family that could afford for them to learn golf.

Just to be clear, relatively few people would say that being a good golf player is somehow a good indicator of intelligence, or mental abilities, or character, or wisdom, or creativity, or any of the other skills one might associate with success in life. Perhaps it does require a certain amount of self-discipline. But if one were assessing self-discipline, there almost certainly are better ways of assessing it than skill in golf, which is a highly confounded measure involving so many different things. But suppose the problem is not just golf, water polo, or lacrosse – sports of the well-to-do and well-connected. Suppose the children of the well-off have the edge in pretty much anything, merely because they are children of the well-off.

3.2   It's All Golf, Really

Were the problem only golf or water polo, perhaps we could write off the problem as one privileging only a small number of students who will go to elite colleges. But it is not. Suppose that much of US (and other societies) is built on the same foundation as that for deciding that really good golf or water polo players are entitled to a Harvard degree.

Ask yourself how often, in your life, have you been faced with multiple-choice problems testing your skill in solving relatively obscure kinds of verbal or mathematical problems? Do problems of the sorts found in standardized tests of intelligence or related abilities really represent people's skills to succeed in, or even cope with, life? Or are they, in some measure, like golf and water polo? Obviously, they are not the same. For the most part, we, as a society and as individual members of that society, value, for children, standardized-test performance more than golf performance. For adults, we do not really care about standardized-test performance, only what it has bought one in terms of a degree.

Suppose, for example, that society decided to create a hierarchy of social classes based on golf skill. Everyone is tested for their golf skills, starting at an early age, and continuing at least until they are adolescents. It does not matter whether they have had an opportunity to play golf; they get to play when they take the test. The situation in golf is analogous to that of students who now take the SAT, ACT, and related tests. Some students are marvelously well-prepared, by dint of their home background and schooling, to take the tests; others are hardly prepared at all. But they all have to take the test and then be compared on its results.

Is there something wrong with these tests, beyond their inherent unfairness? I would argue that there is, and that it is something very unfair – something that shows how truly mindless society has become when it comes to standardized testing. We care about standardized-test scores when what we should care much more about is what young people have to contribute to the survival and thriving of the world as we know it. But we are like proverbial lemmings.

3.3   About Lemmings and Mass Suicide

Consider the lemming, which is a small rodent that is usually found in Arctic regions, often in the frozen tundra or in open grasslands. They are a type of vole, which is a mouse-like creature. Most people probably never even would have heard of lemmings were it not for their reputed tendency to commit mass suicide by jumping, en masse, off cliffs. Most people believe that they do indeed jump off cliffs, and Walt Disney helped to immortalize this belief in a 1958 movie, *White Wilderness*, which faked a scene of lemmings jumping off a cliff to their deaths. As a child, I always wondered why lemmings would commit suicide, but I never cared enough to look it up.

Had I looked it up, I might have discovered that, in fact, lemmings do not commit mass suicide – the common-cultural belief is erroneous, popularized by its having spread not only through the Disney movie but also through common-cultural beliefs that are passed down from one generation to another. In fact, the kind of lemming that has been reputed to commit mass suicide, the Norwegian lemming, does jump off cliffs into water, but that is because these lemmings know how to swim. They jump off cliffs, on occasion, as part of a mass migration when the area they are in runs out of food and some of them need to migrate to find a new source of food.

If this were a book about lemmings, I would go on to describe more about the different kinds of lemmings there are and their varied behaviors. But lemmings are not the topic of this book, so that is it for lemmings except for four lessons to be learned from this story:

1 Lemmings show us, in the context of their species, exactly what intelligence is – the ability to adapt to the environment.
2 Lemmings are not the species that commits mass suicide.
3 Lemmings, rather, are adaptive and move on to another habitat when they run out of food in a given habitat (a practice that can be successful so long as there is another habitat to which to migrate and which they are able to reach).
4 Just because large numbers of people believe something does not make it so; but people, or in this case, filmmakers, will at times go to great lengths to perpetuate common stereotypes, in this case, even faking a scene about lemmings committing mass suicide to make it look like the belief about lemmings is correct.

In this chapter, I will argue that humans, rather than lemmings, are the species committing mass suicide, albeit in a slow-paced unfolding drama. And even worse than with the superstition about lemmings, they are taking down other species with them. Their doing so is at least in part a result of viewing intelligence in terms of IQ instead of in terms of adaptation, not just for any individual, but for the human species, *Homo sapiens*, as a whole. Metaphorically, we care about who plays "golf," or the game of standardized tests, and how well, when what we should care about is species survival.

3.4   Adaptive Intelligence

Way back in 1950, what was then a new Japanese movie, *Rashomon*, made its way to the United States. It won multiple awards, among them, a Golden Globe Award for Best Foreign Film, a Golden Lion Award, and an Academy Honorary Award. The film often appears on a variety of lists of the best movies ever made. For example, *The Guardian* newspaper listed it as the fifth best crime movie of all time,[4] which is impressive given that the movie was not even in the English language in which *The Guardian* is published.

In *Rashomon*, four people describe an event, which would seem to be that a bandit raped a woman in a forest and her husband, a samurai, was killed. But each of the parties describes the event that took place in different, and sometimes mutually inconsistent, or even contradictory ways. In the end, it is hard to tell what happened during the rape, or even if a rape took place.

The concept of intelligence, as described in Chapter 1, has turned out to be somewhat "Rashomon-like." It has been defined, understood, and conceptualized in diverse ways, some of them consistent, others, mutually contradictory.[5] As in the movie *Rashomon*, the accounts seem to be shaded by the self-interest, or at least the ideological predispositions, of those who have sought to characterize intelligence. If one knows the theorists and researchers, one pretty much knows what they are going to say, given their general ideological framework.

As in *Rashomon*, there is a real phenomenon to be explained. But the explanations are as slippery as those in *Rashomon*. For example, as we saw in Chapter 2, intelligence can be viewed as a biologically defined trait, but it also can be viewed as a cultural invention.[6] In this case, the biology of intelligence would depend completely on how a particular culture defines intelligence.[7] Some researchers view intelligence as essentially unitary,[8] whereas others see it as multiple – that is, as there being many intelligences rather than just one.[9]

At some level, intelligence must be biological. When people act, their actions may be stimulated by occurrences in the environment, but the actions stem from activity in the brain. Even cultural variables that affect intelligence, such as diverse ways of raising children, would have to affect whatever biological substrate underlies intelligence or how that substrate operates in the world. But if people are interested in intelligence and wish to understand the nature of intelligence biologically, the brain is not the place to start, even though it might seem to be. All cognitive processes, whether or not involved in intelligence, will necessarily have brain correlates. Correlates are not necessarily causal. Over the course of a child's life from, say, age one to age sixteen, both height and intelligence presumably increase – they are correlated. But height does not cause intelligence and intelligence does not cause height. They both depend on different growth processes. So merely showing that performance on a cognitive or other task is correlated with, and hence, relates to brain functioning is not, in itself, any big deal. One should start with a different level of biology, namely, the evolutionary function of intelligence. On this view, we understand intelligence not only in humans, but in diverse species as a result of their different levels of biological adaptation.[10]

3.5   Two Kinds of Intelligence

Let us consider two kinds of intelligence. One kind is the intelligence as most researchers in the field of intelligence talk about it. This is the kind of intelligence derived from the geographic metaphor (see Chapter 2). The other kind is intelligence as derived from its biologically based definition of adaptation to the environment that goes beyond metaphors (also as discussed in Chapter 2).

3.5.1 General Intelligence (General Cognitive Ability)

Virtually all definitions of intelligence, however they may disagree, agree on one thing – that intelligence must involve the ability to adapt to the environment.[11] Sometimes, the language of the definitions is different. For example, it might be that "it reflects a broader and deeper capability for comprehending our surroundings – 'catching on,' 'making sense' of things, or 'figuring out' what to do" (See Note 5, "Mainstream Science on Intelligence," p. 13). But a common feature of the skills alleged to be involved in intelligence is that they involve, in some way, adaptation to the environment. Such skills might include "learning," "reasoning," "decision making," and/or "problem solving." In each case, one learns, reasons, decides about, or solves problems in the environment in order to adapt to it.

Imagine, for example, a hypothetical group of people who scored highly on intelligence tests formulated by scientists in a particular culture but who then proceeded to act in ways that brought about or at least hastened their own demise as well as the existence of what might have been their future progeny. Such genocidal actions would defy any rational, and certainly biologically based Darwinian definition of intelligence as involving adaptation to the environment.

Consider an example of the importance of adaptive intelligence. The example is science-fictional, but unfortunately, science fiction often has a way of coming true some years after it is written. *1984*,[12] for example, today seems all too real. In the particular fictional serial tale relevant here, that of Superman, as presented in DC Comics, the population of the planet Krypton ignored and actively belittled the warnings of a distinguished scientist, Jor-El, that Krypton was on the verge of exploding and thus vanishing.[13] (In one more recent version of the story, in the movie *Man of Steel*, the tale was that harvesting of minerals from deep inside the planet led to the explosion – something that would never happen on Earth, of course, or would it?) As a result of the people's ignoring the warnings, at least in the original version of the Superman tale, the planet Krypton did indeed explode. All the people of Krypton died except for Jor-El's son, Kal-El, who was sent by his parents in a small rocket ship to Earth. On Earth, Kal-El first became Superboy and later became Superman.

Were the Kryptonians who ignored Jor-El's warning intelligent? Is it intelligent to stick your head into the sand when your life and that of everyone you hold dear is threatened? Whatever their scores on some hypothetical Kryptonian intelligence test, the inhabitants' allowing themselves and their loved ones to die in a predictable explosion would seem, at the very least, inconsistent with, and probably directly contrary to any reasonable definition of intelligence as adaptation. They did not adapt, and so they perished. And the descendants whom they would have created would never come to be.

Allowing the occurrence of a potentially avoidable mass extinction of one's own species, as well as of oneself, would seem to be the ultimate act of biologically maladaptive behavior. It is what the lemmings are supposed to do, but do not do. It is what only humans do. Indeed, later in this chapter, I will suggest that much of the behavior we currently see on Earth is not all so different from that of the residents on the fictional Krypton. The only difference is that the inhabitants of Earth are real.

The main argument of this book is simple: The term "intelligence" has come to be used to describe a psychological construct that is related only vaguely, if it is related at all, to intelligence as adaptation to the environment. The term "intelligence" better should be used in its original sense – to characterize adaptive behavior. Despite the definition of intelligence as involving adaptation, the usual use of the term "intelligence" has little to do with adaptation to the environment, at least in a biological sense. At the very least, *adaptive intelligence* should be distinguished from *general intelligence* in the sense the latter term is usually used.

The word "intelligence" has come to be used, for more than a century, to refer to a fairly standardized set of cognitive abilities. As described in Chapter 2, some of the abilities were first identified by Charles

Spearman, who suggested that there is a general ability that is used for all cognitive tasks and that there also are specific abilities, each relevant to a single task.[14] Louis Thurstone, somewhat later, suggested a more elaborate model, with a series of abilities, such as comprehending verbal material and numerical computations skills.[15] The work of Spearman and Thurstone later was further elaborated upon and systematized by John Carroll, as well as other investigators.[16]

This model deals, more or less, with intelligence as intelligence tests and their proxies measure it.[17] The model encompasses cognitive skills such as those involved in acquiring and using vocabulary, inductive reasoning (reasoning from the specific to the general), spatial visualization (imagining what figures would look like when rotated or otherwise manipulated), memory (remembering strings of digits, letters, words, or pictures), and perceptual speed (how quickly one can process perceptual information).[18] Other abilities, such as deductive reasoning (reasoning from the general the specific), also may be included. Different models of intelligence, in the usual Western sense of the word, involve different levels of differentiation[19] or organization.[20] Nevertheless, the skills highly overlap over models of intelligence and across intelligence tests.[21] The differences among models tend to be in details rather than in any broad conceptualization of what intelligence is.

3.5.2 Adaptive Intelligence

Let us now focus on intelligence in what I suggest is its true biological meaning, as discussed in Chapter 1. Let us then discuss the typical Western conception of "intelligence", only in relation to this biological concept. I am not arguing that intelligence is 100 percent biological. It is not – far from it. Intelligence, using any definition at all, also is influenced by other variables, especially sociocultural ones, as research conducted under the cultural metaphor makes clear (see Chapter 2). But intelligence fundamentally is a matter of adaptive thought and behavior.

In order to avoid confusion in terminology, I will refer to what I am calling intelligence as *adaptive intelligence*. It is intelligence that is used for the purpose of biological (and other forms of) adaptation to the environment. I will distinguish adaptive intelligence from the usual Western conception of *general intelligence* or *general cognitive ability* – the first (highest-order, most general) factor in hierarchical models of cognitive abilities. "General intelligence" may be presented as biological. But in the sense that many Westerners use it, it is largely culturally, not biologically, defined, regardless of whatever claims IQ testers or others may make for it.

In biology, "adaptation" is a "process by which an animal or plant species becomes fitted to its environment; it is the result of natural selection's acting upon heritable variation."[22] I will call this kind of adaptation, *narrow adaptation.*

An alternative view of biological adaptation is to view it as involving preservation only of one's own set of genes, not of the human species in general.[23] The arguments made in this book will apply to either view of biological adaptation, that is, as concerning the species or as concerning one's own set of genes.

The view of intelligence as biological adaptation in a narrow sense oversimplifies what intelligence is. This is the view of intelligence as changing oneself (adapting) to fit the environment. As an example, cockroaches have apparently been on Earth for about 300 million years. At a species level, therefore, they certainly have been very adaptive. Bacteria also have been around an extremely long time. But if cockroaches and bacteria are "intelligent," their "intelligence" would seem to exist in a sense that is more limited than the sense in which we usually refer to intelligence. In this regard, "adaptation" can and should be viewed broadly rather than narrowly. A broad view would involve not only changing oneself to fit the environment (*narrow adaptation*), but also changing or somehow modifying the environment to fit oneself (*shaping the environment*) and finding or creating new environments as needed (*selecting environments*).[24] In this sense, broad adaptation involves somehow making the environment work for you, or else finding a new environment.

Cockroaches, for example, are adaptive to their environments. But their ability to shape and select environments, while impressive, is much more limited than that of those species with more of what I am calling "adaptive intelligence." In the remainder of this chapter and book, I will refer to *adaptation* not just in its narrow sense, which is that of changing oneself to fit the environment. Rather, I will be speaking of adaptation in the broad sense of additionally shaping the environment to fit oneself and selecting new environments as needed in one's life, usually when adaptation and selection fail. Narrow adaptation (changing oneself to fit the environment), plus shaping of existing environments and selection of new environments, is what I will call *broad adaptation.* Humans' level, or at least potential level, of broad adaptation, is what distinguishes humans from other species. But the crucial word here is "potential." Humans seem intent on destroying their own potential and taking down with them the world as we know it.

A conundrum arises from the definition of intelligence as adaptation (adaptive intelligence). This puzzle is a consequence of two outcomes that would appear to be fundamentally incompatible – greater general intelligence, on the one hand; but also associated with that greater general intelligence, maladaptive behavior, on the other hand. This conundrum arises when (a) higher cognitive information-processing capacity (as usually associated with higher general intelligence) is utilized (b) so as to reduce adaptation (as usually associated with lower adaptive intelligence). Let us consider some examples.

First, the consensus of over 95 percent of climate scientists is that humans are acting in ways that worsen levels of global climate change.[25] (I am directly experiencing the results right now as I am writing in Germany.) Emissions of carbon dioxide gas reached an all-time high level in 2018,[26] and most likely went higher by the end of 2019. Indeed, as of September 2019, things were looking very bleak.[27] This human-induced emission of carbon dioxide, leading to global climate change, in combination with other factors, is causing a massive extinction of species, with roughly one million species already extinct or near-extinct and more to come.[28]

One could argue, of course, that intelligence as adaptation applies only to members of one's own species. In this case, some would say, who cares about other species? Such a view is obviously shortsighted. At the very least, other species are essential in the food chain, just so long as humans do not take to eating each other. But in any case, the consequences of global climate change already are resulting in deaths of members of our own species. These deaths are occurring through a variety of weather-related events: increasing temperatures, fierce (Categories 3–5) hurricanes, frequent tornadoes, typhoons, and serious flooding resulting as well from many kinds of extraordinary weather events. It has been estimated that, in future decades, more than a quarter of a million people may die annually because of global climate change.[29] There are few parts of the world that are being totally spared. As I review this chapter, wildfires are burning out of control in many parts of the world, notably, New South Wales in Australia, the Amazon in Brazil, and California and Oregon in the United States.

In the United States, coastlines and even interior areas of states are disappearing.[30] In Germany, where I am now, and elsewhere, people already are dying. In excess of 40,000 people died in Europe during a heat wave in the summer of 2003.[31] Climate change is already driving mass migrations around the globe and these only will get worse – much worse – with the possibility of wars being fought over space and water.[32] The disappearance of potable water is especially frightening, as people can live through bad weather and claustrophobic space conditions, but they cannot live through lack of potable water. The World Bank has estimated that, by 2050, 140 million people might be forced to migrate, making current problems with refugees seem puny.[33]

We know that transfer in problem solving is hard to get under the best of circumstances, even when two problems are essentially the same except for the way they are presented.[34] These are the problems the world faces that must be dealt with. Societies are choosing people to deal with these problems on the basis of whether they can solve multiple-choice test problems, whether we think we would like to have a beer with them, and whether they are good actors, no matter how hypocritical, self-preoccupied, and even mentally ill they may be. Of course, the world went through all this in World War II, but as Santayana is alleged to have noted, those who do not learn from history are doomed to repeat it. That is what is happening now.[35] How good will multiple-choice experts be at solving such large, challenging unstructured problems? It is ironic that g-theorists – those who are adherents of the concept of general intelligence – are so impressed with the generalization of g across a wide range of fairly trivial tasks that have no species-adaptive value – and often little, if any individual-adaptive value. What would be impressive instead is a demonstration of strong generality to much harder problems. Many of the fairly trivial problems to which g shows such high generalization have certain features in common, which distinguish psychometric-test problems from serious real-world adaptive problems. General intelligence predicts many things; one thing it has failed to be shown to predict is who will solve the pressing problems facing the world today.

Table 3.1 shows the relationship between the kinds of problems to which IQ tests and their proxies best generalize and problems to which they presumably generalize less. The g construct can be seen as a limiting case of adaptive intelligence for problems that are of a certain kind. As one moves toward higher levels of the characteristics in the table, the needs of adaptive intelligence start to diverge from the needs for solving IQ-test problems.

The table is, in essence, a theory of task complexity. As tasks become more complex and varied, the relevance of general intelligence becomes less clear because so much more enters into being adaptively intelligent. Others take a different view, seeing general intelligence as becoming more relevant with increasing task complexity.[36] But the kinds of complexity they consider are far from the problems that threaten to destroy the world as we know it, such as lack of potable water, pandemics such as COVID-19, nuclear weapons, and global climate change. These kinds of complexity go

Table 3.1 *Elements of tasks requiring adaptive intelligence*

Level A refers to problems at low, standardized-test-like levels of complexity; Level B refers to problems at high, everyday-life levels of complexity.

I. Level of Pre-Recognition of Problem

A. *Pre-recognized* – one is alerted to the fact that there is a problem to be solved

Example: Any IQ-test problem or problem in school homework

B. *Not pre-recognized* – one is not alerted to the fact that there is a problem to be solved

Example: One has a spot on the skin that may be cancerous but no one has mentioned it and one has no physician appointments upcoming at which its existence might be pointed out – the onus is therefore on oneself to recognize it as a potential problem

Comment: Whereas school and test problems are recognized for students, real-life problems generally are not; one has to recognize when one's intimate relationship is not going well, when one's finances are in peril, when one's job is not working out, etc.

II. Level of Predefinition of Problem

A. *Predefined* – the existence of the problem and what the problem is have been pointed out to one

Examples: Any IQ-test problem; one has a mole that a dermatologist has labeled as cancerous

B. *Not predefined* – one is aware of a problem, but not of exactly what the nature of the problem is

Examples: One's child is crying but one does not know why; a farmer is desperate because it is no longer raining enough to irrigate his cornfields but he does not know why the rain has practically disappeared

Comment: Whereas test and school problems are generally predefined, real-life problems generally are not, such as what it means that the weather is getting hotter or that rain is becoming scarcer.

III. Level of Problem Structure

A. *Highly structured* – there is at least one clear path to solution; the beginning state, end state, and constraints are clearly specifiable

Example: Typical arithmetic word problem on a standardized test

B. *Ill-structured* – there are no clear paths to solution; the beginning state, end state, and constraints are not all clearly specifiable

Example: How can one get a child who is crying for unknown reasons to stop crying?

Comment: Intelligence-test problems are generally highly structured. Serious life problems, such as how to recover from a traumatic personal loss, are generally ill-structured.

IV. Level of Answer(s) Being Presented

A. *Presented* – answer(s) is/are presented along with incorrect answers

Example: Multiple-choice tests

B. *Not presented* – answer(s) is/are not presented

Examples: Essay tests; problem of what to do about a possibly cancerous mole

V. Level of Emotional Involvement

A. *Low level of emotional involvement* – problem involves little or no level of emotional investment

Examples: An IQ-test problem; deciding what to wear for work

B. *High level of emotional involvement* – problem is difficult to solve in part because of emotional investment on the part of the problem-solver

Table 3.1 (*cont.*)

Example: Under what circumstances should the law allow a woman to have an abortion of an unborn child?

Comment: Many life and world problems involve a high level of emotional investment, to the point at which emotional factors are such that people of equal IQ have radically different views regarding solutions; such problems require an infusion of wisdom to reach a solution that has broad acceptability.

VI. Level of Personal Stakes in Outcome

A. *Low Stakes* – the way the problem is solved appears to have little or no importance to the course of one's life

Examples: IQ-test problems; deciding whether to buy a Ford or a Chevrolet of roughly equal price and levels of performance

B. *High Stakes* – the way the problem is solved is extremely important to one's life and may alter the course of one's life

Examples: Whether to get an abortion; whether to quit one's job rather than act unethically; whether to leave a faltering marriage

VII. Level of Technical Expertise Required for Problem Solution

A. *Low Level of Technical Expertise* – one needs relatively little or no technical training to solve the problem

Examples – defining a word or solving a number-series problem on an IQ test; ordering food at a restaurant; treating oneself for a routine headache

B. *High Level of Technical Expertise* – one needs a great deal of technical training to solve the problem

Examples – designing a cell phone; making a violin; doing meaningful research on cancer

Comment: Most IQ-test problems require relatively low levels of technical expertise, at least for those socialized in cultures that routinely use such tests. Most everyday-life problems also require low levels of technical expertise. IQ predicts acquisition and utilization of many kinds of technical expertise, at least up to a point.

VIII. Level of Tacit Knowledge Required for Problem Solving

A. *Low Level of Tacit Knowledge* – one needs relatively little life or job experience to solve the problem

Examples: IQ-test problems; how to tell time; how to boil potatoes; how to peel a banana

B. *High Level of Tacit Knowledge* – one needs to have learned a lot from life and job experience to solve the problem

Examples: How to meet production quotas while still meeting quality-control standards in a factory suffering from high employee turnover; how to treat a patient presenting symptoms of borderline personality disorder

Comment: Problems of consequence for one's life often require a high level of tacit knowledge, a kind of knowledge not well tapped by IQ tests and their proxies. The Wechsler Intelligence Scales have one subtest dealing with tacit knowledge – Comprehension. Standardized-test problems typically require some level of academic knowledge.

IX. Level of Novelty of Problem

A. *Relatively Low Level of Novelty* – the problem is relatively familiar in view of one's past experience

Examples: A vocabulary item on an IQ test; turning on a television; cooking a hamburger

Table 3.1 (*cont.*)

B. *Relatively High Level of Novelty* – the problem is relatively novel in view of one's past experience
Examples: One is buying a house for the first time; one is planning one's financial future for the first time; one is deciding whether to get married to an individual one has known but not lived with; some IQ-test problems, such as challenging Raven Matrix problems
Comment: Problems with relatively high levels of novelty may require creativity to solve, which is measured, but only weakly, by fluid-ability tests.
X. Level of Complexity of Problem
A. *Relatively Lower Level of Complexity* – the problem has relatively few parts or may have more parts, but they are each simple to solve
Examples: Planning for a stroll in the park; planning for a rendezvous with friends at a local restaurant
B. *Relatively Higher Level of Complexity* – the problem has many parts or fewer parts but each part is complex in itself
Examples: Planning for the birth of a child; planning for one's career path
Comment: IQ tests predict performance up to moderate levels of complexity.

Note: These levels are on a continuum. Only high and low levels are shown in the table. Adaptive intelligence is involved at all levels. At the lower levels, adaptive intelligence becomes more similar in its characteristics to what is measured by IQ tests. At the higher levels, it becomes less similar in its characteristics.

far beyond how one can keep the books in a business or how one can make more money for the business.

It is utter folly to believe that the people who are good at solving trivial multiple-choice problems necessarily will be able to solve serious problems in the world. On the contrary, some of them may bring their skills for solving small, structured problems to the solution of large, unstructured problems, and with predictably disastrous results. We have many organizational and political leaders who, through their skill in solving trivial problems, gained admission to, and degrees from prestigious universities, only to prove themselves utterly incompetent at solving the problems they then faced in their jobs. Little wonder, perhaps, that so many CEOs, in fact, went to public colleges rather than prestigious private ones.[37]

It is not just about CEOs. The unfortunate irony in heat waves caused in part by excess carbon emissions is that the economically developed countries, full of well-educated people with high IQs, cause many of the climate-related problems; the economically less well-developed countries, with less well-educated people and thus possibly lower IQs (reflecting, in part, poorer educational opportunities), pay the price because they have fewer means to protect themselves against weather-related and other results of climate change.[38]

This pattern of the less well-off paying the price for the follies of the more well-off is not limited to climate change, of course. When countries such as the United States introduced mass IQ testing to deal with a perceived problem of immigration, it was the poor, the homeless, and the less fortunate, in general, who paid the price.[39] When eugenicists recommended sterilizing people with lower IQs (and when the Nazis actually executed some such people), it was again the less fortunate who paid the price.[40] The historical pattern with respect to IQ-based theory has been that, sometimes, the so-called "intelligent" people come up with the toxic ideas and the people labeled as not so intelligent by their instruments suffer the consequences. Climate change is only one example of a general historical pattern.

One point of view would be that lack of general intelligence and its proxies are the only constructs needed to explain weak action or, in some places, inaction with respect to global climate change. On this view, smart, scientifically literate people would believe in the validity of human-induced climate change whereas not so smart, scientifically illiterate people would not. This view does not hold up, however. Rather, general intelligence and its correlates such as scientific literacy and scientific education are poor predictors of people's views on climate change and related phenomena.[41] Thus, part of the problem of people with high IQs creating the technology that causes problems for themselves and so many others is that having a high IQ is much more helpful in creating potentially destructive technology than it is in recognizing the destructive effects of the technology that one creates.

Ultimately, human-induced climate change, if it is not stopped or greatly reduced, will be enough to destroy humanity as we know it. It no longer takes an asteroid from outer space of the kind that created the climate change and other effects that killed off the dinosaurs. But regrettably, human-induced climate change is just one example of our species-destructive behavior. It is in no way merely a one-off.

A second example of species-destructive behavior is the creation of technology that produces extremely unhealthy amounts of air pollution (which also is linked to, but distinct from, climate change). High levels of air pollution have been linked to roughly 4.2 million human deaths annually, and also to far more cases of severe respiratory and other related illnesses.[42] Let us put the figure of 4.2 million cases into perspective. This number of people exceeds the population level of the second largest city in the United States – Los Angeles, California. Los Angeles, as it happens, ranks #1 in ozone pollution among all cities in the United States.[43] Were air pollution merely irritating psychologically, the situation would be unpleasant but not toxic. But air pollution is potentially deadly. It also causes stunting of cognitive growth in children.[44] Air pollution in India was responsible for over a million deaths in 2017.[45]

How much do problems with global climate change and air pollution – as two examples of current worldly problems – have to do with intelligence? Are they perhaps instead issues to do with avarice, selfishness, ideology, or short-term thinking at the expense of long-term thinking? For those who view intelligence in terms of the general intelligence of the geographic metaphor, this argument would seem to be largely justifiable. But if one instead views intelligence as *adaptive* intelligence, the argument fails because adaptive intelligence, by definition, requires people to act in ways that are biologically adaptive in leading to species survival or, at least, survival of one's own gene pool. Creating conditions for an uninhabitable planet for ourselves, our children, and future generations beyond those children can be viewed only as biologically maladaptive. It really does not matter where such maladaptive behavior falls on the general-intelligence scale. It is contrary to high levels of adaptive intelligence.

Unfortunately, global climate change and significant air pollution are only two of many examples of species-extinguishing behavior on the part of humans. A third such behavior is the fabrication of nuclear weapons. An atomic bomb killed over 100,000 people in Hiroshima, Japan. A separate atomic bomb resulted in the deaths of almost 100,000 people in Nagasaki, Japan.[46] Some would argue that killing those people in Hiroshima and Nagasaki was necessary to save even more people. But how far can one extend this argument with regard to potential future use of nuclear weapons by terrorists or rogue states? Do they also need to teach the world some kind of lesson? Certainly, they think they do. Or what can we make even of the potential use of nuclear weapons by established powers that then will claim that it was necessary to kill off the people in a country to prevent the people in that country from killing off even more people elsewhere? Where does that line of reasoning end?

The explosion of an atomic bomb and even the resulting radioactivity might be only the beginning of the problems with explosion of nuclear devices. Many more people might be killed in the future by the "nuclear winter" that could follow from atomic explosions.[47] As with global warming and pollution, collateral effects often are worse than the direct effects of a particular human-made problem.

Another, fourth dubious accomplishment of Homo sapiens is that the same species has been generally intelligent enough to create antibiotics and also generally unintelligent enough to overuse them and render many of them ineffective. Antibiotic resistance of bacteria poses one of the greatest threats, perhaps the greatest existing threat, to global health.[48] In the United States, drug-resistant bacteria are killing someone every fifteen minutes, many more than were previously thought.[49] On top of all that, there are so-called anti-vaxxers, who oppose vaccinating their children against childhood diseases such as measles. Many of these anti-vaxxers are highly generally intelligent, in the sense of the geographic metaphor. Their opposition to vaccination of children, based on pseudo-science, has led to an epidemic of measles, a disease declared to be eradicated in the year 2000. From January 1 to June 20, 2019, there were 1,077 cases of measles in the United States, the greatest number since 1992.[50] Lest this seem like a benign outcome, consider that measles can lead to severe complications, including pneumonia and encephalitis. Up to one out of twenty children who get measles then proceed to pneumonia, the most common cause of death among children who contract measles.[51] And, as noted in Chapter 1, they often lose their immune memory, meaning that they often become susceptible again to diseases to which they once were immune.[52] If so-called "intelligent" parents are allowing their children to contract measles, there really is something wrong with the conventional conception of intelligence! Were people's beliefs in unfounded conspiracies limited only to measles, society would perhaps be in trouble, but not in serious trouble. Unfortunately, these days, conspiracy tales are daily fodder, and in some media, the rule rather than the exceptions to the rule.[53]

In multiple ways, humans appear to be acting collectively in ways that threaten and sacrifice their own adaptation to the environment. Some of the more generally intelligent humans are creating technology that is destructive to the human and other species, both in the short term and in the long term. Whatever their IQs, how can one square the result of their behavior with intelligence as biological adaptation? It would seem para-doxical, even perverse, that greater general intelligence as evidenced by a thirty-point increase in IQ during the twentieth century[54] would lead to human behavior that ultimately is species self-destructive and thus lower in adaptive intelligence. What good are IQ points if their ultimate outcome is the destruction of the organisms that pride themselves on their high intelligence?

Imagine a situation in 1,000 years, or perhaps 100, or maybe even fewer. Intelligent aliens land on Earth. When they arrive, they find no intelligent life at all, or at least, life that they recognize as intelligent. There are bacteria, some plants, some small insect-like creatures. But the traces of civilization they find could not have been created by any of those creatures. Eventually they stumble on the fact of what happened – that one species (out of millions) essentially destroyed the planet not only for itself but also for some millions of other specie as well. Ironically, they discover, that species considered itself the most intelligent on the planet. Perhaps they might marvel at what egocentric definition of intelligence could self-congratulate a species stupid enough to label itself as the most intelligent species, when in reality it was the only species on the planet stupid enough to destroy its entire world.

How does one resolve the apparent paradox of higher general intelligence being associated with lower adaptive intelligence? Several alternative resolutions could be proposed.

3.6 Alternative Possible Resolutions of the Paradox of Apparent High General Intelligence and Species-Maladaptive Destructiveness

High general intelligence could be viewed as consistent with species-maladaptive destructiveness, or at least as not mutually exclusive, if one could come up with a reasonable resolution of what seems to be a paradox.

3.6.1 Resolution 1: There Is No Paradox – Intelligence Is Distinct from Biological Adaptation

Resolution 1 is that general intelligence is orthogonal with respect to biological adaptation. One simply has nothing to do with the other. If one operationally defines intelligence in terms of scores on intelligence tests and their proxies, then biological adaptation could be viewed as possibly, but not necessarily, correlated with general intelligence. On this view, it is not problematical that when species reach a certain level of intelligence, they may well extinguish themselves. Eventually, in that case, there may be no one left to decide whether Resolution 1 was valid, because everyone may be dead.

This argument, however, is inconsistent with any notion of intelligence as adaptation. Species self-destruction is perhaps the ultimate expression of nonadaptive behavior, both at an individual level and a species level. If intelligence is not for adaptation, what is it for – to do well on IQ tests? To make a lot of money while the world around one burns? To have good health while those around one die because of degradation of air, water, and general living conditions? If there is a reasonable ultimate criterion for intelligence, I suggest, it is not how much money one earns or how high one reaches professionally and certainly not how high one's grades in school are, but rather, the extent to which one acts in biologically adaptable and hence sustainable ways. What good are grades – which so often are used to validate standardized tests – if they produce a toxic world?

3.6.2 There Is No Paradox because Intelligence Has No Purpose in and of Itself

On this view, there is no paradox because intelligence is not purposive. It refers to mental power that can be used for any purpose at all. In this case, intelligence is about means, not about ends. An extremely powerful brain can be put to good use or bad, one might argue.

Imagine an extremely complex machine capable of thinking at a level of complexity and efficiency far beyond that of humans. In a sense, it is an extraordinary accomplishment because of its sheer power. If asked, it could solve any IQ-test problem correctly, no matter how difficult the problem might be. You see the machine busily humming away and you ask the owners, the Super-AI Company, what the machine does. They answer, "Nothing, really." It is thinking powerfully with no end result. Meanwhile, the world around the machine is crumbling and it is attempting to solve none of the problems of that world. Eventually, it will be destroyed because the world will become so hot that its machinery will be fried. But the machine busily hums away. The machine possibly might be able to solve the problem of global climate change but is not engaged in doing so. Is the machine truly intelligent?

I, at least, find it difficult to label such a machine as intelligent, no matter how many IQ-test problems the machine is capable of solving. I believe, as I first stated long ago in my earliest writings on intelligence, that intelligence is purposive – it is not merely a powerful machine but a powerful machine doing something for some purpose.[55] So here, one may encounter a philosophical distinction between intelligence merely being a powerful set of information-processing functions – intelligence as a means but with no need for any ends at all – and intelligence as directed toward doing something. I would argue that an extremely powerful and efficient machine is not intelligent if it is not engaged toward some *meaningful* end. And as intelligence has always been defined in terms of adaptation to the environment, that end should pertain to adaptation.

That is the problem perhaps with high-IQ societies. The members may have high information-processing abilities. But what matters is the end to which those abilities are directed.

Now imagine that, instead of its being a machine, it is a person who has complex thoughts that he or she puts to no use. He or she does fabulously well on IQ tests and their proxies. The person does nothing more. Even his or her grades in school are mediocre. Perhaps the person joins a high-IQ organization, but beyond that, the individual does nothing with their complex thoughts processes. If we label that person "intelligent," then we truly view intelligences simply in terms of the operational definition of intelligence as what IQ tests test. But why do we use these particular tests? What is so special about them that they, as opposed to any other test, should be labeled as measuring "intelligence"? Is solving largely meaningless problems of no consequence to anyone really how we want to define *intelligence*? Such tests certainly measure academic knowledge and abstract analytical reasoning, but are they complete measures of intelligence? No, or at least, not intelligence as adaptation to the environment.

On this view, the current Western preoccupation, at least in some places, with intelligence-test scores and their proxies is misconceived. Suppose such tests do measure, to some extent, mental power and efficiency. If that power and efficiency is like the machine engaged in doing nothing, then in what sense of the word "intelligence" is it truly intelligent? Someone can be a super information processor and yet be unintelligent.

Consider if there truly were musicians playing on the deck of the *Titanic* while the ship was sinking. Were they good musicians? Probably they were at least creditable, if they were hired to play on the *Titanic*. Were they good processors of musical information? Most likely. In Gardner's sense of "musical intelligence," they were "musically intelligent." And they probably were interpersonally intelligent, in Gardner's sense, in that they were trying to calm the passengers. But were they adaptively intelligent? Probably not. At that point, anyone employed by the ship should have realized that their main responsibility was to help save the passengers on the ship. Regardless of their IQs, musicians playing and passengers dancing while a ship is sinking are not engaging in adaptively intelligent behavior – they would have been better off doing anything they could, however little it might be, to help to save the ship and the people on it.

One could argue, of course, that there was nothing anyone could do. But that is simply not true. Even bailing out water from the decks might have helped the ship last just a bit longer in the hope that it might stay above water long enough for rescuers to arrive.

3.6.3 There Is No Paradox: Intelligence Is about Individual, Not Collective Adaptation

Another possible resolution of the paradox is that general intelligence does not pertain to adaptation at the species level or really any other large level. Rather, intelligence concerns adaptation only at the level of the individual. The argument here would be that intelligence comprises the mental power and efficiency that enable individuals to adapt to their individual environments and the sets of circumstances presented within those environments.

To some extent, this resolution seems to be the one that the field of general intelligence has been taken by default. When one looks at the criteria that are used for validating intelligence tests, they are individually achieved performances, including, for example, scores on intelligence tests other than a particular one at issue, scores on achievement tests, school grades, performance ratings achieved by individuals at work, and so forth. This solution is problematical.

First, there is no clear and consistent definition of what constitutes "individual adaptation." As a result, the field has been left with a set of less than fully satisfactory criteria, each of which is supposed to measured individual "adaptation" or "success." In my own past research, I have assumed that although no one of the criteria may be adequate, collectively, the criteria are jointly reasonable.[56] My colleagues and I also have recognized that, to the extent that one defines successful intelligence as achieving one's own meaningful and prosocially appropriate goals in life, this argument is hollow.[57] For many individuals, none of those criteria may be relevant. Someone trying hard and even somewhat effectively trying to save the world from its own madness, for example, may not do particularly well on IQ or achievement tests, may not have had high grades in school, may not be making a lot of money or have a prestigious title, and may not have won any awards (and indeed, may instead have been vilified), and yet have been acting in ways that are adaptively intelligent.

The criteria used to validate tests of intelligence usually appear to have been selected for reasons of variable persuasiveness; but none of the criteria are compelling. All are socioculturally derived. One criterion is ease of measurement. Researchers and practitioners like things that are easy to measure in the context in which they work, such as grade point average (GPA). These data are readily available in most instances. And higher grades would seem to be associated with intelligence – but also with many other things, such as academic motivation, conscientiousness, agreeableness with respect to the desires of one's teachers, obedience to the desires and sometimes the whims of authority figures, and other things. I have argued that good grades in most schools tend to be associated with an "executive" thinking style – that is, willingness to do what one is told and to try to do it well. I have published data to support this assertion.[58] Of course, this same style tends to lead to higher scores on intelligence tests; to some extent, the shared variance between school grades and intelligence-test scores reflects a style of willingness to follow instructions voluntarily and at least somewhat accurately, even on tasks that may have little meaning to those who are doing them.

Criteria for "success" are selected for utilitarian conformity to a typical Western sociocultural norm of success. This kind of logic is illustrated by the statement[59]: "The measurement of intelligence – which has been done primarily by IQ tests – has utilitarian value because it is a reasonably good predictor of grades at school, performance at work, and many other aspects of success in life . . .." (p. 131).[60] The problem is that one person's success is another's failure – making any of the criteria used in the voluminous literature problematical. Is a lot of money success? Some people think so; Jesus and Francis of Assisi, to name two rather distinguished individuals, had the opposite view ("prosperity gospel" notwithstanding). Is getting more education a "success"? In many environments it is; but in other environments, it is associated with failure to get a job, resulting in years of education that lead nowhere. Even in the West, going on in education to a PhD can reduce income, just in case one should view income as a measure of success.[61] Upper class individuals not only "game" tests to measure what they, on average, are good at; they also game the criteria against which the success of the tests and the people who take them are measured.

These criteria and others related to them may well be valued by people in many modernized Western and other cultures but, at the same time, may be valued much less by people living in other cultures, where the tasks required for adaptation to the environment are different and are not oriented so much toward school grades, promotions, money, or whatever.[62] Thus, to state that particular tests measure intelligence because of their high correlations with specific outcomes attained by individuals may tell us all a lot about the kinds of behavior valued by a particular culture (i.e., our own) but not very much about what intelligence really is.

The irony of the psychometric study of intelligence is that it has enabled researchers essentially to "cop out" of solving the problem of just what intelligence is. Are intelligence tests relevant to real-world performance? "Sure," intelligence testers will say, pointing to the usually small to moderate correlations of the tests with real-world performances. But what exactly are

the intelligent people doing that is making them intelligent? In early information-processing research, investigators identified fairly basic mental
processes.[63] Today, they more emphasize working-memory correlates[64] or
perhaps biological correlates.[65] What is not so clear, perhaps because it is so
easy to finesse the problem with correlations, is what intelligent people do in
solving real-world problems that distinguishes what they are doing from
what less intelligent people do. Current accounts of intelligence may tell us
something – that they are applying more of g, or have better working
memories, or process information more efficiently. But that will not help
someone who decides he or she wants to take a smarter approach to
problems, and then asks what he or she can do to accomplish that goal.
And if we cannot do that, to what extent do we really "understand" intelligence as opposed merely to being able to describe entities that correlate
with it?

In cultures other than our own, in the current day, other skills matter
more than those assessed by IQ tests and their proxies. These are the skills
used in hunting and fishing; figuring out how to stay warm enough to
survive and perhaps live comfortably; gathering agricultural products;
avoiding, and when necessary treating, parasitic illnesses; warding off
dangerous predators; or knowing how to navigate large distances without
use of maps, GPS, or similar aids. These skills might be far more important
to intelligence in the sense of environmental adaptation. The skills needed
for avoiding and fighting off predators may be more linked to the practical
than to the analytical aspect of intelligence – the tacit procedural knowledge needed for getting along in the world.[66]

More generally, though, external validation of intelligence tests (correlating test scores against various criteria in the world) invariably has drawn
upon culturally valued criteria. These criteria differ from one culture and
even subculture to another. There is nothing inherently biological or
biologically adaptive about the various correlates that are typically used
as criteria to externally validate intelligence tests. Consider some of these
criteria and just what their significance truly is for external validation.

One criterion frequently used to validate general-intelligence tests
involves correlating scores on a new test of general intelligence with scores
on old, already existing, tests of general intelligence. This criterion is highly
problematical. It assumes the validity of the operational definition that it is
trying to validate. One never can get beyond the existing content of
intelligence tests if one always is validating new tests against existing
tests. No matter what the tests actually measure, this criterion will guarantee that they continue in the same mode. Any new test that measures skills

beyond those in the current tests will be viewed as inadequate because it departs from the old (and by now, outdated) conventions.

Such a procedure hinges upon Edwin Boring's operational definition of intelligence as whatever intelligence tests measure.[67] But this definition is entirely circular, as has been pointed out numerous times by numerous investigators.[68] Essentially, test-constructors create tests to measure intelligence. How do test-constructors know the test measures intelligence? They do so by defining intelligence as whatever the test measures, or by validating the test against other tests that also have been stipulated as measuring intelligence. If people decided that intelligence can be measured by skin tone (as many racists seem, explicitly or implicitly, to have decided), then tests of skin tone would be stipulated to be measuring intelligence and would be validated by one's saying that one test of skin tone correlates highly with other such tests, and therefore they all measure intelligence. If, in some not so hypothetical society, people with lighter (or darker) skin tones were given more advantages in life and those with darker (or lighter) skin tones were deprived of such advantages, one even could show that the test of skin tone predicts societal outcomes that are valued by that society.

Researchers could have amassed hundreds or even thousands of such correlations at high levels – whether for intelligence tests as we know them or for tests of skin tone, for that matter – and yet have no real validation of whether what the tests measure is in fact intelligence. In the case of conventional tests of intelligence, the tests do seem to measure a cognitive construct that has been labeled "general cognitive ability," which is related, for whatever reasons, to success in many scholastic as well as everyday-life challenges. But is the underlying construct *intelligence?* That is not so clear.

Researchers in the field of intelligence have realized ever since the early years of the twentieth century that pretty much all tests of general cognitive ability, whether or not it is truly "intelligence," are highly correlated with each other.[69] That such a correlation "proves" they measure intelligence is a huge leap of faith – it is not tantamount to a proof unless one resorts to Boring-type circularity.

Many seemingly different kinds of abilities tend to cluster together psychometrically – they correlate with each other. This holds for Carroll's model and for the Cattell-Horn-Carroll (CHC) model, as described in Chapter 2, and even in the more radical and pathbreaking work of Howard Gardner. Gardner has identified in his analysis what he alleges are multiple intelligences, or at least, multiple domains of cognitive functioning.[70] The fact that people who have particular levels of cognitive skills in a given domain (e.g., mathematical skills) tend to have high levels of cognitive skills in other domains (e.g., spatial skills) suggests that the skills form a general factor of something. But that something is not necessarily a general factor of intelligence as adaptation. There are general factors of many things, such as athletic or musical ability. The fact that there is a general factor of something does not mean that it is a factor of general *intelligence*.

A second and even more common criterion against which intelligence tests are validated is GPA, or related measures. But quality of GPA at any level of schooling is a weak and, in some ways, implausible criterion for validating a test of intelligence.[71] The tradition of using GPA and related measures as a criterion is probably in part an historical accident. It derives in part from Alfred Binet and Theodore Simon's use of school performance as a criterion for validating the usefulness of a test of intelligence.[72]

School grades are, of course, easy to collect. But in many and diverse cultures, the academic aspect of school performance is not particularly valued; as noted earlier, it even may be viewed as a distraction from life and thus be devalued.[73] Furthermore, some cultures do not have formal schooling, or at least anything that many Westerners would recognize as schooling. For example, most of us would be reluctant to send our children to a school in which instruction consists solely of memorizing a religious book. In any case, in the course of human history, formal schooling is a fairly recent invention. Using school grades as a criterion against which to validate an intelligence test is a representation of a system of cultural values. According to these values, school grades are important in life and are a valid indicator of intelligence. Moreover, in much of life, it is not enough or may even be counterproductive merely to do what one does to get a high GPA, namely, doing what one is told to do and doing it well. Innovative people are innovative precisely because they do not do what they are told.[74] It is not clear that school grades tell one what one would want to know about who will succeed in life, especially in times when creativity matters so much to forward advancement in society.[75]

A third criterion for validating intelligence tests has been age, which was the original basis for computing scores on the Stanford–Binet intelligence scales, which compared mental age to chronological age. Binet, sensibly, recognized that, up to a point, intelligence should increase with age. But it is not unique, of course, in increasing with age. Height, weight, and other biological markers also may increase with age. At some point, some of these markers, such as height, stop increasing or actually may decrease, but then, so apparently does intelligence. Age may have some value through the teenage years as a criterion against which to validate intelligence tests, but it loses value after those years, and people's intelligence tends to decrease, at different rates for different people and different abilities, in adulthood.[76]

A fourth criterion against which intelligence tests are validated is the potpourri of measures that are constituted as professional success. These criteria, like academic criterion measures, are very culturally bound. How important is annual income, and to whom? How does one compare annual incomes across professions and even across regions of the country? Is a salary of $100,000 in San Francisco worth anything like what it is worth in Jackson, Mississippi? Is the title of CEO the same in a 5-person business as in a 5,000-person business? Is a CEO's work more important and more requiring of intelligence than the work of a teacher of children with intellectual disabilities? Is societally sanctioned success in all jobs a key indicator of intelligence? In general, what kinds of value systems lead some jobs (e.g., investment banker) to be considered to be more highly related to intelligence than other jobs (e.g., teacher)? Why do we even pay investment bankers more than teachers? Might one imagine a culture in which rank orders are reversed, such as one in which being a successful teacher is more valued than being an investment banker? How can success be measured, in any case? For example, a doctor who joins Doctors without Borders will make much less money and will experience, for many, less prestige than would a cosmetic surgeon; but who does more good? How, really, does one measure the success of people, all of whom have different goals in life? Occupational success is culturally defined. Even within a culture, it is hard to define success. Is an attorney who gets murderers declared "not-guilty" because of technicalities "successful," even if he makes a lot of money? How about a well-paid accountant who files false but persuasive tax returns for wealthy clients?

Of course, there is no one perfect criterion against which to validate intelligence tests. As a result, it is sensible to use multiple criteria in validation. As no one criterion is perfect, one could argue that, if scores on intelligence tests correlate with a number of different high-stakes variables, such correlations then show that the tests must measure intelligence. But, in fact, the criteria typically reported in intelligence-test manuals and published research articles *all* are culturally bound. They are relevant to measures based on experts' implicit theories of intelligence in particular cultural settings. Their relation to biological or even cultural adaptation is much less clear.

In sum, individual adaptation is a biologically vacuous concept. Evolutionary biologists scarcely pay attention at all to individuals, because their goal is to understand adaptation at collective levels, such as at the levels of species or phyla. The focus that psychologists – at least, North American and European ones – have placed on individual adaptation to culturally-defined measures of success reflects a strong cultural bias toward individualism as opposed to collectivism.[77] Individualism, globally, reflects a minority position. In many societies, individuals are viewed as of relatively little importance in that their purpose is in serving collective interests. For example, some African, Central American, South American, and especially Asian, societies tend to be more collectivist in their orientation than are European and North American ones.[78] In a collectivist culture, criteria for assessing the validity of a test of intelligence or of related skills emphasizing accomplishments of individuals might seem oxymoronic. Individuals in collectivist cultures might even have difficulty taking intelligence tests if the assumption of the testing is that collaboration is unethical and therefore impermissible.[79] The preference for individualism in the typical Western conception of intelligence is demonstrated by the likelihood that someone who is in a prestigious, high-paying managerial job who destroys the environment as part of that job (for example, his job involves polluting a lake, river, or ocean) might well be viewed, by the usual Western criteria, as being generally intelligent, perhaps very intelligent if he or she is able to hide the pollution.

3.6.4 Intelligence Is Ultimately Self-Destructive

One possible explanation of the destructive behavior of humans might be that intelligent life, by its nature, is intrinsically self-destructive – that once it reaches a certain point of advancement, it turns on, and, ultimately, destroys itself.[80] This explanation has been suggested as a potential resolution to the so-called *Fermi paradox*. This paradox concerns why, given the vastness of the universe, extraterrestrial species have not visited Earth (at least to our knowledge).[81] The reason then might be that species, as they advance in complexity, are ultimately self-annihilating. For example, advanced species experience industrialization, which leads to climate change and related problems, and then these and other problems ultimately kill off the species before they reach the point of interstellar or possibly even merely interplanetary space travel. This is sometimes called the *self-destruction hypothesis*.[82]

The self-destruction hypothesis is not entirely adequate, in at least one sense. This is that the self-destruction hypothesis fails to explain how intelligence, which by its traditional definition is adaptive, ultimately can be fatally maladaptive for any species, no matter how "advanced." If a set of skills – such as those involved in industrialization to the point of environmental collapse – is actually maladaptive, then it would seem that almost any labeled description would apply better to that set of skills than that of "intelligence," which, by definition, is adaptive to the environment.

3.6.5 Constructs Other Than Intelligence *Better Explain Why People Act Against Their and Their Species' Biological Interests*

Another possibility for understanding maladaptive behavior is that constructs different from intelligence would best explain why people act against their own and their species' biological or other interests. Examples of some other constructs would include greed, narcissism, Machiavellianism, and psychopathy (the last three constituting the so-called "dark triad" of personality). Perhaps people's self-destructiveness may be best understood in terms of a continuum of wisdom-related behavior.[83] In particular, destructive behavior of any kind is associated with lack of wisdom, which can be conceived of as *foolishness*.[84] At an even more extreme level, such behavior can be viewed as showing the opposite of wisdom, *toxicity*.[85] Viewed in this way, an individual can be "intelligent" in the traditional Western sense, but unwise, foolish, or even toxic. He or she can be seriously lacking in adaptive intelligence. Toxic leaders, as an example, frequently encourage people to act against their own best interests and to act in ways that harm or even destroy the natural environment upon which the generations of the future will depend. Current toxic leaders in corporations and in politics are busily lowering standards for their companies and countries.[86] They also are failing in preserving the environment, mortgaging future generations for the imagined sake of the well-off in the present generation.

I tried in my earlier augmented theory of successful intelligence to resolve the paradox of destructive intelligent people by including wisdom within my augmented theory of successful intelligence.[87] The idea in this theory is that people who act in ways to harm others and the environment for their own interests or for the interests of their perceived in-group, or progeny, would be downgraded with respect to evaluations of their level of successful intelligence because of their support of biologically and environmentally maladaptive causes. This augmented theory of successful intelligence goes beyond the theory of general intelligence. It claims that, in order to be fully adaptive, intelligence requires not only the analytical skills that are measured by standardized tests and that constitute general intelligence, but also, in addition, creative, practical, and wisdom-based skills.

Creative skills are those involved in generating ideas and products that are novel and, in some way, useful.[88] Analytical skills are involved in ascertaining the quality or applicability of these ideas or products.[89] Practical skills are involved in implementing the ideas and also in persuading others that the ideas or products are valuable and somehow useful ones.[90] Wisdom-based skills are involved in using one's creative, analytical, and practical skills to achieve a common good, by balancing one's own, others', and larger interests, over the long as well as the short term, through the application of positive ethical values.[91] *Adaptive intelligence is the wise use of creative, analytical, and practical skills for the purpose of broad environmental adaptation (including narrow adaptation to environments, shaping of environments, and selection of new environments.)* Adaptive intelligence, then, requires the use of one's knowledge and abilities for the common good, balancing one's own with others' and larger interests, over the long and short terms, through the infusion of positive ethical values.

The common good is an elusive concept because diverse people have a different notion of what it is. But often this is because they choose to define the common good in terms of their own self-interest or the interests of their "tribe." Even religious people, who should know better, can succumb to defining the common good in terms of members of their own religious groups; countries can define the common good in terms of their own self-interest (as in the thinking of "America-Firsters"), and often not even of everyone in the country but rather only of those who are members of particular groups. The common good refers to everyone for whom one has any responsibility at all, and as the world becomes more globalized, the list of people for whom one has some responsibility increases. We can never be sure of what the common good is, but we at least can try our best to achieve it.

According to the augmented theory of successful intelligence, if a person's creative, analytical, and/or practical skills are used toward dark ends,[92] that would be reflected in a reduced assessment of the person's overall level of successful intelligence.

The solution offered by the earlier augmented theory of successful intelligence is, I believe, at best, partially successful. According to this theory, someone who acts against his or her own, as well as against others' biological adaptive interests, still can do fairly well on some kind of composite successful-intelligence scale. The person is "dinged" for the lack of wisdom but not for lack of creative, analytical, or practical intelligence. Unless wisdom is viewed as a necessary condition for high levels of successful intelligence, extremely unwise and destructive people can be viewed as fairly high in successful intelligence. Suppose, for example, a malevolent yet clever person were highly creative in devising a nuclear or biological weapon that could destroy most or even all of human civilization, highly analytical in making sure it works, highly practical in making certain that it can be delivered flawlessly, but nevertheless extremely unwise in having undertaken the project and then executed it in the first place. That person still might be viewed as, on the whole, quite successfully intelligent. This would be so despite the potential of the nuclear weapon to destroy all of humanity. That said, those psychologists or others who view intelligence through the substantially narrower psychometric lens of "general intelligence" almost certainly will reject the notion of successful intelligence. It would not, for them, properly dignify *g*, or general intelligence. The notion of relying on general intelligence is a hard habit to break.

To summarize, if one cannot adapt, then one is not truly intelligent. Adaptation is a necessary condition for intelligence. This, incidentally, is a primary way in which Howard Gardner and I, although we both have proposed systems theories of intelligence, disagree. From the standpoint of this book, a set of skills should be labeled as "intelligence" only if they are necessary for adaptation. Gardner labels as "intelligences" skill sets that are not necessary for adaptation. For example, he speaks of bodily-kinesthetic skills as comprising an "intelligence." But one can have very intelligent people – the late Stephen Hawking and the late Helen Keller come to mind – who have severely deficient bodily-kinesthetic skills but who nevertheless manage very well to adapt to the environment and, in fact, who make outstanding contributions to that environment.

In contrast, without creative skills, one could not think in novel ways, and would be utterly stymied by any new situation that arose in life. Without analytical skills, one would be unable to analyze options available to oneself and repeatedly would make terrible decisions in life. Without practical skills, one could not get one's work done or get along with others. And without wisdom-based skills, one might well become wholly egocentric, looking out only for oneself at everyone else's expense. One might succeed for a while, but eventually others likely would turn on one when they realized that one was concerned only with one's self-interest.

3.7 Is the Typical Western Conception of Intelligence Actually Intelligence?

Considering the available evidence, I would argue that the assertion that so-called *g*-related phenomena are really and truly "intelligence" is based on a flimsy house of cards.

First, the fact that IQ tests, proxies of IQ tests, and their various subtests intercorrelate with (relate to) each other suggests only that they measure related cognitive (and other) skills. These intercorrelations do not necessarily mean that those cognitive skills fully (or even, necessarily, partially) constitute intelligence. The tests seem to do a poor job of measuring the kinds of critical thinking that would lead people to make good judgments in their everyday lives. For example, as I write these words (May 6, 2020), states in the US are opening up in the midst of a raging COVID-19 pandemic. It is clear that many of them merely will have to shut down again after the virus spreads still further and more lethally (which, when I review these words on August 6, 2020, only three months later, is exactly what has happened). There seem to be serious gaps in critical thinking.

Second, the fact that IQ tests and their proxies yield a general factor and a hierarchical structure under the general factor also does not tell us that the tests actually measure intelligence. That is, this factorial structure implies merely that the tests measure a set of related cognitive and other related abilities. The reification of these abilities into "intelligence" is nothing more than an assertion.

Third, the undisputed fact that IQ tests and their proxies correlate with many and diverse kinds of behavior[93] tells us that general cognitive ability (so-called "GCA") has many and diverse real-world correlates that many people, at least in many Western societies, think are important, such as school grades. People in other cultural settings may value other outcomes, as was discussed above. Certainly, in many Western societies, GCA is culturally important.[94] Nothing here is intended to dispute that assertion. But is GCA intelligence in any biologically adaptive, as opposed to a particularly culturally adaptive, sense? That is not at all clear.

Fourth, some researchers or readers might take the discovery of brain correlates between GCA and various aspects of brain functioning as a kind of proof that general cognitive ability is indeed intelligence. But such correlations have no dispositive value whatsoever. *Any* cognitive skills or, for that matter, any emotional or other psychological function, will have correlates of brain functioning. No one, presumably, would dispute that cognitive activity originates in anything other than the brain, or at least, in the central nervous system. The fact that behavior is brain-based does not mean that the behavior is "intelligent." Almost all behavior, except reflexes, whether intelligent or not, is brain mediated in some way. That would include behavior that is unrelated to intelligence, or even behavior that we might call "stupid."

So, then, what is intelligence in its true biological sense? Thought and behavior are intelligent, in a biological sense, by virtue of their being biologically adaptive. True intelligence is adaptive intelligence. It is not clear that *any* of the various demonstrations by psychometricians and other psychologists show that what they are labeling "intelligence" is truly adaptive in a biological sense. Biologically adaptive behavior helps a species (or gene pool) survive and thrive through adaptation to, shaping of, and selection of environments that the organism faces. Humans are not necessarily the best species at adaptation to the environment, at least in a narrow sense. Bacteria and cockroaches have been in existence, and almost certainly will continue to be in existence, much longer than humans. But humans are, at least, arguably unique in their superior ability jointly to balance narrow adaptation to, shaping, and selection of environments.

Unfortunately, humans often have used their cognitive and other skills to shape the environment in biologically and altogether *maladaptive* ways. If an extraterrestrial were to land on Earth, or even if an Earth person were to look at the condition of the planet objectively, either individual might conclude that human contributions to global climate change, air pollution, groundwater pollution, nuclear weapons, and bacterial resistance to antibiotics, among other things, tell us far more about human intelligence – or its lack thereof – than do human scores on tests of IQ. Why is the ability to solve a reading-comprehension problem, a spatial-visualization problem using abstract figures, or a number-series problem a better indicator of intelligence than is the ability to think of ways to manage a company to benefit all stakeholders or to mitigate worldwide disasters? Why should school grades be more important criteria against which to validate intelligence tests than problem solutions and decisions that could make the difference between environmental preservation and destruction? Should we not be emphasizing, in our schools at all levels, the development of *adaptive intelligence* at least as much as the development of general intelligence? Adaptive intelligence, much more than general intelligence, might help ensure that all stakeholders in the well-being of the world, and most of all, our progeny, are able to benefit from whatever contributions we can make to the world.

One could argue, of course, that issues such as mitigating global climate change or air pollution are political, moral, ethical, or values issues. It is not clear why preventing the destruction of the species would be a values issue. Do we really need to trade off the value of preserving species diversity to the value of killing off millions of species? Deciding to ask test-takers what number comes next in a series of numbers or what a rotated shape looks like is also a matter of values as to what to test. What value system would lead people to decide that solving number-series problems or solving spatial problems, which are problems pretty much unlike any people are likely to encounter in their lives, is more relevant to intelligence than biological adaptation – preservation of one's own health and even life, the health and life of one's progeny, and also the health and life of our species and of other species?

If society views intelligence as adaptive, it should focus on *adaptive intelligence* – biologically based behavior that preserves the world for ourselves and for future generations and that recognizes the relation between biology and the ecological niches in which we (as well as so many other species) live.[95]

The main points I have made in this chapter are not unique to me or my way of thinking. Researchers who study the extremes of intelligence have long held similar ideas. Arguably, they have made more insights about intelligence than those who study the continuum of intelligence as a whole. Consider both extremes of the intellectual spectrum.

At one end, the American Association on Intellectual and Developmental Disabilities (AAIDD), formerly the American Association on Mental Retardation (AAMR), defines intellectual disability both in terms of what I have called in this chapter "general intelligence" and in terms similar to what I have called "practical intelligence," which is a major component of adaptive intelligence. They take the broader kind of view that has been lacking in the field of intelligence as a whole. The association defines "*intellectual disability* [a]s a disability characterized by significant limitations in both intellectual functioning and in adaptive behavior, which covers many everyday social and practical skills. This disability originates before the age of 18" (https://aaidd .org/intellectual-disability/definition). In this definition, "*intellectual functioning* – also called intelligence – refers to general mental capacity, such as learning, reasoning, problem solving, and so on." Furthermore, "*adaptive behavior* is the collection of conceptual, social, and practical skills that are learned and performed by people in their everyday lives." The association does not use terms such as "practical intelligence" or "adaptive intelligence," but it clearly is referring to sets of skills that the association views as different from those constituting general intelligence. On this view, we cannot fully and rightfully understand individuals' intellectual functioning without going beyond the concept of general intelligence.

This idea was proposed years ago, by one of the great leaders, now deceased, in the field of intellectual disability, Edward Zigler.[96] Zigler recognized that many people with traditional intellectual disabilities essentially have to cultivate practical, adaptive abilities to cope with their lack of abstract analytical skills. In terms of the augmented theory of successful intelligence, one would say that they find a way of compensating for their weaknesses as well as of capitalizing on their strengths.

At the other end of the spectrum, the National Association for Gifted Children (NAGC) has noted that children are designated as gifted when their ability is significantly above the average level for their age. Giftedness may manifest itself in a number of different ways, including domains such as the intellectual, creative, artistic, or leadership domains, or in specific academic fields including language arts, mathematics, or science (www .nagc.org/resources-publications/resources/what-giftedness). The NAGC, like the AAIDD, has pointed out that a broad definition of intellectual functioning needs to be more encompassing than would be possible simply by relying on general intelligence. Adaptation to the environment requires more than general intelligence, and more than IQ or related constructs. It requires a broader conception of intelligence, what is referred to here as *adaptive intelligence*. If society recognizes and values the importance of broad and not just narrow adaptation to the environment, it may be in a better position to head off the destructive and potentially self-annihilating path on which humanity has set itself with its various misadventures. This may sound like a pessimistic view but it actually is an optimistic one. There still is hope, if society recognizes it is on the wrong course.

Why would organizations that look at the extremes of intelligence adopt a broader view of intelligence than those that look at intelligence more generally? Perhaps it is because, as Howard Gardner recognized in presenting his theory of multiple intelligences, one learns a lot by looking at limiting cases. No one ever transformed the world, at least for the better, solely as a result of his or her IQ points. If people are truly gifted, not merely labeled as "gifted," they make a positive difference in some meaningful way.[97] They do not merely have a strength; they capitalize on it. Similarly, people with intellectual disabilities, by virtue of their life circumstances, need to find ways to compensate for their weaknesses. Truth is, so do we all.

General-intelligence theory is a theory of means. In contrast, adaptive intelligence is a theory of means applied to adaptive ends.

3.8 Objections to and Responses from the Theory of Adaptive Intelligence

Consider now some of the objections that might be posed with regard to the theory of adaptive intelligence.

3.8.1 Potential Objection #1: The Theory Includes Too Much in the Concept of Intelligence

A common objection to this theory, as well as to Gardner's and my own earlier theory of successful intelligence, is that these theories include too much in intelligence. The issue then becomes one of how one decides what is "too much." In practice, "too much" typically means that the theory goes outside the scope of what is normally measured on psychometric tests of intelligence and what is characterized by psychometric theories of intelligence.[98] If one is relying on previous conceptions of intelligence to validate new conceptions, then one can see how researchers would come to such a conclusion. Moreover, the empirical evidence in favor of some broader theories is scanty.[99] The number of researchers exploring broader views is paltry compared with the number exploring the well-worn path set out by g-theory.

This view of "too broad" relies on what experts on intelligence have been believing for years, namely, that what is measured in intelligence tests now is what should be in intelligence tests of the future. It harks back to Boring's theory, as presented earlier, of intelligence being what intelligence tests measure. With Boring as a basis, theories derived post hoc from such measures, such as Carroll's (discussed in Chapter 2), form the basis for what is allowed or not allowed in a theory. Suppose, instead, however, that we use a different and external criterion to decide what is "too broad." That criterion harks back to the almost universal definition of intelligence as adaptation to the environment, as discussed. Then what should be included in a theory or measure of intelligence is determined not by what psychometricians (i.e., "testers") included in the past, but rather by what skills are needed for adapting to environments – past, present, and future, as the skills may vary by epoch as well as by culture. In that case, I would argue, a broader conception of intelligence is not only desirable but even necessary. Those adhering to a psychometric view – and those whose validation of their ideas depends on a psychometric view (e.g., biological psychologists finding brain correlates of IQ-test performance or information-processing psychologists, including myself in earlier years, validating their components of information processing against such tests),[100] can never break outside a box of their own creation – what Thomas Kuhn referred to as a paradigm of normal science.[101] Because their theoretical work resides in a closed box, anything outside the box seems outside the purview of what is allowable to include in a definition or to study under the rubric of intelligence

Adaptation to the environment – even if limited to cognitive adaptations – certainly involves more than the knowledge and analytical skills included in the conventional definition of intelligence.

3.8.2 Potential Objection #2: The Theory Is Too Philosophical

A second objection might be that the theory is too philosophical – that discussing what is adaptive is like discussing how many angels can dance on the head of a pin. But there is nothing really philosophical, for example, about one of the headlines in the news the very day I am writing this sentence: The city of Chennai, India, a city of 7 million (and thus just slightly smaller in population than New York City, itself the most heavily populated city in the United States), has essentially run out of water.[102] Although there is a bit to be pumped out, almost all water now has to be brought into the city. If the monsoons come this year – they did not come last year – there still may be hope. If not, then people soon will be leaving the city in droves. The exodus already has begun. What field besides the entrenched field of intelligence research would look at the skills needed to solve a problem such as "2, 5, 9, 14, . . .?" as critical to intelligence but the skills needed to solve the water problem in Chennai – and tens of thousands of problems like it – as too broad, too philosophical or policy-oriented, or just too big to be included in a concept of intelligence? If intelligence is concerned with adaptation to the environment, certainly solving the problem of the near-disappearance of water for 9 million people takes precedence over a number-series problem. Or if the skills in the number-series problem are supposed somehow to be relevant to solving the water problem, one might wonder why intelligent people who can solve number-series problems allowed things to reach this point in the first place.

3.8.3 Potential Objection #3: The Theory Is Prescriptive, Telling People What to Do

The theory is like other information-processing theories in specifying steps of processing information in solving problems, but it is prescriptive beyond those theories in one key sense – that the goal of adaptive intelligence is, indeed, adaptation to the environment at a larger level than just the individual. Consider a hypothetical "thought experiment."

Are you, perhaps, familiar with the Super-Evil School of Biological Terrorism? Probably not, because the school does not really exist. But never mind. This hypothetical school only wants the best, so it admits students by IQ. To ensure that the test is useful, the school does a validity study. It finds that the IQ test predicts first-year grades at the school with a validity coefficient of 0.65. The school concludes that the test is a good measure of intelligence. In this respect, it follows the now time-"honored" way of viewing correlation coefficients of a test with some kind of academic performance as a signal of what is intelligence and what is not.

A year later, the students in the same hypothetical class succeed in a group project to create a biological agent that kills people and for which, if there is an antidote, it is only potential because it simply does not yet exist. The class releases the agent and all humans on Earth die. That is it – kaput. All human life on Earth vanishes.

The question: Was the IQ test a valid measure of intelligence? From the typical Western standpoint, I believe the answer would be yes. The students were very intelligent in figuring out a destructive biological agent with no known antidote. They even figured out how to deliver it. From the standpoint of the theory of adaptive intelligence, however, the students were not adaptively intelligent because they unwisely acted maladaptively – against the common human good – when they destroyed humanity.

3.8.4 Potential Objection #4: The Theory Assumes That the Theorist's Ethical Judgments Are the Correct Ethical Judgments

When I spoke to a Cornell-student audience about adaptive intelligence, one student in the audience suggested that I was imposing my ethical values on others. On his view, ethical values are different from intelligence and really ought not to be included in the concept. For example, he pointed out, some people such as myself may oppose pollution, but others may favor it, and still others may not care. At the time, I responded that I was unaware of anyone who actually favored pollution or at least higher carbon emissions, but that was before I read an article that shows that a scientist actually has concluded that higher levels of carbon dioxide are good for us humans.[103] Well, that certainly is a novel point of view!

Obviously, people have different values. Although there may be relatively few, besides William Happer, who are in favor of higher CO_2 levels in the world, there may be quite a few who believe that the trade-off between higher CO_2 levels and industrialization favors the world's having higher CO_2 levels. In the short term, such a scenario certainly seems like a trade-off between one good (better air) and another (more industrialization). But in the long term, are there really two valid sides to the story?

A study found that someone buying a house with a thirty-year mortgage today might want to think twice in terms of location. The study, by the Union of Concerned Scientists, found that more than 300,000 coastal homes, worth well over $100 billion, are at risk of being fully or partially underwater by 2045. By the end of the twenty-first century, more than 2.4 million homes, worth more than $1 trillion, are anticipated to be fully or partially under water.[104] Some people believe that projections of climate change are designed to be provocative but not necessarily accurate. Actually, indications are that these projections have *underestimated* rates of climate change.[105]

Today, the most prominent activists for controlling climate change are young people,[106] because they are the ones who best recognize those the current adult generations are mortgaging not only their own futures, but that of the young people who will have to cope with the future results of climate change. Unfortunately, a not uncommon reaction is that of a relative of mine, who, in response to threats to the future, commented (to one of his children): "I don't care because I won't be around to have to deal with them."

Is the loss of life, property, tax base, and land mass really a matter of differing ethical points of view? This view just is too reminiscent, I believe, of those who have defended massacres or genocides as a matter for those in the affected countries to judge in ethical terms.[107] I would argue that, in sticking with intelligence tests that present number-series or symbol-copying tasks, one is not avoiding ethical judgment but rather making it by default. It is an ethical judgment, and I believe a compromised one, that what people do with their cognitive power just does not matter for the concept of intelligence. On this view, it is fully ethical to identify as "intelligent" people who may choose, by dint of their high intelligence, to destroy the environment on which the rest of us (and they, themselves, and their progeny) depend.

3.8.5 Potential Objection #5: Adaptive Intelligence Cannot Be Efficaciously Measured

The field of intelligence, more perhaps than any other field in psychology, has lived (and for some, died) on issues of measurement. Whereas other fields have certainly made measurement of constructs an important focus, no other field, to my knowledge, has produced a set of tests and then spent over a century trying to justify why the tests should be at the theoretical and practical center of the field.

An understandable concern, therefore, would be that approaches to intelligence other than the psychometric one simply have not provided the sound basis of measurement that the psychometric approach has provided.[108] It is hard to argue with this concern. However, as always, there is an alternative point of view.

First, psychometric researchers and, especially those working in companies that sell standardized tests, have spent countless hours developing, trying out, and analyzing data from standardized tests of intelligence. They have spent a tiny fraction of that time investigating alternative or supplementary ability-based measures, presumably because of their confidence that the existing psychometric paradigm is the best one. But one cannot really create new paradigms unless one is willing to make a serious investment in them, something that testing researchers and companies have been loath to do. More common are articles explaining why the psychometric approach as traditionally formulated is best and why alternative approaches do not, could not, and will not work.[109]

Certainly, in psychometric terms, the existing armamentarium of standardized tests is what we have to offer that has been painstakingly constructed and validated. But it has been clear for over half-a-century that the tests work better for some than for others and that group differences reflect in part the very different socialization experiences children from different cultures, socially defined races, and socioeconomic backgrounds have.[110]

Most researchers trained in the psychometric tradition have been, so far as I can tell, such unquestioning boosters of the traditional psychometric approach and so opposed to attempts to question that traditional approach that they have made, I believe, little progress in changing a century-old tradition. If one imagines medicine still using tests from the early twentieth century, one would be alarmed, especially if one's own future, or the future of a family member, were at stake. Why, then, would we be any less concerned about a psychological or educational approach that has changed so little from a century ago?

In Chapter 4, I will describe some of the efforts my collaborators and I have made to measure successful intelligence[111] and I also will describe what further efforts might look like to transform these measures into measures of adaptive intelligence. But the complacency of much of the psychometric establishment and their lock on testing not only in the United States but elsewhere leave me skeptical that they will want to change much, given how little they have changed in a century. Houses will sink underwater, people will die from climate change and pollution, and they will go on measuring intelligence with the same kinds of items they have for a century. They are the modern-day musicians on the *Titanic*.

3.8.6 Potential Objection #6: Adaptive Intelligence Lacks a Research Base

The idea of intelligence as adaptation to the environment is extremely old and can be found even in the 1921 symposium on the nature of intelligence cited at the beginning of this chapter. Two contributors, S. S. Colvin and R. Pintner, both explicitly referred to adaptation to the environment in their definitions. Other contributors implicitly made the same reference.

But the concept of "adaptive intelligence" as I refer to it in this book is new. I have previously written about it only once.[112] Thus, although there is a fairly extensive research base on my previous concept of successful intelligence, there is not yet a research base for adaptive intelligence. I would hope that this book might stimulate the production of such a research base, from myself, of course, but also from others.

3.8.7 Potential Objection #7: It Solves a Problem That Does Not Exist, Given That We Already Know What Intelligence Is

We only think we know what intelligence is, in the sense that those who have entered the field have been willing to accept a set of somewhat arbitrary criteria for defining intelligence: (a) a general factor of intelligence atop a hierarchy of abilities, (b) abilities limited to what intelligence tests have measured before, and (c) correlations with a variety of real-world criteria. The construct elicited, I believe, qualifies as some kind of fairly general cognitive ability, as noted earlier. But is it intelligence in the sense of adaptation to the environment? It is, only if one takes the usual external criteria – correlations with various individual measures of culturally defined success as showing that the construct is *intelligence*. Intelligence also correlates with health measures such as longevity,[113] but so would conscientiousness and simply doing what is medically sound because one is told to do it. This is not to downplay the importance of general cognitive ability. It is merely to point out that if everyone attends only to his or her own school grades, income, job prestige, and longevity, among other things, the world will be in trouble – which it currently is because of a lack of concern about adaptation for all over the longer haul. Oddly, conventional intelligence tests are not even particularly good predictors of these conventional criteria.

3.8.8 Potential Objection #8: Intelligence Is Individual; Collective Intelligence Is Something Else Entirely and Hence Is Not Relevant to Accounts of Intelligence

Adaptive intelligence is both an individual construct and a collective one. It involves individual people trying to attain a common good – to "lift all boats" – and it involves humans, collectively, doing what it takes to avoid the behaviors in which we have engaged that are resulting in the extinction of species and, ultimately, our own species. People usually think of intelligence as individual and think of group intelligence[114] or collective intelligence[115] as exotic. But perhaps this customary way of thinking is wrong, or at least, shortsighted. As Thomas Malone and Anita Wooley (see Note 107) and Steven Sloman and Philip Fernbach[116] have pointed out, almost all of our serious uses of intelligence are based on our making use of the intelligence of others. We constantly rely on what others before us have done, appropriating their knowledge without really understanding it.

How many of us know how to construct a toilet, a dishwasher, a washing machine, a cell phone, a television, a computer, a house, a car, or any of the multifarious conveniences that we use in everyday life? How much of our knowledge even of our own fields of specialization comes from our own work, and how much from the work of others? We often think we know things, but really, we have only the vaguest idea of them. For example, even schoolchildren know that Mt Everest is the tallest mountain in the world, but only because others have told them. How many of us have ever seen Mt Everest, or even if we had, personally verified that it is the tallest mountain in the world? We know that astronauts walked on the moon, but only because others told us. We know that turning on our computer will start the computer, but what happens inside the computer? And we know about the world, but mostly through reading and assorted media that convey to us information that we barely understand but accept as valid. Much of the information is far from valid, but we have little, if any way of challenging it. Intelligence is and always has been a collective as well as an individual phenomenon. And we are now at a point in civilization at which, if we do not acknowledge its collective nature, we will watch as the world as we know it collapses because we were unwilling to recognize the role that collective *adaptive intelligence* needs to play in keeping it livable for the generations to come and even for our own generation.

3.8.9 Potential Objection #9: Most Problems Do Not Require Complex Judgments about Biological Adaptation or the Future of the World, so All This Talk of Adaptive Intelligence Is Beside the Point

Many problems, it is true, lack a wisdom component, in that they do not concern competing interests. But then, there are many problems that do have a wisdom component and people do not see that component or even try to see it. For example, when Facebook was created, it probably was seen as combining a set of technical challenges with a set of marketing challenges. Subsequent events have made clear that the founders were challenged with respect to the ethical dilemmas and sheer destructive power it would unleash.[117] They still are, their high IQs notwithstanding.[118]

Not every decision we make is of the magnitude of the founding and maintenance of Facebook. But many of our actions have implications for our own and others' futures that, at the time, we just do not think about. For example, sea animals, even very large ones, are now being found dead with large amounts of plastic in their bodies.[119] When companies have manufactured plastic bottles, or other companies have bought them for their beverages, or consumers have bought them as convenient holders of their beverages, they probably have not thought about their effects on sea animals. But how about the effects of plastics directly on us? Mass production of plastics began only six decades ago, a tiny fraction of the time animals have inhabited the Earth. In that time, 8.3 billion metric tons of plastics, or more than 9 trillion tons (in US measurement) have been produced. Less 10 percent of this plastic is recycled, meaning that the rest enters the environment.[120] This would not be so bad if plastic degraded quickly. But an average plastic bottle takes at least 450 years to degrade and some plastic bottles are estimated to take as long as 1,000 years to degrade.[121]

Some people might be unsympathetic to whales, despite the importance of whales to the food chain. But perhaps, then, they are more sympathetic to themselves. The average person consumes between 126 and 142 plastic particles a day and inhales another 132–170 plastic particles per day.[122] On average, people are consuming 39,000 to 52,000 particles of microplastics a year. If one counts inhalation, the number of particles exceeds 74,000.[123]

Seafood is the major source of microplastics, as so much plastic ends up in the sea. Phthalates, used to make many plastics, have been found to induce malignancies of the breast and of the prostate.[124] Bisphenol A (BPA), found in some plastics, can interfere with reproductive hormones.[125] All of this might sound a bit far-fetched in terms of everyday life. How many people, after all, get cancer? Actually, a lot. But one statistic should concern everyone: Men's sperm counts have roughly halved since the 1970s.[126] Sperm counts are falling almost everywhere.[127] More couples are having trouble conceiving as a result. It may not be an apocalypse yet, but the trends are troubling. There is no consensus as to why this is happening. But with more than 80,000 chemicals registered for use, only a small proportion of which have been tested for safety,[128] one has to wonder just how intelligent we are being in safeguarding the future of the environment and of ourselves.

How wisely do we use our creative, analytical, and practical skills in our everyday lives? How many bad situations do we get ourselves into, or let others get us into, that could have been avoidable had we thought more wisely? For almost all of us, the answer, I suspect, is "quite a few." Adaptive intelligence is not just a set of skills for manufacturers or software developers or politicians. It is a set of skills we all need to make the world better not just for other species, and not just for other people, but also for ourselves.

3.8.10 Potential Objection #10: Even Though the Skills Involved in Intelligence May Change in Emphasis Across Time or Space, g Is Relevant to All of Those Emphases – Probably More so Than Anything Else

Clearly, general intelligence is relevant to many things, as mentioned repeatedly throughout this book. But g has proven to be a total bust in terms of preserving the world for future generations. If two extra standard deviations worth of IQ points in the twentieth century were not enough to move us toward creating a more viable world instead of one that is continually degrading, g, upon which IQ is largely based, cannot be *the* answer and may not even be *an* answer. We need something more. I suggest that something more is adaptive intelligence.

Our societal emphasis on general intelligence reflects the incredibly individualistic, narrow, and short-term thinking not only of people in general (what else is new?), but of researchers in the field of intelligence, who, if anyone, should know better.

3.8.11 Potential Objection #11: Nothing Is Going to Change Anyway, so Why Bother?

In a strange way, this is the strongest objection. I have been trying to change the way society conceives of intelligence for over forty years; so has

Howard Gardner. Nothing has really changed. Even education, with so many researchers and developers trying to change things, has barely budged at all except in sometimes cosmetic ways. What is the point? Until very recently, I felt like a total failure in my career, for many reasons, chief among which was that, after forty+ years, little has changed. There are cracks – some colleges and universities going test-optional – but often the reasons for the changes have little to do with doing the right thing and a lot to do with gaining financial momentum. Today, COVID-19 is resulting in changes in testing that none of our efforts have come close to matching. Recently, I gave a talk in Boston and mentioned how Gardner and I and many others had failed. A member of the audience begged to differ, suggesting that as long as we keep trying, we have not failed. He was right. I may not change things but perhaps someone after me will. We all have to keep trying because time is not on humanity's side. Eventually, people either will realize this, or there will be no people left to realize this or anything else.

3.9   Implications for Action

There are at least three implications of the proposed theory for action.

First, psychologists, in particular, and society, in general, have to consider more seriously what they mean by the term "intelligence." General intelligence may be general across a number of seemingly diverse domains of skills – verbal, mathematical, spatial, and so on. But it may not be general when it comes to what, biologically, matters the most: the propagation and ultimate biological success of our own species or gene pools. In a world not threatened by products of general intelligence, this lack of generality might matter less. But in a world threatened by global climate change, food shortages, water shortages, pollution, nuclear bombs, extreme poverty, and so many other things, it matters greatly that the so-called "generality" of general intelligence *does* not extend to those things that really matter in the long term. We have to stop sticking our heads in the sand.

Second, educational institutions at all levels need to be more reflective and conscientious in the skills they assess through their various testing programs. Overwhelmingly, assessment programs emphasize cognitive and educational skills associated with individual success as traditionally defined in typical Western schooling. We have built a closed system where we value things that matter primarily or even exclusively only in the short run in a modern Western system of values. But those things often have little importance for sustaining the world as we have known it. More importantly, they will not matter for creating a future world as we will want to know it. If we care about the preservation of our own and millions of other species, we must change what and how we assess. As a start, we need tests that measure creative, practical, and wisdom-based skills as applied to significant problems.[129] We cannot go on pretending that solving sterile multiple-choice problems of no consequence is more important than solving real-world problems that face individuals and humanity as a whole.

Third, educational institutions need to reconsider what and how they teach what they teach. At present, the curriculum is highly skewed toward teaching to tests that measure narrow proxies of general intelligence.[130] Schools should take on the responsibility for teaching skills that develop not only general intelligence but also adaptive intelligence.[131] This is the kind of intelligence that the world needs if it is to be preserved as a place in which humans and millions of other species can live, thrive, and flourish.

Notes

1. Kottasova, I. (2019). Germany's temperature record smashed as Europe's heat wave intensifies. *CNN*, June 26. https://cnn.it/39V4D8i
2. Chandra, S. (2019). Are parts of India becoming too hot for humans? *CNN*, July 4. https://cnn.it/3hZveDO
3. Sternberg, R. J. (2019). A theory of adaptive intelligence and its relation to general intelligence. *Journal of Intelligence.* https://doi.org/10.3390/jintelligence7040023
4. Gilbey, R. (2010). Rashomon: No. 5 best crime film of all time. *The Guardian*, October 17. www.theguardian.com/film/2010/oct/17/rashomon-crime
5. "Intelligence and its measurement": A symposium (1921). *Journal of Educational Psychology*, 12, 123–47, 195–216, 271–5; Snyderman, M., & Rothman, S. (1987). Survey of expert opinion on intelligence and aptitude testing. *American Psychologist*, 42(2), 137–44. doi: 10.1037/0003-066X.42.2.137; Gottfredson, L. S. (1997). Mainstream science on intelligence: An editorial with 52 signatories, history, and bibliography. *Intelligence*, 24, 13–23. https://bit.ly/2PhpI3f
6. Haier, R. J. (2016). *The neuroscience of intelligence*. New York: Cambridge University Press.
7. Berry, J. W. (1974). Radical cultural relativism and the concept of intelligence. In J. W. Berry, & P. R. Dasen (Eds.), *Culture and cognition: Readings in cross-cultural psychology* (pp. 225–9). London: Methuen.
8. Jensen, A. R. (1998). *The g factor*. Westport, CT: Greenwood-Praeger.
9. Gardner, H. (2011). *Frames of mind: The theory of multiple intelligences*. New York: Basic.

10. Jerison, H. J. (1982). The evolution of biological intelligence. In R. J. Sternberg (Ed.), *Handbook of human intelligence* (pp. 723–91). New York: Cambridge University Press; Sternberg, R. J., & Kaufman, J. C. (Eds.) (2001). *The evolution of intelligence*. Mahwah, NJ: Lawrence Erlbaum Associates.

11. Neisser, U., Boodoo, G., Bouchard, T. J. Jr., et al. (1996). Intelligence: Knowns and unknowns. *American Psychologist, 51*(2), 77–101, 96.

12. Orwell, G. (1950). *1984*. New York: Signet.

13. Action Comics. (1938). Superman. *Action Comics*. Issue 1, June, pp. 1–13. New York: DC Comics.

14. Spearman, C. (1927). *The abilities of man*. New York: Macmillan.

15. Thurstone, L. (1938). *Primary mental abilities*. Chicago, IL: University of Chicago Press.

16. Carroll, J. B. (1993). *Human cognitive abilities: A survey of factor-analytic studies*. New York: Cambridge University Press; Schneider, W. J., & McGrew, K. S. (2012). The Cattell-Horn-Carroll model of intelligence. In D. P. Flanagan, & P. L. Harrison (Eds.), *Contemporary intellectual assessment: Theories, tests, and issues* (3rd ed., pp. 99–144). New York: Guilford Press.

17. Urbina, S. (2011). Tests of intelligence. In R. J. Sternberg, & S. B. Kaufman (Eds.), *Cambridge handbook of intelligence* (pp. 20–38). New York: Cambridge University Press; DeBoeck, P., Gore, B., Gonzalez, T., & San Martin, E. (2020). An alternative view on the measurement of intelligence and its history. In R. J. Sternberg (Ed.), *Cambridge handbook of intelligence* (2nd ed., pp. 47–74). New York: Cambridge University Press.

18. Willis, J. O., Dumont, R., & Kaufman, A. S. (2011). Factor-analytic models of intelligence. In R. J. Sternberg, & S. B. Kaufman (Eds.), *Cambridge handbook of intelligence* (pp. 39–57). New York: Cambridge University Press.

19. Sternberg, R. J. (Ed.) (2018). *The nature of human intelligence*. New York: Cambridge University Press.

20. Johnson, W., & Bouchard, T. J. (2005). The structure of human intelligence: It is verbal, perceptual, and image rotation (VPR), not fluid and crystallized intelligence. *Intelligence, 33*, 393–416.

21. Sternberg, R. J. (1983). Components of human intelligence. *Cognition, 15*, 1–48.

22. Gittleman, J. L. (2018). Adaptation: Biology and physiology. *Encyclopedia Britannica,* April 26. www.britannica.com/science/adaptation-biology-and-physiology

23. Dawkins, R. (2016). *The selfish gene* (4th ed.). New York: Oxford University Press.

24. Sternberg, R. J. (1988). *The triarchic mind: A new theory of human intelligence*. New York: Viking.

25. The 97% consensus on global warming. *Skeptical Science.* https://bit.ly/33mDCJm

26. Harvey, C. (2018). CO_2 emissions reached an all-time high in 2018. *Scientific American*, December 6. https://bit.ly/3i3TMLX

27. Mulvaney, K. (2019). Climate change report card: These countries are reaching targets. *National Geographic*, September 19. https://on.natgeo.com/2XqM5Yu

28. Fears, D. (2019). One million species face extinction, UN report says. And humans will suffer as a result. *Washington Post*, May 6. https://wapo.st/3k6dVCO

29. Rettner, R. (2019). More than 250,000 people may die each year due to climate change. *Live Science*, January 17. www.livescience.com/64535-climate-change-health-deaths.html

30. Rush, E. (2018). Rising seas: "Florida is about to be wiped off the map." *The Guardian*, June 26. https://bit.ly/2BT9c6i; Kolbert, E. (2019). Louisiana's disappearing cost. *The New Yorker*, April 1. https://bit.ly/3k6ZJK4; Xia, R. (2019). The California coast is disappearing under the rising sea. Our choices are grim. *Los Angeles Times*, July 7. https://lat.ms/39PN1ui

31. Der Spiegel Staff (2018). Is Germany's heat wave a preview of the future? *Der Spiegel*, August 7. https://bit.ly/2XlR9NN

32. Turrentine, J. (2019). Climate change is already driving mass migration around the globe. *National Resources Defense Council*, January 25. https://on.nrdc.org/39YGHRq

33. United Nations Climate Change. (2017). Climate change is a key driver of migration and food insecurity. *United Nations*, October 16. https://unfccc.int/news/climate-change-is-a-key-driver-of-migration-and-food-insecurity; World Bank Group. (2018). Climate change could force over 140 million to migrate within countries by 2050: *World Bank Report*, March 19. https://bit.ly/3i1lTeB

34. Gick, M. L., & Holyoak, K. L. (1983). Schema induction and analogical transfer. *Cognitive Psychology*, 15, 1–38.

35. IEP. (N.D.). George Santayana (1863–1952). *Internet Encyclopedia of Philosophy (IEP)*. www.iep.utm.edu/santayan/

36. Sackett, P. R., Shewach, O. R., & Dahlke, J. A. (2020). The predictive value of general intelligence. *Human intelligence: An introduction* (pp. 415–42). New York: Cambridge University Press.

37. Schwanhausser, M. (2007). Forget the Ivy League: Most valley CEOs went public. *The Mercury News,* November 27. https://bayareane.ws/39OuEpG

38. Oxfam. (2015). Extreme carbon inequality. *Oxfam Media Briefing*, December 2. https://bit.ly/3gpW1c8

39. Saini, A. (2019). *Superior: The return of race science*. New York: Beacon Press.

40. Gould, S. J. (1996). *The mismeasure of man* (rev. and expanded ed.). New York: W. W. Norton.

41. Kahan, D. M., Peters, E., Wittlin, M. et al. (2012). The polarizing impact of science literacy and numeracy on perceived climate change risks. *Nature Climate Change*, 2, 732–5. www.nature.com/articles/nclimate1547

42. World Health Organization. (2019). *Air pollution.* www.who.int/airpollution/en/

43. American Lung Association. (2019). *Most polluted cities.* https://bit.ly/2EF4ES0

44. Williams, S. (2018). Air pollution linked to decline in cognitive performance. *The Scientist*, August 28. https://bit.ly/3olOOUN; Zhang X., Chen, X., & Zhang, X. (2018). The impact of air pollution on cognitive performance. *PNAS*, 115(37), 9193–7. www.pnas.org/content/115/37/9193

45. Goldhill, O. (2018). Air pollution in India caused 1.2 million deaths last year. *Quartz*, December 8. https://bit.ly/3if2De3

46. Children of the Atomic Bomb. (N.D.). *Hiroshima and Nagasaki death toll.* www.aasc.ucla.edu/cab/200708230009.html

47. Baum, S. (2015). The risk of nuclear winter. *Federation of American Scientists*, May 29. https://fas.org/pir-pubs/risk-nuclear-winter/

48. World Health Organization. (2018). Antibiotic resistance. *WHO*, February 5. https://bit.ly/33nDlWK

49. Cohen, E., & Kounang, N. (2019). Every 15 minutes, someone in the US dies of a drug-resistant superbug. *CNN*, November 16. https://cnn.it/31d1Lj4

50. Centers for Disease Control and Prevention (CDC). (2019). Measles cases and outbreaks. *CDC*, June 24. www.cdc.gov/measles/cases-outbreaks.html

51. Centers for Disease Control and Prevention (CDC). (2019). Complications of measles. *CDC*, June 13. https://bit.ly/3i4ceEk

52. Guglielmi, G. (2019). Measles erases immune "memory" for other diseases. *Nature*, October 31. www.nature.com/articles/d41586-019-03324-7

53. Walker, J. (2014). *The United States of paranoia: A conspiracy theory.* New York: Harper Perennial; Brotherton, R. (2017). *Suspicious minds.* New York: Bloomsbury Sigma.

54. Flynn, J. R. (2013). *Intelligence and human progress: The story of what was hidden in our genes.* London: Elsevier.

55. Sternberg, R. J. (1977). *Intelligence, information processing, and analogical reasoning: The componential analysis of human abilities.* Hillsdale, NJ: Erlbaum.

56. Sternberg, R. J., Forsythe, G. B., Hedlund, J. et al. (2000). *Practical intelligence in everyday life.* New York: Cambridge University Press.

57. Sternberg, R. J. (in press). The augmented theory of successful intelligence. In R. J. Sternberg (Ed.), *Cambridge handbook of intelligence* (2nd ed.).New York: Cambridge University Press.

58. Sternberg, R. J., & Grigorenko, E. L. (1995). Styles of thinking in school. *European Journal for High Ability*, 6(2), 201–19; Sternberg, R. J. (1997). *Thinking styles.* New York: Cambridge University Press.

59. Nisbett, R. E., Aronson, J., Blair, C. et al. (2012). Intelligence: New findings and theoretical developments. *American Psychologist*, 67(2), 130–59. doi: 10.1037/a0026699

60. See also Herrnstein, R. J., & Murray, C. (1994). *The bell curve.* New York: Free Press; as cited by Nisbett et al. (Note 41); Gottfredson, L. S. (1997). Mainstream science on intelligence: An editorial with 52 signatories, history, and bibliography. *Intelligence*, 24, 13–23. http://dx.doi.org/10.1016/S0160-2896(97)90011-8

61. "Why doing a PhD is often a waste of time." *The Economist*, December 27. https://bit.ly/31bkRWI

62. Sternberg, R. J., Nokes, K., Geissler, P. W. et al. (2001). The relationship between academic and practical intelligence: A case study in Kenya. *Intelligence*, 29, 401–18; Grigorenko, E. L., Meier, E., Lipka, J. et al. (2004). Academic and practical intelligence: A case study of the Yup'ik in Alaska. *Learning and Individual Differences*, 14, 183–207.

63. Hunt, E. B. (1978). Mechanics of verbal ability. *Psychological Review*, 85, 109–30; Sternberg, R. J. (1979). The nature of mental abilities. *American Psychologist*, 34, 214–30; Hunt, E. B. (1980). Intelligence as an information-processing concept. *British Journal of Psychology*, 71, 449–74.

64. Conway, A., & Kovacs, K. (in press). Working memory and intelligence. In R. J. Sternberg (Ed.), *Cambridge handbook of intelligence*. New York: Cambridge University Press.

65. Haier, R. J. (in press). The biological basis of intelligence. In R. J. Sternberg (Ed.), *Cambridge handbook of intelligence*. New York: Cambridge University Press.

66. Sternberg, R. J., & Hedlund, J. (2002). Practical intelligence, g, and work psychology. *Human Performance* 15(1/2), 143–60; Wagner, R. K. (2011). Practical intelligence. In R. J. Sternberg, & S. B. Kaufman (Eds.), *Cambridge handbook of intelligence* (pp. 550–63). New York: Cambridge University Press; Hedlund, J. (in press). Practical intelligence. In R. J. Sternberg (Ed.), *Cambridge handbook of intelligence*. New York: Cambridge University Press.

67. Boring, E. G. (1923). Intelligence as the tests measure it. *New Republic*, 36, 35–7.

68. Sternberg, R. J. (1985). Human intelligence: The model is the message. *Science*, 230, 1111–18; Sternberg, R. J. (1990). *Metaphors of mind*. New York: Cambridge University Press.

69. Spearman, C. (1904). *"General intelligence,"* objectively determined and measured. *American Journal of Psychology*, 15(2), 201–93.

70. Gardner, H. (2011). *Frames of mind: The theory of multiple intelligences*. New York: Basic Books.

71. Sternberg, R. J. (1985). *Beyond IQ: A triarchic theory of human intelligence*. New York: Cambridge University Press.

72. Binet, A., & Simon, T. (1916). *The development of intelligence in children* (E. S. Kite, trans.). Baltimore, MD: Williams & Wilkins.

73. Sternberg, R. J. (2004). Culture and intelligence. *American Psychologist*, 59(5), 325–38.

74. Sternberg, R. J. (2018) Creative giftedness is not just what creativity tests test: Implications of a triangular theory of creativity for understanding creative giftedness. *Roeper Review*, 40(3), 158–65. doi: 10.1080/02783193.2018.1467248

75. Kaufman, J. C., & Sternberg, R. J. (2019). *Cambridge handbook of creativity* (2nd ed.). New York: Cambridge University Press.

76. Hertzog, C. (in press). Intelligence in adulthood. In R. J. Sternberg (Ed.), *Cambridge handbook of intelligence* (2nd ed.). New York: Cambridge University Press.

77. Triandis, H. (1995). *Individualism & collectivism.* Boulder, CO: Westview; Markus, H. R., & Conner, A. (2014). *Clash: How to thrive in a multicultural world.* New York: Plume.
78. Nisbett, R. E. (1994). *The geography of thought: How Asians and Westerners think differently . . . and why.* New York: Free Press; Sternberg, R. J. (2007). Intelligence and culture. In S. Kitayama, & D. Cohen (Eds.), *Handbook of cultural psychology* (pp. 547–68). New York: Guilford Press.
79. Greenfield, P. M. (1997). You can't take it with you: Why ability assessments don't cross cultures. *American Psychologist, 52,* 1115–24; Rogoff, B. (2003). *The cultural nature of human development.* New York: Oxford University Press.
80. Shklovski, I. S., & Sagan, C. (1966). *Intelligent life in the universe.* San Francisco, CA: Holden-Day; Spektor, B. (2018). 9 strange, scientific excuses for why humans haven't found aliens yet. *Live Science,* July 31. www .livescience.com/63208-alien-life-excuses.html
81. Howell, E. (2018). Fermi paradox: Where are the Aliens? *Space.com,* April 27. www.space.com/25325-fermi-paradox.html
82. Hart, M. H. (1975). "Explanation for the absence of extraterrestrials on Earth." *Quarterly Journal of the Royal Astronomical Society, 16,* 128–35.
83. Sternberg, R. J., & Jordan, J. (Eds.) (2005). *Handbook of wisdom: Psychological perspectives.* New York: Cambridge University Press; Sternberg, R. J. (2019). Introduction to the Cambridge handbook of wisdom: Race to Samarra: The critical importance of wisdom in the world today. In R. J. Sternberg, & J. Glueck (Eds.), *Cambridge handbook of wisdom* (pp. 3–9). New York: Cambridge University Press; Sternberg, R. J., & Glueck, J. (Eds.) (2019). *Cambridge handbook of wisdom.* New York: Cambridge University Press.
84. Sternberg, R. J. (2005). Foolishness. In R. J. Sternberg, & J. Jordan (Eds.), *Handbook of wisdom: Psychological perspectives* (pp. 331–52). New York: Cambridge University Press.
85. Sternberg, R. J. (2018). Wisdom, foolishness, and toxicity in human development. *Research in Human Development, 15,* 200–10. doi: 10.1080/ 15427609.2018.1491216
86. Thomas, A. (2018). 3 highly toxic leaders you should avoid at all costs. *Inc. com,* March 30. https://bit.ly/3olk8TA
87. Sternberg, R. J. (in press). The augmented theory of successful intelligence. In R. J. Sternberg (Ed.), *Cambridge handbook of intelligence* (2nd ed.). New York: Cambridge University Press.
88. Kaufman, J. C., & Sternberg, R. J. (Eds.) (2019). *Cambridge handbook of creativity.* New York: Cambridge University Press.
89. Sternberg, R. J. (1997). *Successful intelligence.* New York: Plume.
90. Sternberg, R. J., & Wagner, R. K. (Eds.) (1986). *Practical intelligence: Nature and origins of competence in the everyday world.* New York: Cambridge University Press.
91. Sternberg, R. J. (1998). A balance theory of wisdom. *Review of General Psychology, 2,* 347–65.

92. Cropley, D. H., Cropley, A. J., Kaufman, J. C., & Runco, M. A. (Eds.) (2010). *The dark side of creativity*. New York: Cambridge University Press; Sternberg, R. J. (2010). The dark side of creativity and how to combat it. In D. H. Cropley, A. J. Cropley, J. C. Kaufman, & M. A. Runco (Eds.), *The dark side of creativity* (pp. 316–28). New York: Cambridge University Press.

93. Deary, I. J., & Whalley, L. J. (2008) *A lifetime of intelligence*. Washington, DC: American Psychological Association.

94. Sackett, P. R., Shewach, O. R., & Dahlke, J. A. (in press). The predictive value of general intelligence. In R. J. Sternberg (Ed.), *Human intelligence: An introduction*. New York: Cambridge University Press.

95. Ceci, S. J. (1996). *On intelligence ... more or less: A biological treatise on intellectual development*. Cambridge, MA: Harvard University Press; Sternberg, R. J., & Grigorenko E. L. (2001). Degree of embeddedness of ecological systems as a measure of ease of adaptation to the environment. In E. L. Grigorenko, & R. J. Sternberg (Eds.), *Family environment and intellectual functioning: A life-span perspective* (pp. 243–62). Mahwah, NJ: Lawrence Erlbaum Associates; Sternberg, R. J. (2003). Biological intelligence. In R. J. Sternberg, & E. L. Grigorenko (Eds.), *The psychology of abilities, competencies, and expertise* (pp. 240–62). New York: Cambridge University Press.

96. Zigler, E., & Seitz, V. (1982). Social policy and intelligence. In R. J. Sternberg (Ed.), *Handbook of human intelligence* (pp. 586–641). New York: Cambridge University Press. Zigler, E. (1986). Intelligence: A developmental approach. In R. J. Sternberg, & D. K. Detterman (Eds.), *What is intelligence?* (pp. 149–52). Norwood, NJ: Ablex Publishing.

97. Sternberg, R. J. (1993). The concept of "giftedness": A pentagonal implicit theory. In G. R. Bock, & K. Ackrill (Eds.), *The origins and development of high ability* (pp. 5–21). Chichester: CIBA Foundation; Sternberg, R. J., & Zhang, L. F. (1995). What do we mean by "giftedness"? A pentagonal implicit theory. *Gifted Child Quarterly*, 39(2), 88–94.

98. Hunt, E. (2010). *Human intelligence*. New York: Cambridge University Press; McGreal, S. A. (2013). The illusory theory of multiple intelligences. *Psychology Today*, November 23. https://bit.ly/3opywdD

99. Visser, B. A., Ashton, M. C., & Vernon, P. A. (2006). Beyond *g*: Putting multiple intelligences theory to the test. *Intelligence*, 34(5), 487–502.

100. Sternberg, R. J. (1978). Componential investigations of human intelligence. In A. Lesgold, J. Pellegrino, S. Fokkema, & R. Glaser (Eds.), *Cognitive psychology and instruction* (pp. 277–98). New York: Plenum.

101. Kuhn, T. S. (1970). *The structure of scientific revolutions* (2nd ed.). Chicago, IL: University of Chicago Press.

102. Masih, N., & Slater, J. (2019). As a major Indian city runs out of water, 9 million people pray for rain. *Washington Post*, June 28. https://wapo.st/3opoc2e

103. Okeson, S. (2019). Trump scientist insists that "carbon dioxide is good for you." *Raw Story*, July 1. https://bit.ly/3gpiUw5

104. Union of Concerned Scientists. (2018). Underwater: Rising seas, chronic floods, and the implications for US costal real estate. *UCS*, June 18. https://bit.ly/3iox5Iz

105. How the IPCC is more likely to underestimate the climate response. *Skeptical Science.* https://bit.ly/2Di7qMC

106. Winston, A. (2019). Young people are leading the way on climate change, and companies need to pay attention. *Harvard Business Review*, March 26. https://bit.ly/39T2fif

107. Sternberg, R. J., & Sternberg, K. (2008). *The nature of hate.* New York: Cambridge University Press.

108. Mackintosh, N. J. (2011). *IQ and human intelligence.* New York: Oxford University Press.

109. Sternberg, R. J., & Williams, W. M. (1998). You proved our point better than we did: A reply to our critics. *American Psychologist*, 53, 576–7.

110. Daley, C. E., & Onwuegbuzie, A. J. (in press). Race and intelligence: It's not a black and white issue. In R. J. Sternberg (Ed.), *Cambridge handbook of intelligence.* New York: Cambridge University Press; Suzuki, L. A., Larson-Konar, D., Short, E. L., & Lee, C. S. (in press). Racial and ethnic group differences in intelligence in the United States: Multicultural perspectives. In R. J. Sternberg (Ed.), *Cambridge handbook of intelligence* (2nd ed.). New York: Cambridge University Press.

111. Sternberg, R. J. (2010). *College admissions for the 21st century.* Cambridge, MA: Harvard University Press.

112. Sternberg, R. J. (2019). *Adaptive intelligence.* Article submitted for publication.

113. Deary, I. J., Whiteman, M. C., Starr, J. M., Whalley, L. J., & Fox, H. C. (2004). The impact of childhood intelligence on later life: Following up the Scottish Mental Surveys of 1932 and 1947. *Journal of Personality and Social Psychology*, 86, 130–47.

114. Williams, W. M., & Sternberg, R. J. (1988). Group intelligence: Why some groups are better than others. *Intelligence*, 12, 351–77.

115. Malone, T. W., & Wooley, A. W. (in press). Collective intelligence. In R. J. Sternberg (Ed.), *Cambridge handbook of intelligence* (2nd ed.). New York: Cambridge University Press.

116. Sloman, S., & Fernbach, P. (2018). *The knowledge illusion: Why we never think alone.* New York: Riverhead Books.

117. Phipps, S. (2014). Facebook's big problem: ethical blindness. *InfoWorld*, June 30. https://bit.ly/2CiESlI; Blum, R. (2017). Facebook's little ethics problem. *Gatestone Institute*, June 7. www.gatestoneinstitute.org/10457/facebook-ethics

118. Olen, H. (2019). Mark Zuckerberg flounders before Congress. *Washington Post*, October 24. https://wapo.st/39TEOoM

119. Daly, N. (2018). For animals, plastic is turning the ocean into a minefield. *National Geographic*, June. https://on.natgeo.com/39Vv3Xh

120. Parker, L. (2018). A whopping 91% of plastic isn't recycled. *National Geographic*, December 20. https://on.natgeo.com/300KP9X

121. Postconsumers. (2011). How long does it take a plastic bottle to biodegrade? *Postconsumers*, October 31. https://bit.ly/33kTwUI
122. Young, L. (2019). Here's how much plastic you might be eating every day. *Global News*, June 5. https://bit.ly/3gCetyt
123. Gibbens, S. (2019). You eat thousands of bits of plastic every year. *National Geographic*, June 5. https://on.natgeo.com/30lTTfW
124. Hsieh, T. H., Tsai, C. F., Hsu, C. Y. et al. (2012). Phthalates induce proliferation and invasiveness of estrogen receptor-negative breast cancer through the AhR/HDAC6/c-Myc signaling pathway. *FASEB Journal*, 26(2), 778–87. www.ncbi.nlm.nih.gov/pubmed/22049059
125. Rochester, J. R. (2013). Bisphenol A and human health: A review of the literature. *Reproductive Toxicology*, 42, 132–55.
126. Belluz, J. (2019). Sperm counts are falling. This isn't the reproductive apocalypse – yet. *Vox*, May 30. https://bit.ly/33la5zT
127. Fetters, A. (2018). Sperm counts continue to fall. *The Atlantic*, October 12. https://bit.ly/3if63xp
128. Scialla, M. (2016). It could take centuries for EPA to test all the unregulated chemicals under a new landmark bill. *PBS*, June 22. https://to.pbs.org/2Xk4WEf
129. Sternberg, R. J., & Grigorenko, E. L. (2004). WICS: A model for selecting students for nationally competitive scholarships. In A. S. Ilchman, W. F. Ilchman, & M. H. Tolar (Eds.), *The lucky few and the worthy many. Scholarship competitions and the world's future leaders.* (pp. 32–61). Bloomington, IN: Indiana University Press.
130. Frey, M. C., & Detterman, D. K. (2004). Scholastic assessment or g? The relationship between the scholastic assessment test and general cognitive ability. *Psychological Science*, 15, 373–8; Koenig, K. A., Frey, M. C., & Detterman, D. K. (2008). ACT and general cognitive ability. *Intelligence*, 36, 153–60.
131. Sternberg, R. J., Jarvin, L., & Grigorenko, E. L. (2009). *Teaching for wisdom, intelligence, creativity, and success.* Thousand Oaks, CA: Corwin; Sternberg, R. J., & Hagen, E. S. (2019). Teaching for wisdom. In R. J. Sternberg, & Glueck, J. (Eds.),*Cambridge handbook of wisdom* (pp. 372–406). New York: Cambridge University Press.

CHAPTER 4

Why General Intelligence May Be Unhelpful, or Detrimental, in Times of Instability, and for that Matter, in Other Times as Well

General intelligence is helpful for many things, as you saw in Chapter 3. But are there circumstances under which it is ill-suited – under which it might actually hinder performance? That is the question I will explore with you in this chapter.

Let us start with a quick review of a major theory of intelligence, that proposed by Raymond Cattell, and variants of which are still popular today.[1] Most contemporary theories of intelligence, such as those of John B. Carroll[2] and of Kevin McGrew and colleagues,[3] all are based, at least in part, on Cattell's theory.

Let us review Cattell's theory. The basic idea is simple. There are two principal kinds of intelligence, fluid intelligence and crystallized intelligence.

Fluid intelligence comprises your ability to engage in abstract reasoning – to perceive relationships and then apply these relationships as needed. A variety of tests commonly are used to measure fluid intelligence. One is number series, where you might be asked what the next number is in the following series of numbers: 2, 10, 13, 21, 24, . . .? (32). Sometimes test-takers instead see a series of letters or geometric objects. A second possible test would be word classifications, such as: Which word does not belong with the others?: turquoise, sapphire, aquamarine, emerald, lapis lazuli (emerald). A third possible test would be analogies, such as COW : MAMMAL :: FROG : ? (AMPHIBIAN). With classifications and analogies, geometric objects also may be used.

Crystallized intelligence basically comprises the knowledge and acquired cognitive skills you have built up over the course of your lifetime. Tests commonly used to measure crystallized intelligence include vocabulary and general information. So, you might be asked what the word "exacerbate" means (to make worse); or you might be asked what the name of the temperature scale is that has a temperature of absolute 0 degrees in which there truly is no heat at all (Kelvin).

In Cattell's theory, crystallized intelligence develops from fluid intelligence. That is, one builds up one's knowledge base through learning and thinking, which require fluid intelligence. Although Cattell believed it possible to construct a culture-free, or at least, culture-fair test of intelligence,[4] psychologists now realize that this is not possible, at least given what we know today. All current testing is culture-based in some way. For example, in some cultures, particularly those with typical Western schooling, children develop familiarity with the kinds of abstract geometric objects featured in the Cattell intelligence tests, whereas in other cultures, they do not.[5] Even the act of taking a test is a cultural act. In some cultures, there are no intelligence and achievement tests. Indeed, they are a recent invention.

Testers make assumptions about taking tests that may not be shared by those taking the tests. For example, I once conducted a study with a colleague on analogical reasoning in young children.[6] There were three groups of children – in grades two, four, and six. The results for the second-graders were bizarre. A number of students got no problems correct, even though the problems were not particularly difficult. When we looked at the test booklets, we discovered what had happened. The students were youngsters in a Hebrew Day School that conducted instruction in English in the morning and Hebrew in the afternoon. We tested in the afternoon. As Hebrew is read right to left and the testing was when the students normally would be reading Hebrew, they read the problems right to left.

There are no pure tests of anything, at least, not at the present. For example, all the fluid-intelligence tests described above draw on cultural knowledge. To solve the number series, you have to be conversant with numbers and how to manipulate them; to solve the word-classification problems, you need knowledge about various kinds of gemstones; and to solve the analogy, you have to know the various classifications of animals, and which animals fall into which classes.

It has been recognized for many years that levels of crystallized and fluid intelligence correlate positively with many aspects of human performance.[7] At the same time, the correlation is not always positive, and even can be negative in special circumstances, such as in cultures that particularly value skills other than academic ones.[8] But our use of conventional intelligence measures to create societal pyramids, where those who score better on tests go higher on the pyramid and those who score worse go lower on the pyramid, may be a mistake, perhaps even a serious one. Consider why.

4.1 Is Fluid Intelligence Exactly What It Is Cracked Up to Be?

I would like to suggest that fluid intelligence is not all it is cracked up to be. Consider first the role of speed. Almost all tests of fluid intelligence are speeded, but at what cost?

4.1.1 *The Speed Factor*

For me, the first indication of problems with fluid-ability tests came in a study I performed many years ago in my doctoral dissertation.[9] I was analyzing scores on speeded tests of analogical reasoning. The analogies were presented via a machine (called a "tachistoscope") that would display items and then measure how quickly test-takers could solve the problems. Many of the results were as expected. For example, on average, test-takers who solved the problems more quickly also performed better on conventional tests of intelligence. This finding is scarcely surprising, because our test items were highly speeded, as are many items on conventional standardized tests of intelligence and allied abilities. Because both kinds of items – conventional test items and our particular test items – were speeded, a correlation was almost built in – it would seem hard not to get a positive correlation for two highly speeded tests of complex reasoning.

Yet, when we broke down performance on the test items into component processes of analogical reasoning, the picture was more complex. One component of information processing, *encoding*, showed the opposite of the pattern we had expected. In particular, the higher test-scorers spent *more* time encoding stimulus items than did the lower test-scorers. In other words, the high-scorers were looking more carefully than the lower-scorers at exactly what was in the items and what it all meant, before they started solving the problems. In this way, they were more likely to ensure that they were solving the problem actually presented rather than what they might have thought, quickly, was the problem, even though it was not. This result was especially extraordinary because the tests were speeded and test-takers got credit for being quick, not for being slow. But they also got credit for being accurate, and the smarter participants recognized this. They thus spent more time encoding the terms of the test items.

When we test for fluid intelligence, then, we might be making a mistake if we emphasize time limits and quick solutions too much. Life's serious problems are rarely ones we can solve quickly – in a matter of a few seconds or even a few minutes. Why, then, would we expect people taking tests to be as fast as possible? Might it be better, for many serious adaptive problems in life, to take the time to make sure that the problem one is solving is really the problem that needs to be solved? Who has not been in a situation in which they spent serious time on a problem, only to discover that the problem they were trying to solve was the wrong one?

That could have been a quirky finding except for another finding that emerged soon thereafter. A colleague and I were studying analogical reasoning in children and looked at the development of the information-processing components of reasoning by analogy. What did we find? We found that, as children got older, they got faster, on average, on all components of analogical reasoning except for, you guessed it, encoding. They actually became slower in encoding.[10] Once again, merely speeding tests of intelligence on the notion that faster is smarter greatly oversimplifies things. We are measuring general intelligence in a way that may be counterproductive, falsely assuming that the faster you are, the smarter you are.[11] How many people do you know who, for real-world adaptive problems, just respond quickly and impulsively? Are you impressed with their intelligence? Do you really want to respect people who make split-second decisions about whom to marry, when to have children, how to invest money, when to buy a house, and so forth?

Those two findings might have been just lucky coincidences except for a third finding. In a study I did, we were looking at how people solve problems requiring intelligence, particularly problems that were quite novel to them.[12] I used experimental techniques to isolate two basic processes of problem-solving, which I called global planning and local planning. *Global planning* is what you do when you are first starting to solve a problem. It is the planning you do up front to make sure that you have a pretty well-developed strategy for solving a problem. People who do not do much global planning just jump into solving a problem without much advance thought about what they are going to do or why they are going to do it. Initial encoding of stimuli is an important part of global planning. In contrast, *local planning* is the planning you do at the various steps along the way. This is the planning you to make sure you are staying on track. If you do not do sufficient global planning, you are likely to do more local planning, as you will tend to get lost along the way or lose track of what you are doing. And what did we find? Same as before. The more intelligent participants spent *more* time on global planning than did the less intelligent participants; but they spent less time on local planning.

What these results all suggest is that, although it is desirable to have the ability to think quickly, as Carroll and many others have pointed out in their theories of intelligence, thinking and especially acting quickly can be a huge mistake. Other cultures recognize this fact.[13] For some reason, many Western cultures have been slow to recognize that their emphasis on doing things fast can be counterproductive.

I was writing to a colleague just earlier today on the pressure in academia, my field, to produce published articles. CVs of current applicants for assistant professorships look like the CVs of applicants for associate or even full professorships from when I was just starting my career (in 1975). With so much pressure to hurry up and publish, are these individuals really going to be doing their best work? When I was applying for a job, I had a book contract and a dissertation. That would probably get me hired exactly nowhere today. But the book turned out to be a Citation Classic. Would I, or the field, have been better off if I had written a bunch of small articles that probably would have had little or no impact at all?

Today, many parents recognize that their children have a lot to offer but the children are not necessarily the fastest workers around. If the parents have the resources and the child has a learning disability or something resembling a learning disability, the parents may attempt to get a disability diagnosis from a licensed psychologist or other specialist attesting to the disability. The children then get extra time not only on standardized tests, but on many tests given in school. They may also get other special services. The system is heavily tilted toward parents who can afford to get diagnoses (which are expensive) and who live in school districts that provide high levels of services to children with disabilities.[14] The system would be so much better off if *all* children got extra time. In the end, it is quality of thinking rather than speed of thinking that matters in most adaptive situations. Of course, there are exceptions. Air traffic controllers do not have the luxury of time. If you are heading toward an accident on the highway, you do not have a lot of extra time to think. But for the most part, adaptive real-world problems are best solved with deliberation rather than in haste.

The bottom line is that our emphasis on speed in thinking about fluid intelligence is generally misplaced. Regrettably, society has been very slow in acting upon the realization that speed is often not important. In this case, speed is of the essence!

4.1.2   Entrenchment

There is another problem, I believe, with tests of fluid intelligence. This problem, like the speed problem, goes to the heart of what the tests measure. This problem is that the tests, for all their supposed emphasis on novelty, actually measure a fairly conventional form of thinking.

Think for a moment about the way that tests of fluid intelligence measure fluid ability, using problems such as series problems, classification problems, analogies, and also, sometimes, matrix problems in which one is presented with a two-dimensional array of geometric figures and one has to fill in a missing figure. All these tests measure your ability to discern patterns and then, in some way, to extrapolate from those patterns. In the case of a famous test of fluid intelligence – perhaps the most famous test – *Raven's Progressive Matrices* – the whole test consists of discerning patterns in matrices and filling in the missing geometric form.[15]

Certainly, the ability to discern patterns and then extrapolate beyond them is important and even matters for some forms of creativity, generally, those that work within an existing paradigm. But consider why this focus on discerning patterns might be a problem.

All our knowledge, in science and everything else, is limited. A problem, though, is that we tend to believe that, as things have been in the past, so they will be in the future. The ability to spot and extrapolate from existing patterns is extremely useful, so long as those patterns actually will continue to exist in the future. But that is not always the case. The most radical forms of creativity involve breaking away from existing patterns, not merely extrapolating from them.[16]

A colleague and I observed this firsthand in a study we did on practical intelligence in Russia just after the breakup of the Soviet Union.[17] Before the breakup, there were people in a wide variety of professions who had the talent and skills – and the sheer fluid intelligence – to make a successful go of things. But after the breakup of the country, the living situation for many people became very chaotic. The skills many of them had before, such as of being a scholar, became devalued. Many professors found that they were not even being paid, for example. Rather suddenly, practical and especially entrepreneurial skills came into very high demand. A whole new "upper class" emerged quite suddenly, with many of those previously in the upper class, or at least the upper middle class, sinking rapidly. The patterns of the past were not repeating themselves. People who drew on past patterns and tried to extrapolate them were just out of luck. We found practical intelligence to be more important for health-related outcomes than was the more academic side of intelligence, in particular, fluid intelligence. Moreover, the kind of creativity that mattered now was not extrapolating past patterns but establishing new ones.

The same sequence of events is being repeated today, in multiple ways, in the United States. When I was young, there was a real premium on being able to do fast and accurate arithmetic computation. Schools valued it. Oddly, they still do, as my nine-year-old (as of today!) triplets show me day after day. People who were good at computation could become accountants or at least accounting clerks, or really go into any profession where facility with numbers mattered. Today, very few people who are adults need a high level of skill in fast, accurate arithmetic computation. The nature of intelligence has changed.[18] The importance of computation just is not what it used to be. Intelligence tests like the SRA *Primary Mental Abilities* that used to measure arithmetic computation probably would not today.

The main problem with fluid-ability tests measuring pattern processing is the assumption that patterns that have worked in the past will work in the future. People who are adept or even extremely adept at handling past patterns may not be those who best can adjust to new patterns. A former colleague, Peter Frensch, and I saw this in a study we performed comparing expert and novice performance in a card game, bridge.[19] The experts were obviously much better than the novices. No surprise there. But what we were interested in was the effect of making changes in the game on their performance.

In one condition, we made only minor, surface-structural changes in the game. Names of suits – clubs, diamonds, hearts, spades – were changed to neologisms, such as *gleebs* and *fricks*. When we made this minor change, both experts and novices were briefly affected for the worse, but both also quickly recovered. The change made virtually no long-term difference. In another condition, however, we changed something more fundamental – which player went first after the bidding period of the game was over. Instead of the high bidder going first, we created a situation in which the low bidder went first. This change was more deep-structural and profound. The change affected experts more than novices and experts continued to show effects even after the initial period when they first got used to playing the game with the new rule. The take-away message was that experts, while advantaged by their deeper knowledge and understanding of the game, are disadvantaged by that same knowledge. In a word, they become *entrenched*.

The potential horror of entrenchment is being seen in the global response to the COVID-19 pandemic. Many of the public-health measures that were in place for the past have not proven to work well when actually implemented in the present to combat this pandemic. The US had a pandemic response team that President Trump disbanded. The public-health community warned the politicians that new measures were needed to combat the pandemic. The politicians, in many instances, were oblivi-ous, and some of them saw it in the same way they always have seen crises – as an opportunity further to polarize the country politically. Why waste a crisis? The result has been, as of August 7, 2020, more than 160,000 deaths, many of them due to ideological bickering over whether to wear masks or engage in social distancing. Many of these politicians and their followers are well-educated and almost certainly had the high ability-test scores needed to get into the universities they attended. Their IQs appear not to have helped. So much for the thirty-point leap in IQs during the twentieth century. The politicians and many of their followers reacted in the same entrenched way they so often react: Never lose an opportunity to turn a crisis into an ideologically polarizing event, even if thousands die in the process. For them, right to life seems to apply to the unborn but not to the living. Is this a matter of intelligence as well as of politics? It is if you believe that intelligence is the ability to adapt to the environment and you see behavior that is not only self-injurious but also potentially fatal to others as matters of individual and collective adaptation to the environment.

Intelligence tests and their proxies, such as the SAT, ACT, and the GRE, are tests of a particular kind of expertise. They measure somewhat general cognitive skills and knowledge. Someone who is good at taking the tests will be good at other kinds of things that require the same expertise. But what if the required expertise in a society changes, as in Russia after the fall of the Soviet Union, or after an economic crisis such as that of 2008, or as of right now as a result of climate change or COVID-19? Will the same people who are able to understand and exploit existing patterns be those who can understand and exploit wholly new patterns? Or will their entrenchment get in their way? Clearly, it *does* get in the way. Look at Australia burning.

Gestalt psychologists early in the twentieth century – Kurt Koffka, Max Wertheimer, Wolgang Kohler, and others – recognized the importance of what has since come to be called mental set or, in German, *Einstellung*. These terms refer to a mechanized state of mind in which one continues to solve problems much in the same way one did before, even after better methods of problem-solving become available or even after the old methods of problem-solving no longer work. For example, Abraham

Luchins studied the effects of mental set on solving problems involving multiple water jugs. One had to transfer water from one jug to another in a series of moves.[20]

In one group, an experimental group, participants were given five problems for practice, followed by four test problems. A control group received the same test problems but without the practice problems. The practice problems all could be solved using a single formula. The test problems required a different formula. Those who had practiced on a first formula found it difficult to switch to a new formula. In other words, having practice actually hindered performance.

Many of us have had the same experience in certain forms of athletics. We developed our play, say, serving a tennis ball in a certain way, or swinging a golf club in a certain way. We then learn that the way we are swinging is nonoptimal. Changing our game may seem harder than it was just to learn how to play the game in the first place. I have a bit of this problem playing the cello. I do not hold the bow quite correctly, as it turns out. But I find it quite difficult to switch to the correct way of holding the bow, even though my incorrect way almost certainly impedes my cello playing over the long haul. In learning foreign languages, if a new language is too similar to what we know, but not entirely similar, sometimes we have difficulty distinguishing the rules of the new language from those of the old.

The implications of these results are important for society. On the one hand, we want experts, not amateurs, to handle serious problems as they arise.[21] Current distrust of experts and even scorning of what they have to offer is a great loss to society when experts are replaced by amateurs or, worse, flatterers who get by simply by being obsequious to those in command. But experts, despite their knowledge, have a weakness, namely, their tendency to rely on past patterns that have led to success. They function well – until, perhaps, the rules of the game change in a deep-structural way.

The changes can occur quickly. As I write, Cory Booker just dropped out of the running to be selected as the Democratic candidate for president in the 2020 election. One of the things that was asked about Booker was something that, just a few years ago, would have seemed odd: Was Booker too nice, too positive, too upbeat?[22] Barack Obama ran twice on a positive, upbeat message, and won both times. Both those were different times. In 2012 and 2016, many people were looking for a positive message. In 2020, Democrats, whose support Booker needed to win the nomination, were looking, it seems, for one thing above all others – the ability to beat the incumbent president and reverse the course on which the incumbent set the country.[23] They were angry, and had little interest in a candidate who was too sunny and upbeat. In the same way, the strategies that were used to win the 2016 election might well not have worked in an earlier election.

One might like to believe that there is something special about politics, but I would suggest there is nothing special at all. In every field, the skills change that are needed to succeed over time, and the question of longevity for a given person is whether he or she will be able to maintain those skills needed for success over an extended period of time, even as their exact identities change. Just as with arithmetic computation, the skills that once were important may cease to be important and other skills may become more important in their stead. For example, although arithmetic computation is less important than it once was, and so is spelling because of spellcheckers, information-retrieval and information-evaluation skills have become much more important than they once were.

In the past, one had editors, producers, and libraries to evaluate the validity of material to be presented to the public. Much of that is gone. With the rise of the Internet, each user is pretty much on his or her own to retrieve and evaluate material.[24] And many internet users are failing in the use of these evaluation skills. Worse, many people do not care if what they read or hear is true or not.[25] The very most basic assumption of the Enlightenment – that the difference between truth and falsehood matters – is being called into question in a post-truth age. As a result, political candidates who hope to make inroads by pointing out that a rival candidate lies may be sorely disappointed with the result. Unlike in past times, many voters may just not care – odd as that may sound.

What are some other professions that are being affected by deep-structural changes? Well, radiologists are one. Radiologists are trained to interpret X-rays and other diagnostic images. That has been pretty much the definition of their job. But more and more, artificial intelligence (AI) has become better at detecting cancer in X-rays than are radiologists.[26] This means that, fundamentally, the job of a radiologist is likely to change radically in a very short period of time; or else, radiologists may become relics. Of course, the same challenges have faced lawyers.

Attendance at law schools has plummeted, in large part because so much legal work is now being done either by AI or by outsourcing to other countries, such as India.[27] Of course, much of what accountants once did by hand or by a handheld calculator is now being done by computer, and researchers of many different kinds, including student researchers, find that they are making far fewer trips to their libraries as much of their research can be done online rather than in the library stacks. Change in jobs has become a constant and even jobs themselves are changing at a rapid pace. There is little market any more for those making buggy whips, washboards, clothes lines, or, for that matter, many kinds of conventional passenger cars.

The implication of these changes is that identifying intelligent people by assessing their ability to discern and understand past patterns may be, to some extent, a mistake. We need people who will have the skills of the future, not the skills of the past. Severe age discrimination in hiring in Silicon Valley and elsewhere is rife. As one plastic surgeon, Larry Fan, was quoted as saying, "'In Silicon Valley, it's commonly believed that if you're over the age of 35, you're seen as over the hill.'"[28] This view reflects the recognition that yesterday's experts may not be the experts of tomorrow or even those who are worth being consulted.[29] What the world needs is people, young or old, who can, in the words of the Gestalt psychologists, break set.

The problem for discriminatory hiring processes is that the ability to break set is not necessarily a function of age. Some young people are stuck in the patterns they learned in school or at home. In fact, they may well be the individuals who had the highest scores on standardized tests, which largely measure people's ability to deal with given patterns rather than to break out of these patterns. None of the existing standardized tests used for educational purposes provides an adequate measure of creative intelligence – the ability to cope with true novelty and to provide new solutions to old problems as well as new problems.

If what we need are set-breakers – those who are adaptively intelligent for the future, not just for the past – then we need to think about testing people's ability to break set. The Luchins water-jug problems provided one way of doing this, and researchers in the Gestalt tradition and related traditions have thought above ways of measuring not only set-breaking but insightful-thinking skills in general.[30] What are some other ways, besides water jugs, to measure the ability to think in nonentrenched ways – to break set?

In some of my research, my colleagues and I presented experimental participants with relatively novel kinds of reasoning problems that, although novel, had a single best answer. One was what we called a "conceptual projection problem."[31] Participants might be told that, as they know, some objects are green and others blue. But we also suggested, following Nelson Goodman's new riddle of induction,[32] that still other objects might be labeled as "grue," meaning green until the year 3000 (the year 2000 was used in the original studies, because they were done before the year 2000) and blue thereafter, or instead, "bleen," meaning blue until the year 3000 and green thereafter (again, the year 2000 was used in the original studies). Or, in a different instantiation of the new riddle of induction, they might be told that there are four kinds of people on the planet Kyron: "blens," who are born young and die young; "kwefs," who are born old and die old; "balts," who are born young and die old; and "prosses," who are born old and die young.[33] The task of the participants in the research was to predict future states from past states, given incomplete information. The task was hard but eventually participants learned to solve the problems.

In another set of studies, participants were given more standard and conventional kinds of inductive-reasoning problems, such as analogies, classifications, and series completions. They were told to solve the problems, but there was a wrinkle. Preceding the problems were either conventional premises (such as "Suppose that dancers wear shoes") or novel premises ("Suppose that dancers eat shoes"). The participants were asked to solve the problems as though the counterfactual premises were true.[34]

In these studies, correlations with conventional kinds of tests of fluid intelligence depended on how novel or nonentrenched our items were. The more novel our items, the higher the correlations of these tests with scores on successively more novel conventional tests. These results suggested that so-called "fluid intelligence"[35] is not exactly a single thing, but rather on a continuum of novelty. As items becomes more novel, they begin to favor certain individuals more but to favor other individuals less.

When response times on the relatively novel problems were analyzed, some components measured the creative or novelty-dealing aspect of intelligence better than others. For example, in the "grue-bleen" task as described earlier, those information-processing components requiring people to switch from conventional "green-blue thinking" to novel "grue-bleen thinking" and then back again to conventional "green-blue thinking" again were a particularly good measure of the ability to cope with novelty.

In sum, some individuals can handle small but not large amounts of novelty; others can handle more novelty. Even hard items on conventional matrix tests may represent high novelty levels of novelty for those tests, but not high levels of novelty relative to the kinds of unusual problems people sometimes need to solve in their lives, especially in times of crises.

The problems we used in these studies are not unique in their possibilities. For example, Thomas Ward and his colleagues have used a number of different tasks to measure nonentrenched thinking.[36] In one of these tasks, researchers asked participants to draw pictures of aliens from outer space.[37] There was a wide range of kinds of pictures. But the large majority of the pictures had a head, arms, legs, and a symmetrical structure. In other words, asked to imagine life on other planets, the life bore a very close resemblance to life on Earth (with the possible addition of other features, such as antennae, unusual eyes, and the like). People have difficulty breaking out of their old conceptual structures. These conceptual structures form the basis for crystallized intelligence. But fluid-intelligence tests often challenge the ability to cope with novelty only for forms of novelty that are somewhat routine. That is, they may have hard items, but the hard items may challenge working memory and conventional reasoning processes more than they challenge the skills needed to deal with a radical departure from everyday-life routine.

4.1.3 Crystallized Intelligence

I once was contacted by a man who planned to become the smartest person in the world. I asked him how he planned to achieve this goal, and he told me that he planned to achieve it by reading the *Encyclopedia Britannica* cover to cover. He even planned to write a book about it, and he did indeed write the book.[38] I never read the book but it does receive four stars on Amazon.com, averaged from 420 ratings, so I guess a lot of other people did read the book. I tried to discourage him, as, apparently, did many others, but he was determined, and whether or not he became the smartest person in the world, he obviously made some serious money from the royalties off the book.

If one were to consider the way in which crystallized intelligence is defined, in terms of acquired knowledge base, the man's plan would seem to make some sense. The main tests of crystallized intelligence on the Wechsler Intelligence Scales, perhaps the most venerated in the history of intelligence testing, are *Vocabulary* and *General Information*. Reading an encyclopedia cover to cover certainly should help one on both of those fronts, so long as the amount of general information in the encyclopedia does not overwhelm one. But what is knowledge worth having?

Literary detective Sherlock Holmes, when queried by Dr. Watson about his ignorance on many matters of everyday life, including that the Earth revolves around the sun, indicated he did not want to waste brain cells on unnecessary information.[39] Holmes suggested that the brain is like an empty palace, in which one can arrange the furniture as one likes. The implication was that if one clutters up the palace with unnecessary furniture, especially furniture that one does not need, one will be unable to reach the furniture that is really important.

Holmes's theory of the brain was not correct, but it is true that, as we get older, our ability to retrieve information may decrease in part because we have so much information that we cannot find what we need. Whatever may be the case, Holmes knew almost everything there was to know about crime. He was not, however, brilliant merely because he knew so much about crime. Rather, Holmes was brilliant because of the inferences he could make from what he knew. He observed things that others missed and related them to the plentiful knowledge he had about what mattered to him.

What is wrong, perhaps seriously wrong with tests of crystallized intelligence such as vocabulary and general information is, first, that they measure what you know rather than whether (like Sherlock Holmes) you can use it to good effect; second, that the knowledge is often knowledge that does not matter to you any more than what heavenly body revolves around what heavenly body mattered to Holmes; third, that what is measured is the old knowledge you have acquired rather than your ability to acquire new knowledge that builds on the old; and fourth and finally, that the tests are hopelessly biased. Let us look at each of these issues in turn.

What you know matters much less for adaptive intelligence than how you use it. Reading the *Encyclopedia Britannica* did not make A. J. Jacobs the smartest person in the world – far from it. Even if Jacobs memorized the whole encyclopedia, he still would not be the smartest person in the world. And that still would be true if he got a perfect score on the Wechsler Intelligence Scale General Information subtest. What matters in life is not merely what you know but how you use it. Scott Morrison, the Prime Minister of Australia, has admitted that global climate is a problem for the world and for Australia. He knows that twenty-six people have died as of January 14, 2020, and that as many as a billion nonhuman animals may have died as well.[40] His problem is not lack of knowledge, but rather, lack of ability or inclination to use that knowledge. Smart people can act in very foolish ways, as he shows.[41] So many people have IQs and waste them, or use them to bad ends. It is a mystery, at least to me, why so many people care more about the ability to think complexly about matters of absolutely no consequence than the ability to think about important matters of great consequence. It is backward and perhaps pathetic to view the ability to think blithely about largely meaningless trivia as more important than the ability to think productively about serious issues. The basis for measuring intelligence should be the ability to solve real, consequential problems, not the ability to solve trivial, meaningless ones. If we value the latter, then we promote the futures of more people who will be experts at applying their cognitive skills to problems of no consequence.

Similarly, in the United States, it matters little that most likely almost every member of Congress knew that, as of December 16, 2019, the president of the United States had made over 15,400 false public statements[42] (and well over 20,000 by the summer of 2020), certainly a record that no other president from the past would even begin to approach. (This is not a matter of political opinion, but rather of public record.) What matters is that legislators have lied about his lying and about many other things he has done, such as his attempt to solicit foreign interference in the 2020 election.[43] This is, again, not a matter of political party. Democrats and Republicans both lied about the lack of success of the war in Afghanistan.[44] Knowledge is useless if it is not used to productive and meaningful ends. Intelligence tests that merely measure knowledge miss the whole point of intelligence as adaptation, which is that knowledge matters only if it is used to good effect.

Adaptive intelligence depends on that particular knowledge that matters for adaptation. This statement seems almost trivial, right? Of course, adaptive intelligence depends on knowledge that matters for adaptation. Yet, many tests of intelligence and their proxies measure, or have measured in the past, knowledge that does not matter. Unless you are an architect or an engineer or a surveyor or someone else who regularly does trigonometrically-based measurements, how often have you used what you learned in trigonometry (just in case you ever took it)? Do you even remember what a cosine or a cosecant is? Do you want to? There is nothing wrong with learning this stuff. But if we want to teach for adaptive intelligence, that is perhaps not where we should start. A better start might be understanding how marketers take advantage of our ignorance of probability and statistics to fool us into buying products we do not need and believing utter blatant falsehoods such as those propagated by antivaxxers. Much more harm is being done today by ignorant people misusing statistics than by people misusing cotangents – again, unless you are in a field that needs these things, such as civil engineering!

4.1.4   Stored Knowledge versus Knowledge Acquisition

Some of our renowned world and corporate leaders today may be in various stages of cognitive decay. They are old enough and they have enough predatory enablers who will try to hide it for them. But until the middle to latter stages of cognitive decay, people retain a great deal of their crystallized intelligence – their knowledge base. Their ability to acquire new knowledge is more limited, however. Worse, one does not have to enter the stage of cognitive decay to be unable meaningfully to learn new information. One just has to have the attitude that some of our leaders seem to have – "It does not matter whether I can learn anything new; I do not want or need to."

The problem is that some people may once have been good learners, or even not such great learners, but then they stop learning and just keep repeating the same mistakes. Perhaps it means something when a president of a country has filed for corporate bankruptcy not once or twice, but rather six times.[45] That does not sound like learning from experience. Of course, such behavior is not limited to Republicans. A former president, a Democrat, repeatedly got into trouble over extramarital affairs that ended badly, with one of them leading to his impeachment.[46] Politicians are not alone in making mistakes. Many of us keep making the same mistakes, over and over – including, at times, me among them – failing to learn from experience – which shows just how limited the usefulness of crystallized intelligence can be in everyday life.

The issue for adaptive intelligence is not what we know, but what we learn from experience and how we put what we learn into action. There are still leaders who are in denial about global climate change: What more do they need to know to teach them that the world has not already taught them, or at least, tried to teach them? There are also leaders whose behavior results in painful and unnecessary deaths, such as in the attacks in Myanmar against the Rohingya.[47] And unfortunately, bad, irresponsible, and even evil behavior is contagious.[48] The experience of fascism in the events leading up to World War II taught us that. For those who cannot understand how people could be so mentally vacuous as to follow Hitler, Mussolini, or Stalin, they only have to look to the present day to see that nothing has changed. The lessons of history seem too rarely to be learned. It is not what you know: It is what you do about it. A large vocabulary or store of general information means nothing if you ignore it, or worse, use it to destroy the institutions that hold humanity and the rest of the world together.

4.1.5 Group Bias

The final problem with crystallized intelligence is so obvious that many people miss it. That problem is: Whose crystallized intelligence? That is, whose knowledge should we be measuring? As cultural psychologists have shown, over and over again, people in different cultures have very different kinds of knowledge that are important for their own adaptation.[49] If you are a Yup'ik Native American in an Alaskan fishing village, knowledge of hunting, ice fishing, and spatial navigation in frozen tundra is much more important for adaptation than information about literary or political figures. If you are living in sub-Saharan Africa, knowledge of how to avoid, if possible, or, if not, treat malaria is more important than knowledge of cosines. But even in the mainland United States, if you are a dairy farmer, you need to know how to eke out a living farming at a time that milk prices are plummeting.[50] If you are a coal miner, your knowledge about techniques of coal mining may soon be worth little or nothing to you.[51]

It may sound like these crises only apply to those who live in developing countries or who are employed in working-class jobs. After all, we all know that toll collectors and secretaries have been on the way out for a long time. But tell that to lawyers, discussed above, who cannot find jobs and have yet to pay off enormous law-school debt,[52] or to bankers and especially mortgage-loans officers, or to accountants (for whom much of the work is now being done by computers).[53] So the cultural problems are not just between countries but also within countries. What knowledge counts as "crystallized intelligence" for the purpose of testing? Presumably, the knowledge everyone should have. But who is to decide that? And even if everyone should have it, is it equally important to everyone? And does everyone have the same opportunity to learn it? In practice, the people who decide are those who have profited from the present socioeconomic system. They scarcely are representative of the United States or of the world. Rather, they represent the status quo, as do the tests they create. Their tests often tend to reflect what got them to where they are, or what they think got them there. And when so-called comparisons of intelligence are done around the world, they inevitably serve as ego trips for those who hold power and get to define, or believe they get to define, what intelligence should be not only for themselves, but for everyone else.

4.2 Conclusion

Thomas Kuhn believed that there are two kinds of science: normal science and revolutionary science.[54] Sciences go through periods of normal science, with scientists each sharing assumptions and methods and adding incrementally to existing knowledge. Then, every so often, the scientists or, more likely, their students recognize that things are not holding together. So, one or more scientists creates a revolution, challenging assumptions that the scientists often did not even realize they had. Physics, for example, has gone through such a revolution with relativity theory and also with quantum theory. Genetics represented such a revolution, as has epigenetics.

The field of intelligence research has not undergone such a revolution, or at least, not successfully. The bad thing is that many in it think it has. And I once contributed to that way of thinking. I thought, in the 1970s, that the cognitive-information-processing approach represented a whole new approach to intelligence;[55] it did not. It merely related new information processing components to old psychometric factors. It was more of the same. The ultimate criterion was an array of scores on psychometric tests. Brain researchers today perhaps think they are revolutionary; they are wrong too. It is more of the same. They are relating information processing in various areas of the brain to the same psychometric factors.[56] Again, the ultimate criterion is the old psychometric tests. The biological approach is actually old, in any case. Scholars have been relating head size to intelligence for a long time![57] The problem is that as long as we keep relating our new measures to old ones – and validating them in terms of their correlations with these old measures – we are stuck in the same old same old.

Maybe at one time, it did not matter if scientists studying intelligence thought they were revolutionary or not. Academia is largely a game, anyway: Scholars publish, trying to be noticed, hoping to be the ones who are cited instead of their rivals. Today, however, we just do not have time to limit ourselves to publishing games. The world is in jeopardy. The fires in Brazil, Australia, California, and many other places tell us that. So do the hurricanes and the rising temperatures and the areas that once got rain but no longer do. So do newly arising authoritarian governments in various parts of the world. So does COVID-19.

It is not "intelligent" to have an elephant in a room and pretend it is not there. Neither fluid intelligence nor crystallized intelligence is enough, it appears, to cope with the adaptive problems facing the world today. It is for that reason that I believe we need to think and act in terms of adaptive intelligence. We have a world to save while we still can. Academic games have not and will not save the world. Neither will the people who are chosen for leadership positions as a result of the intelligence tests and their proxies that have proved to be collateral damage of these games. We need to measure and teach for adaptive intelligence, as discussed in Chapter 5.

Notes

1. Cattell, R. B. (1971). *Abilities: Their structure, growth, and action.* Boston, MA: Houghton-Mifflin.
2. Carroll, J. B. (1993). *Human cognitive abilities: A survey of factor-analytic studies.* New York: Cambridge University Press.
3. McGrew, K. S. (2005). The Cattell-Horn-Carroll theory of cognitive abilities. In D. P. Flanagan, & P. L. Harrison (Eds.), *Contemporary intellectual assessment: Theories, tests, and issues* (2nd ed., pp. 136–81). New York: Guilford Press; McGrew, K. S. (2009). CHC theory and the human cognitive abilities project: Standing on the shoulders of the giants of psychometric intelligence research. *Intelligence, 37*, 1–10.
4. Cattell, R. (1949). *Culture Free Intelligence Test,* Scale 1, Handbook. Champaign, IL: Institute of Personality and Ability Testing.
5. Sternberg, R. J. (2012). Intelligence in its cultural context. In M. Gelfand, C.-Y. Chiu, & Y.-Y. Hong (Eds.), *Advances in cultures and psychology* (Vol. 2, pp. 205–48). New York: Oxford University Press.
6. Sternberg, R. J., & Rifkin, B. (1979). The development of analogical reasoning processes. *Journal of Experimental Child Psychology, 27*, 195–232.
7. Sackett, P. R., Shewach, O. R., & Dahlke, J. A. (2020). The predictive value of general intelligence. In R. J. Sternberg (Ed.), *Human intelligence: An introduction* (pp. 381–414). New York: Cambridge University Press.
8. Sternberg, R. J., Nokes, K., Geissler, P. W. et al. (2001). The relationship between academic and practical intelligence: A case study in Kenya. *Intelligence, 29*, 401–18.
9. Sternberg, R. J. (1977). *Intelligence, information processing, and analogical reasoning: The componential analysis of human abilities.* Hillsdale, NJ: Lawrence Erlbaum Associates.
10. Sternberg, R. J., & Rifkin, B. (1979). The development of analogical reasoning processes. *Journal of Experimental Child Psychology, 27*, 195–232.
11. Nettelbeck, T., Zwalf, O., & Stough, C. (2020). Basic processes of intelligence. In R. J. Sternberg (Ed.), *Cambridge handbook of intelligence* (2nd ed., pp. 471–503). New York: Cambridge University Press.
12. Sternberg, R. J. (1981). Intelligence and nonentrenchment. *Journal of Educational Psychology, 73*, 1–16.
13. Sternberg, R. J. (2004). Culture and intelligence. *American Psychologist, 59*(5), 325–38.
14. Sternberg, R. J., & Grigorenko, E. L. (1999). *Our labeled children: What every parent and teacher needs to know about learning disabilities.* Reading, MA: Perseus Publishing Group.
15. Raven, J. C., Court, J. H., & Raven, J. (1992). *Manual for Raven's Progressive Matrices and Mill Hill Vocabulary Scales.* Oxford: Oxford Psychologists Press.
16. Sternberg, R. J., Kaufman, J. C., & Pretz, J. E. (2002). *The creativity conundrum: A propulsion model of kinds of creative contributions.* New York: Psychology Press.

17. Grigorenko, E. L., & Sternberg, R. J. (2001). Analytical, creative, and practical intelligence as predictors of self–reported adaptive functioning: A case study in Russia. *Intelligence*, 29, 57–73.
18. Greenfield, P. M. (2020). Historical evolution of intelligence. In R. J. Sternberg (Ed.), *Cambridge handbook of intelligence* (2nd ed., pp. 916–39). New York: Cambridge University Press.
19. Frensch, P. A., & Sternberg, R. J. (1989). Expertise and intelligent thinking: When is it worse to know better? In R. J. Sternberg (Ed.), *Advances in the psychology of human intelligence* (Vol. 5, pp. 157–88). Hillsdale, NJ: Lawrence Erlbaum Associates.
20. Luchins, A. S. (1942). Mechanization in problem solving: The effect of Einstellung. *Psychological Monographs*, 54(6), i–95. doi: 10.1037/h0093502
21. Nichols, T. (2018). *The death of expertise*. New York: Oxford University Press.
22. Martin, J., & Corasiniti, N. (2018). Is Cory Booker too nice? (And is that bad?) *New York Times*, June 25. https://nyti.ms/2Oy71aU
23. Martin, J. (2019). Who's best to beat Trump? 7 answers when 7 Democrats debate. *New York Times*, December 19. https://nyti.ms/3eArgiX
24. Carr, N. (2008). Is Google making us stupid? *The Atlantic*, July/August. https://bit.ly/391aqbI
25. Resnick, B. (2017). Trump supporters know Trump lies. They just don't care. *The Atlantic*, July 10. https://bit.ly/3olXPMk; Effron, D. A. (2018). Why Trump supporters don't mind his lies. *New York Times*, April 28. https://nyti.ms/2OtkpNL
26. Sandoiu, A. (2019). Artificial intelligence better than humans at spotting lung cancer. *Medical News Today*, May 20. https://bit.ly/3fAuKmJ; Ryan, B. (2020). Google's AI can detect breast cancer better than radiologists. *Cancer Health*, January 9. https://bit.ly/2B4eGuv
27. Forbes Magazine. (2017). The first law school casualty: More to come? *Forbes*, April 21. https://bit.ly/2ClERO3; Savkar, V. (2019). How will artificial intelligence change law schools? *Above the Law*, June 20. https://bit.ly/3fCZOSP
28. Holly, P. (2020). In Silicon Valley, some men say cosmetic procedures are essential to a career. *Washington Post*, January 9. https://wapo.st/2ClF6Zt
29. Meyer, C. (N.D.). Dirty little secrets about ageism in Silicon Valley. *Menlo Partners Staffing*. https://bit.ly/30gIhtj
30. Sternberg, R. J., & Davidson, J. E. (Eds.) (1994). *The nature of insight*. Cambridge, MA: MIT Press.
31. Sternberg, R. J. (1982). Natural, unnatural, and supernatural concepts. *Cognitive Psychology*, 14, 451–88; Tetewsky, S. J., & Sternberg, R. J. (1986). Conceptual and lexical determinants of nonentrenched thinking. *Journal of Memory and Language*, 25, 202–25.
32. Goodman, N. (1983). *Fact, fiction, and forecast* (rev. ed.). Cambridge, MA: Harvard University Press.
33. Sternberg, R. J. (1982). Nonentrenchment in the assessment of intellectual giftedness. *Gifted Child Quarterly*, 26, 63–7.

34. Sternberg, R. J., & Gastel, J. (1989a). Coping with novelty in human intelligence: An empirical investigation. *Intelligence*, 13, 187–97; Sternberg, R. J., & Gastel, J. (1989b). If dancers ate their shoes: Inductive reasoning with factual and counterfactual premises. *Memory and Cognition*, 17, 1–10.

35. Cattell, R. B., & Cattell, H. E. P. (1973). *Measuring intelligence with the Culture Fair Tests.* Champaign, IL: Institute for Personality and Ability Testing.

36. Ward, T. B., & Kolomyts, Y. (2019). Creative cognition. In J. C. Kaufman, & R. J. Sternberg (Eds.), *Cambridge handbook of creativity* (2nd ed., pp. 175–99). New York: Cambridge University Press.

37. Ward, T. B. (1994). Structured imagination: The role of conceptual structure in exemplar generation. *Cognitive Psychology*, 27, 1–40.

38. Jacobs, A. J. (2005). *The know-it-all: One man's humble quest to become the smartest person in the world.* New York: Simon & Schuster.

39. Doyle, A. C. (1886). *A study in scarlet.* London: Ward Lock & Co.

40. Wright, S. (2020). Australian fires imperil populations of green bees, honeyeaters, and potoroos. *Wall Street Journal*, January 14. https://on.wsj.com/3fwoxoZ

41. Sternberg, R. J. (2004). Why smart people can be so foolish. *European Psychologist*, 9(3), 145–50; Sternberg, R. J. (2005). Foolishness. In R. J. Sternberg, & J. Jordan (Eds.), *Handbook of wisdom: Psychological perspectives* (pp. 331–52). New York: Cambridge University Press.

42. Kessler, G., Rizzo, S., & Kelly, M. (2019). President Trump has made 15,413 false or misleading claims over 1,055 days. *Washington Post*, December 16. https://wapo.st/391AF1G

43. Wolf, Z. B., & O'Key, S. (2019). The Trump-Ukraine impeachment inquiry report, annotated. *CNN.com*, December 3. https://cnn.it/2Wuzcfw

44. Whitlock, C. (2019). The Afghanistan papers: At war with the truth. *Washington Post*, December 9. https://wapo.st/3jhNcmH

45. Lee, M. (2016). Fact check: Has Trump declared bankruptcy four or six times? *Washington Post*, September 26. https://wapo.st/3fzkZp6

46. Graham, D. A., & Murphy, C. (2018). The Clinton impeachment, as told by the people who lived it. *The Atlantic*, December. https://bit.ly/2CIzNmw

47. Barron, L. (2018). More than 43,000 Rohingya parents may be missing. Experts fear they are dead. *Time*, March 8. https://bit.ly/32sDl7k

48. Egan, T. (2020). Trump's evil is contagious. *New York Times*, January 17. https://nyti.ms/3h5b1ff

49. Sternberg, R. J. (2007). Intelligence and culture. In S. Kitayama, & D. Cohen (Eds.), *Handbook of cultural psychology* (pp. 547–68). New York: Guilford Press ; Heine, S. J. (2020). *Cultural psychology* (4th ed.). New York: W. W. Norton.

50. Barrett, R. (2020). Dairy farmers are in crisis – and it could change Wisconsin forever. *Milwaukee Journal Sentinel*, January 7. https://bit.ly/30yKamu

51. Evans, G. (2019). A toxic crisis in America's coal country. *BBC*, February 11. https://bbc.in/2WoOwKk; Sengupta, S., & Eddy, M. (2020). How hard is it

to quit coal? For Germany, 18 years and $44 billion. *New York Times*, January 17. https://nyti.ms/30kTVn5

52. Bertman, R. (2019). Lawyers graduate with more student debt and less income than expected. *Student Loan Planner*, April 29. https://bit.ly/2ZCvz9k

53. Burdick, M. (2017). The accounting industry's death is great news for your business. *Entrepreneur.com*, August 17. www.entrepreneur.com/article/298649

54. Kuhn, T. S. (2012). *The structure of scientific revolutions* (50th anniversary edition). Chicago, IL: University of Chicago Press.

55. Sternberg, R. J. (1977). *Intelligence, information processing, and analogical reasoning: The componential analysis of human abilities.* Hillsdale, NJ: Lawrence Erlbaum Associates.

56. Haier, R. J. (2020). The biological basis of intelligence. In R. J. Sternberg (Ed.), *Cambridge handbook of intelligence* (2nd ed., pp. 451–68). New York: Cambridge University Press.

57. Sternberg, R. J. (1990). *Metaphors of mind.* New York: Cambridge University Press.

CHAPTER 5

History of the Theory of Adaptive Intelligence

In order fully to understand adaptive intelligence, it would be useful to understand its history, at least as it has evolved from my own research. The history is summarized in Table 5.1. The chain of events started with what I called "componential analysis."

5.1 Prehistory

The prehistory of my work on adaptive intelligence began for me in elementary school during the 1950s, when paper-and-pencil IQ tests were part and parcel of what many schools did. My elementary school in New Jersey administered them every year or two. And I routinely bombed the tests. As a result, my teachers thought I was stupid; I thought I was stupid; I acted stupidly; my teachers were happy that their expectations were met; and I was happy they were happy. But then, in fourth grade, I had a teacher, Mrs. Alexa, who thought there was more to me than an IQ test score. As a result of her encouragement, I went from being a so-so student to being a good one. But exactly what was that "more" – that might have been in me or in anyone? That is what I have spent most of my career trying to discover.

5.2 Componential Analysis

My early work to break away from the lockstep of factor analysis and IQ testing was based on a system of analysis I devised in the 1970s, *componential analysis*. The idea was that the methodology would uncover the mental components of information processing underlying human intelligence.

The late John B. Carroll and I both independently suggested that one should not start in understanding intelligence with relatively simple laboratory tasks,[1] but rather with the actual cognitive tasks one finds on intelligence tests. Carroll referred to the approach as viewing psychometric tests

Table 5.1 *Evolution of the theory of adaptive intelligence*

Stage 1: Componential Theory of Intelligence (Late 1970s through Early 1980s)
Intelligence can be understood in terms of components of information processing.
Representative book: *Intelligence, information processing, and analogical reasoning: The componential analysis of human abilities* (1977)
Stage 2: Triarchic Theory of Intelligence (Mid-1980s through Mid-1990s)
Intelligence can be understood in terms of analytical, creative, and practical abilities.
Representative books: *Beyond IQ: A triarchic theory of human intelligence* (1985)
Metaphors of mind: Conceptions of the nature of intelligence (1990)
Stage 3: Theory of Successful Intelligence (Late 1990s through Early 2000s)
Intelligence can be understood in terms of capitalization on strengths and correction or compensation for weaknesses in analytical, creative, and practical abilities
Representative books: *Successful intelligence: A new theory of intelligence* (1996)
Teaching for successful intelligence (2000)
Stage 4: Augmented Theory of Successful Intelligence (Mid-2000s through Mid-2010s)
Intelligence also needs to be understood in terms of wisdom
Representative books: *Wisdom, intelligence, and creativity synthesized* (2003)
College admissions for the 21st century (2010)
What universities can be (2016)
Stage 5: Theory of Adaptive Intelligence (Late 2010s–)
Intelligence needs to be understood in terms of adaptation to the environment through the wise use of analytical, creative, and practical abilities
Representative book: *Adaptive intelligence* (2020) [this book]

as cognitive tasks. I referred to the approach, as mentioned above, as componential analysis. It also came to be known as the *cognitive-components approach*. A similar suggestion was made by the late Earl Hunt.[2] Something was in the air.

I believe that something was related, at a basic level, to what I am now calling adaptive intelligence. But it was a much more primitive notion of adaptive intelligence. The idea was that adaptation is not something that is just a hypothetical construct residing, metaphorically, somewhere in the head. It is related to people thinking something – to their having particular thoughts that lead them to act in one way versus another. Our question, in the computational metaphor (see Chapter 2), was what do people do when they adapt?

In particular, I believed I could identify, through componential analysis:

1   *Components of information processing.* These, I believed at the time, are the fundamental units of intelligence. On this view, psychometric test scores are merely unspecified combinations of information-processing components. So are the "factors" (supposedly underlying sources of

individual differences on psychometric tests) that underlie the test scores. For example, "inductive reasoning," on this view, is not a single thing. Rather, it is a combination of a number of elementary cognitive-processing components for dealing with information. The difference between factors and components is that factors typically are obtained by analyzing individual differences in performance across people, whereas components are obtained by analyzing differences in the way people solve items on a test. In other words, are you looking at which people are smarter or which items are harder to solve? An example of a component would be *encoding*, whereby one takes a stimulus on a page, say, "a," and figures out what it is, in this case, the letter *a*.

2 *Strategies into which components combine.* These strategies are how components combine. How, exactly, does a person solve an analogy? How does he or she get from beginning to end? What is the exact sequence of thought processes that the individual goes through from the time he or she first sees the problem to the time he or she solves the problem? Or how does one, really, solve any problem, such as how to dress for a job interview, or how to convince one's children to say "no" to junk food, or how to get to work when one's usual route is closed for construction and there are no "detour" signs?

3 *Mental representations underlying the components and strategies.* How does the person represent information about a particular problem in his or her head? What does the mental representation look like? For example, a representation might be verbal – using words. Or it might be propositional – using some kind of fundamental structure under-lying combinations of words. Or the mental representation might be spatial – a series of mental pictures of sorts that enable the person to visualize concepts and how they are related. For example, when we try to remember what someone said whom we just met, we probably will rely on a verbal representation of some sort, going over the words the person spoke, or at least our recollection of those words. When we try to remember which of two people we met was taller, we probably will rely on a spatial representation. We might also use a spatial representa-tion to imagine how to drive from our current location to the local supermarket or drug store. If we are trying to solve a mathematical problem, such as how much change we owe a customer who has made a purchase, we likely will rely on a numerical representation.

4 *Component times and error rates.* By modeling individual data, it is possible to specify rather precisely how much time each component

process took (its "latency"). It also would be possible to say how susceptible it was to error (its "error rate"). The idea would be that these latencies and error rates would be much more fundamental than any kind of factor score. For example, how long does it take to recognize that "a" is the letter *a*?

5 *Profile of strengths and weaknesses.* A major goal of componential analysis was to help individuals identify profiles of strengths and weaknesses. What is the individual good at? Where is there more room for improvement? Moreover, how can one devise techniques to improve performance on the various components? What kinds of strategies help people optimize their performance?

At the time, componential analysis was a precursor to my attempt to study intelligence as adaptation.

First, I wanted to move psychologists away from IQ-based ideas of intelligence. The tests had done so much harm historically.[3] I was, myself, one of those people who, when I was young, muffed IQ tests as a result of test anxiety. Certainly, there must be something better. Second, suppose the distribution of who was favored by tests and who was not favored were random. Perhaps then things would be better. But the distribution of errors is far from random. The people who are hurt by IQ and other standardized tests tend to be those on the margins of society. They never have had the fortune to receive the kinds of socialization and schooling that would enable them to maximize their scores on IQ and related tests. So, IQ tests, instead of providing opportunities, often end up squelching opportunities. They may leave behind those who might hope to leave the margins of society and become more central parts of it. There are always exceptions: Some people who might be left behind profit from standardized tests of IQ and related constructs. There are just too many people who do not profit.

Third, IQ tests and their proxies (SAT, ACT, GRE, LSAT, etc.) can lead to seriously defective conclusions. They can lie not only about levels of abilities, but also about patterns of abilities. The result can be poor decisions regarding appropriate curricula and even job placements.

It would be easy to blame testing companies – ETS, ACT, the College Board, Pearson – for the huge over-reliance on standardized tests one finds in the world of today. It is not much different from the world of 1975, when I first started at Yale as an assistant professor. I think that would be an oversimplification, however. The problem is systemic: It is not just with one company or even several.

Why has the testing industry been so slow to change? There are a number of factors that gravitate against changes in tests. They will be discussed in detail in Chapter 6. But a huge problem is the emphasis in our higher educational system on perceived *"initial value"* rather than *"value added."* The colleges and universities, at least in the United States, tend to prefer students who have had so many advantages that, if the school did little or nothing, the students still would perform well. In the ideal, schools and universities would be judged for the value they add to students as a result of the education they provide. Instead, the schools are judged on initial value – how the students look on the standardized tests they took before admission. As a result, a school could teach students very little or nothing – could add little value – and still look good because of high initial test scores.

As a result, the tests launder socioeconomic class. Although the correlations of scores with socioeconomic status (SES) are not perfect, students of higher SES generally get better academic preparation. Such students have more access to tutors. They are more likely to be able to afford test-preparation books and courses. The students are also more likely to be test-wise. So, the elite class benefits, on average, and has little incentive to see things change.

If you look at the content of the tests, you will discover that the tests predict future academic success for a very simple reason. They are measures of past academic success. So-called "ability" tests and "achievement" tests are not different in kind. They both measure largely the same academic knowledge and skills. The ability tests simply measure knowledge and skills that a student might have acquired slightly earlier. So, the labels "ability" and "achievement" are largely arbitrary. When I was younger, the morning section of the SAT used to be called the "aptitude" part. The afternoon section was called the "achievement" part to emphasize that the tests were not measuring the same thing. Actually, largely, they are measuring the same thing. That is why the tests correlate so very highly with each other. Those designations were later dropped because they were, at their heart, so fundamentally wrong. The afternoon tests did and do measure more specific content knowledge acquired in schooling. But the morning tests also measure content knowledge and skills largely acquired during the course of a student's schooling.

People (like me) who come from relatively uneducated households tend, on average, to be at a disadvantage on these tests. The home environments often do not include the high level of cognitively-oriented activities developing those academic and test-taking skills that would be found in many homes with more educated parents. Parents like mine would not even have known what these activities might be. Hence, I was left with a lot of time to watch television. That said, not all educated parents provide their children with homes that stress educational accomplishment.

Consider, as one example, the common verbal-analogies test. This test is a feature of many IQ tests. There is even one test used for graduate admissions and other purposes, the *Miller Analogies Test*, that is composed exclusively of analogies. The tests are supposed to measure verbal reasoning. But much of the difficulty of verbal analogies resides in vocabulary and general information. Before solving the items, one must know what the words mean. So, does a low score on a verbal-analogies test indicate a reasoning problem? Or does it indicate a vocabulary/general-information problem? There is no way of knowing from the score. A low score may represent a deficiency in reasoning. Or it may represent a non-native background or an English-as-a-foreign-language problem.

As a second example, many spatial problems requiring mental rotation of objects can be solved spatially. The problems, though, also can be solved verbally by talking one's way through the answer. However, it matters how someone got to a particular score. Someone who is genuinely strong in spatial skills might well make an excellent air traffic controller. But someone who solves spatial problems verbally might become overwhelmed on the very hard spatial problems requiring a quick response that confront air traffic controllers.

Some tests do not even measure what they seem to measure. For example, consider syllogism problems ("All schnoogles are schneegles. Some schneegles are schnagles. Are there any schnoogles who are not schnagles?"; or "Schneegles are heavier than schnoogles. Schnoogles are not as heavy as Schnagles. Can you tell which are heaviest?"). These deductive-reasoning problems appear to be measuring straight deductive (general to specific) reasoning. But, in fact, performance on them is often highly correlated with spatial ability. So, one might conclude someone who has trouble with these problems does not reason well, when in fact, they just do not visualize well or have good spatial working memory.

Charles Spearman, the early intelligence theorist, believed that analogical reasoning forms the basis for intelligent thinking.[4] I took that to heart early in my career. I started studying intelligence by using stimuli in analogies called "People Pieces."[5] They were pictures of people that varied in color (blue, red), height (tall, short), girth (fat, thin), and sex (male, female). By using the People Pieces, I was able systematically to vary the difficulty of the analogies I created. The analogies were of the form A : B ::

C : D1 D2 (where D1 and D2 were alternative answer options). The idea was to have four sources of difficulty in an analogy. The first source of difficulty was the distance (difference) between terms A and B. The greater the distance, the harder the analogy and the longer the thinking would take. The second source was the distance between A and C. Third was the distance between C and the ideal D term (which was always the same as the distance between A and B). And the final source of difficulty was the distance between the answer options, D1 and D2. Now that I had experimental materials, I needed to come up with some kind of cognitive model for how people solved the analogies. I was working backward. I was going from materials to hypotheses. In a purer form of science, I would have been going from hypotheses to materials.

The model of analogical reasoning I devised was that there are seven major cognitive processes people use in solving analogies. Consider, for example, the analogy, TALL : SHORT :: HEAVY : (a) LIGHT, (b) WEIGHTLESS. The cognitive processes are:

1 *Encoding.* The individual sees *"tall."* That experience brings to mind whatever features he or she has stored away that are associated with being tall. Then the individual encodes into working memory (memory for current processing) the word *"short."*

2 *Inference.* The individual figures out the relation between *tall* and *short.* Presumably, he or she is likely to infer that the relation is one of *opposite.*

3 *Mapping.* The individual carries over to the second half of the analogy the relation from the first half of the analogy.

4 *Application.* The individual applies the relation he or she inferred in the first half of the analogy (this case, *opposites*) to the second half of the analogy. *Short* is the opposite of *tall* as what is the opposite of *heavy?*

5 *Comparison.* The individual compares the answer options to determine which is best (or, in the case of two answer options, better). Which is a better opposite for *heavy, light,* or *weightless?*

6 *Justification.* If the best (or better) option appears nonoptimal, the analogy-solver decides if the best (better) option is good enough to be chosen as the "correct" answer. In this case, *light* and *weightless* are both initially plausible, but *weightless* is not an opposite of *heavy* so the correct answer must be *light.*

7 *Preparation-Response.* This is one's preparation to solve the analogy – any analogy – and one's actual response using a button on an answer panel. (In a prediction equation, it is measured as a mathematical

constant – it is everything else statistically that the above six processes do not account for.)

This work built directly on Spearman's model, mentioned above. His model had only three processes. The first was "apprehension of experience" (what I have called "encoding"). The second was "eduction of relations" (what I have called "inference"). The third was "eduction of correlates" (what I have called "application").

The dissertation actually involved three studies. The first was with the People Piece analogies. The second was with verbal analogies, which used words. And the third was with geometric analogies, using abstract geometric forms like squares and triangles and so forth. The advantage of the People Piece stimuli was that one objectively could count features and feature changes. For example, one could count the number of features that changed from the A term to the B term, or from the A term to the C term. A disadvantage of the People Pieces was that the analogies were extremely easy. They also were somewhat lacking in ecological validity (seeming real-life application). In real life, one usually has to figure out what the features are of stimuli. They do not stand out so clearly (as, e.g., tall vs. short or fat vs. thin). For the verbal and geometric analogies, as there were no clear objective features, therefore, I had different participants generate ratings of stimulus complexity and feature overlap. I then used these ratings as the basis for analyzing the data.

There was one other feature of the design. In order better to separate out the various components (inference, application, etc.), I used a method I called the method of "precueing." That is, each trial occurred in two parts. In the first part of the trial, the participant saw either zero, one, two, or three terms of the analogy. The first part of the trial would display either no terms; or just the first term (A); or just the first and second terms (A : B); or just the first, second, and third terms (A : B :: C). In the second part of the trial, the participant always saw the whole analogy. The participant initially would look at the first part of the trial. Then the participant would push a button indicating he or she was ready for the second part of the trial. The assumption was straightforward. It was that, in the first part of the trial, the participant would do all possible operations on the analogy terms that were visible. Then, in the second part of the trial, he or she would process whatever was left to process. In this way, it was possible to separate out processing earlier during solution of the analogy from processing later during the solution of the analogy.

In addition to solving analogies, participants in the studies also took a battery of psychometric tests. The tests measured three kinds of skills. The first were inductive-reasoning skills. These skills are sometimes referred to as "fluid intelligence." The second kind were vocabulary skills. These skills sometimes are called "crystallized intelligence." The third kind were perceptual-speed skills. These are essentially clerical skills. An inductive-reasoning test might ask participants, for example, which of a number of geometric forms does not belong with the others. A vocabulary test might ask participants what the word "ameliorate" means. The participants would see five answer options, and then choose the best. A perceptual-speed test might show long strings of letters. Participants would draw a slash through the letter each time they saw either an "i" or a "t."

The inductive-reasoning tests were used for what sometimes is called *convergent validation*. These are tests with which the components of information processing *should* correlate. That is, one would hope that scores on the analogies task would show a significant correlation with scores on the psychometric inductive-reasoning tasks. After all, analogical reasoning is itself an inductive-reasoning task. One also might expect some degree of correlation with vocabulary. Extent of vocabulary is a measure of intelligence. But the correlation with vocabulary should be lower. This is because a vocabulary test represents a measure of a different kind of intelligence. It measures crystallized rather than fluid intelligence. The perceptual-speed tasks were used for what sometimes is called *discriminant validation*. These are tests with which the components of analogical reasoning should correlate minimally, if at all. That is, one would expect the scores on the analogies task to show only a small correlation with the perceptual-speed tasks (because both tasks are speeded). But the correlation should indeed be small. Analogies tasks measure higher order processing, not basic-level perceptual speed.

I tested alternative information-processing models. The goal was to determine which model best characterized how people solve analogies. These models initially were in the form of flowcharts. These flowcharts showed each of the steps the problem-solver would have to take to solve the analogies. The details of the models are not, at least here, all so important. I also needed to quantify each model. In this way, I could determine the relative validity of each model. I used a linear model – so-called "multiple-regression modeling" – to test the models against each other. This just means each process could be weighted to indicate how important it was to solving the analogies.

Each component of information processing could be assigned a statistical parameter. Each parameter then corresponded to the time taken by that component of information processing. Thus, for example, there would be a statistical parameter for encoding time. There would be another one for inference time. There would be still another one for mapping time, and so on. But I was measuring not only response times, but also error rates. So, there was also a statistical parameter corresponding to the probability of one's making an error during each process. Hence, there was an error parameter for encoding, representing the probability of making an error in that process. Each component of information processing had an error parameter assigned to it. Thus, there were two sets of parameters. One set was for reaction times, the other set was for error rates.

There was one other complication of sorts. It was possible to model group reaction-time and error-rate data. But also, it was possible to model individual reaction-time and error-rate data. That is, one could construct an averaged model over all participants or at least large numbers of participants. Or one could construct a model based just on the data for a single individual. The individual models were especially important. It was through these individual models that one could isolate the parameters that one ultimately would correlate with scores on the psychometric ability tests.

The best model accounted for 92 percent of the variance in the reaction-time data. (That is like a pie chart 92 percent filled in. That is a pretty good prediction! It means that of all the sources of differences in difficulty across analogy item types, 92 percent of them were explained.) Fits for error data were lower but still respectable.

The averaged model fits for the verbal and geometric analogies were not quite as good. But they were still quite good. The lower model fits were to be expected. The People Pieces had countable features. The verbal and geometric analogies did not. Instead of countable features, I was using subjective ratings of feature changes, as described earlier. These ratings inevitably would be imprecise. Moreover, participants presumably mostly encoded People Pieces in the same way. They were all tall or short, fat or thin, and so on. Participants might encode verbal or geometric analyses in any of a number of ways. For instance, the word "right" in a verbal analogy might refer to a direction. Or it might refer to someone's or something's being correct. Or it might refer to a privilege everyone should have, and so on.

The results were very nice. But they were by no means perfect. Because I did individual modeling of data, it was possible to obtain parameter estimates (which I called "component scores") for each individual. These scores were times taken for each of encoding, inference, mapping, application, comparison, justification, and preparation-response. (Justification was relevant only for the verbal and geometric analogies. The People Piece analogies always had an "exactly right" answer because the features were objective determined.)

For the People Pieces and geometric analogies, the correlations were as expected. There were reasonable (usually, about 0.3 level) correlations of the reasoning component scores (inference, mapping, application, comparison, justification) with the inductive-reasoning tests. There were only trivial correlations with the perceptual-speed tests. The verbal analogies predictably showed more of a correlation with vocabulary. As anticipated, the People Piece and geometric analogies component scores did not show much correlation with vocabulary. Those were the "good news" correlations. The bad news was that the highest correlation with the inductive-reasoning psychometric tests was for the preparation-response component score. This score was intended to be a kind of residual, or wastebasket, score. It clearly was not. It would not be until some years later that I came to understand why the correlation was highest for this component. At the point that I got the data, this correlation was a warning sign that something was going on in the data that I did not understand. A typical intelligence theorist might say, with good humor, that I had gone back in time. Through this so-called residual component, I had rediscovered so-called general intelligence, or "*g*."

There was one other correlation that was of particular interest. Keep in mind that the information-processing component scores were expressed in terms of reaction time (number of milliseconds per operation). Correlations of the component scores with psychometric ability-test scores therefore were generally negative. That is, the longer you took to execute an operation, the lower was your reasoning ability, in general. One component score, however, showed the opposite pattern. As mentioned in Chapter 4, this component score was encoding. The longer participants took in encoding, the better their overall inductive-reasoning scores were. In other words, with respect to encoding, slow was good. Why might this be?

Although I had not predicted the result, its interpretation seemed straightforward and generalizable. When you solve problems, your optimal strategy is to spend *more* time in encoding the terms of the problem you are solving. In that way, you will be able to spend *less* time operating on those encodings. In other words, first make sure you understand the terms of a problem. Only then proceed to operate on those terms. This result applies to practically any kind of problem. How many times has any of us rushed into solving a problem, only later to figure out that the problem we have solved is not the right problem? That is, we mis-encoded the problem. Spending more time encoding helps prevent this situation from arising.

Although the result might seem like no big deal, it flew in the face of many people then and now who have argued that intelligence is partly, or largely, about mental speed. Arthur Jensen and his colleagues took the simplest approach. Jensen argued that the basic source of individual differences in intelligence was in speed of neuronal conduction.[6] Today, the current version of the Wechsler Intelligence Scales, such as the WAIS-V, have several subtests measuring mental speed. Most intelligence tests are speeded. And many current researchers still measure mental speed as a key component of intelligence.[7] In other words, people are smart because their nervous systems are efficient. The more efficient their nervous systems, the smarter they are.

Jensen suggested measuring speed of neuronal conduction indirectly. He did this by assessing people's choice-reaction times. For example, you might be told to push one key if you heard a high-pitched tone. You would be asked to push another key if you heard a low-pitched tone. Here, the faster the people were in the choice-reaction-time task (in which one had to pick one of two or more answers quickly), the smarter they were alleged to be. It was never entirely clear whether choice-reaction-time actually measures speed of neuronal conduction. But at least to believers in Jensen's position, the supposition seemed plausible. Although Jensen is deceased, his position remains popular among some aficionados of mental-speed research.

Why do so many intelligence researchers believe mental speed to be so important to intelligence? I suspect it is because, culturally, we in North America value quickness. I have argued that the association between mental speed and intelligence is largely culturally derived. Westerners place an emphasis on getting things done quickly. They have a "folk conception" of intelligence that emphasizes speed. So, they look into the head for intelligent people to be doing things quickly. In other cultures, this emphasis on speed is lacking. In some cultures, the opposite belief dominates. People believe that smart people are slow, reflective, and deliberate, rather than quick (as in the proverb "Haste makes waste"). These cultures would be less likely to produce psychological scientists who come up with theories that just happen to correspond to our common-cultural stereotypes. As shown earlier, our beliefs about intelligence (and practically everything else) are culturally shaped. We do not even realize this to be the case. We assume that what is true of our cultural values is not merely a matter of cultural values. Rather, we think, it is what is true for all times and all places.

The problem of encoding is known to testers. When test-constructors construct multiple-choice answer options, they purposely construct the wrong answers to be alluring. At least some of them are correct answers to the solution of the wrong problem. That is, the answers will appear to be correct if the test-taker mis-encodes the problem. Here, as elsewhere, test-takers should be sure they solve the right problem. Sometimes, when people take standardized tests, they expect themselves to do much better than they do. Their failed expectation may result from their choosing distracters that are correct answers to the wrong problems.

I believe that the problem of mis-encoding applies to the field of intelligence as a whole. Unreflectively – giving the matter almost no thought at all, really – people assume that intelligence is what IQ tests really measure. The people do not take the time to ask themselves whether, in their experience, high-IQ people really are the ones who best adapt to the environment and learn from experience. Rather, they are told this is the case. Then they may accept the answer as true because it comes from supposed authorities. In informal logic, this is known as the fallacy of "appeal to authority."

I expanded componential analysis to a variety of different kinds of tasks. For example, I suggested that the same components used to solve analogies also could be used to solve classification problems, series-completion problems, and matrix problems.[8] In matrix problems, participants are presented with a matrix of geometric figures and have to say which of several figures should go in an empty hole in the matrix. I also applied componential analysis to deductive-reasoning problems such as syllogisms. And I applied it to verbal-comprehension problems – figuring out meanings of made-up words presented in context, such as "The *blen* arose in the morning on the horizon."

An example of one of the kinds of syllogism problems we used is called a "linear syllogism."[9] An example would be, "John is taller than Pete. Pete is taller than Dick. Who is shortest?" I devised very elaborate flowchart models to describe how people solved these problems. Herbert Clark previously had proposed that people solved the problems propositionally (largely using verbal processing).[10] In contrast, Janellen Huttenlocher had proposed that people solve them largely spatially (constructing a linear spatial array in their heads).[11] My own model was a mixed model. It suggested that Clark and Huttenlocher were both not quite correct. Rather, people use both propositional and spatial mental representations in solving the problems. The results were good. In my model, the components of information processing that were supposed to correlate with verbal psychometric tests correlated with verbal tests. And the components that were supposed to correlate with spatial psychometric tests did indeed correlate with the spatial tests.

Unfortunately, there was a problem in the model of linear syllogistic reasoning, which applied not only to my model, but to most information-processing and psychometric models of abilities as well. The problem was the assumption that everyone taking a test solved the problems in the same way. Averaged information-processing models and factorial psychometric models both assume that, although there are differences in how well people solve problems, nevertheless, they all use the same strategies in solving the problems. But this assumption is wrong. My collaborator Evelyn Weil and I found that, although most people used a mixture of linguistic and spatial processes in solving linear syllogisms, some use exclusively linguistic processes and others use exclusively spatial processes.[12] Later, Jerry Ketron and I discovered that there are also differences in strategies for analogical reasoning.[13] These results had a serious implication, although the field, preferring easier data analyses and simpler models, never really acknowledged them. The implication is that our group-averaged models are in part, or even largely, lies. They may apply to lots of people, but they also may apply to no people at all.[14] In other words, it may be that that the averaged data suggest a strategy no one used because, say, half of people used one strategy, another half, another strategy, which, on average, looks like a strategy no one used.

I later proposed an extension of the componential theory. What I had been studying, I suggested, were what I now would call *performance components*. These are the components of information processing that execute tasks – that get them done. These are components like those of which I spoke earlier. They include encoding, inference, mapping, application, and so on. But my data on a variety of reasoning tasks suggested that these components were not, contrary to my original expectation, the ones that were most central to intelligence. What I realized after seeing the data was that these components had to have received some kind of direction. They did not just "happen." There had to be some kind of what in cognitive psychology is called a "central executive function." It would select which components to use and how actually to use them.

I labeled the central executive processes *metacomponents*.[15] These are components that plan, monitor, and evaluate one's information processing. They are constant across all test items. They therefore enter into the constant parameter of the regression equation. That is, you need them for solving all problems. So, they cannot be separated out for one problem versus another. Metacomponents (and other kinds of components) do not apply only to test problems. They apply to all the problems we face in life.

Recognizing the existence of a problem. The first thing you need to do is even to recognize that there is a problem. This step may sound trivial. But without it, no problem can be solved. On a standardized test or in a textbook, a problem is placed in front of you. You are told to solve it. But this is, of course, not the way real life works. In everyday life, most of the time, there is no one to tell you that you have a problem to solve. You have to figure that out for yourself. For instance, countries sometimes start to die because their governments are so corrupt. Yet nothing happens. The corrupt government does everything it can to hide the existence of the corruption problem. So, citizens do not recognize that there is a problem.

Failure to recognize problems is one of the causes of many of the world's ills, especially with regard to adaptation to the environment. A good example is lead in the environment. In the United States, lead was added to gasoline until 1995; lead was allowed in water pipes until 1986; it was outlawed in paint only in 1978. Lead is still found in some jewelry, food, soil, and elsewhere. Lead is an extremely deadly environmental toxin.

Consider some facts from the World Health Organization.[16] Exposure to lead is particularly hazardous and, in any amount, toxic to children. The effects are cumulative. Lead exposure can lead to coma, convulsions, reduction in intelligence and even intellectual deficiency (mental retardation), reduced attention span, antisocial behavior, anemia, hypertension, kidney impairment, damage to the reproductive organs, and even death. As late as 2016, lead is believed to have been responsible for 540,000 deaths worldwide, and of course damage to individuals that did not result in death was far more widespread. It does not take particularly high levels of lead exposure to lead to adverse consequences, especially in children, but also in adults. The lead is stored in the body and the damage is irreversible.

The question then is when scientific evidence first appeared that lead is toxic. The first evidence that lead is toxic appears to have been discovered in the second century BC, and its toxicity has been recognized ever since.[17] By the 1970s, there was strong scientific evidence of the toxicity of lead; it nevertheless continued to be used widely. A serious adaptive problem existed; many people and organizations chose not to recognize it. That is a lack of adaptive intelligence, as no society benefits by having sick and dying children with organ problems, reduced intellectual capacity, and behavioral problems.

A second example of a long-standing nearly unrecognized problem is income disparity in the United States and elsewhere. Similarly, problems of climate change cannot be addressed if they are not even recognized as problems.

The greatest problem that the world is failing to recognize, I believe, may be the creep of tribalism, whose awful consequences were shown in two world wars. Tribalism occurs when one's membership in a tribe becomes more important than truth, whether it is in politics, economics, social policy, or, for that matter, the science of intelligence. Tribalism seeks to preserve a world view, no matter how counterfactual, ridiculous, dangerous, and even self-defeating, simply to retain a sense of internal coherence and meaning.[18]

It is tribalism that is destroying the US, the UK, and many other countries from within, and it is tribalism that keeps intelligence researchers focused on their narrow view of intelligence that totally ignores humans' stupid and species-suicidal path. It focuses on the short term at the expense of the long term, and focuses on safety in numbers – if so many people believe something, how could it be wrong? Tribalists try to expose themselves only to arguments that support their own presuppositions and point of view and dismiss arguments out of hand that oppose their point of view.

Dictatorships have brutal ways of suppressing tribalism, or perceived tribalism. But democracies are ill-equipped to deal with tribalism, and the results have become increasingly clear as dictatorships gain ascendance as democracies tear themselves apart with their internal fights, often abetted by the dictatorships.[19]

Defining the nature of the problem. After you figure out that there is a problem, you have to define the nature of the problem. For example, a country may find that even though it has what appear to be adequate tax revenues, it does not have sufficient funds to pay its expenses. Corrupt government officials will dream up every explanation they can think of for the shortfall. They may attribute it to people not paying taxes, enemies that need to be kept in abeyance, or to extraordinary expenses. Their goal is for citizens not to define the problem as one of corruption.

Defining the nature of a problem also applies to environmental adaptation. For years, unscrupulous tobacco-industry executives claimed that there was some doubt as to whether cigarettes cause cancer. They tried to create plausible doubt.[20] And they succeeded for a long time – until they did not. In much the same way, executives in the sugar industry tried to hide the baleful effects of sugar and to switch the blame to fat.[21] For many years, nutritional guidelines and many diet books[22] demonized fat and largely gave sugar a pass or downplayed its harmful effects.[23] The same thing is now happening with human-induced climate change, where some political administrations are purposely trying to obscure the fact that climate change is in large part a result of hydrocarbons in the atmosphere, or does not exist, or is actually healthful, thereby hoping to benefit hydrocarbon industries at the expense of people's health.[24] The claim is that scientists have gotten things wrong on climate change. They have, but not as the cynical politicians would make it out to be. They thought climate change would move much slower than it actually has.[25]

These examples point out how people, presumably with high IQs, have deliberately and knowingly falsified scientific evidence and then succeeded in convincing millions of people, at least some of whom presumably have high IQs, of deliberately falsified definitions of problems. These problems are quite different from vocabulary drills or arithmetic problems or number-series completions, in that they are complex, ill-defined, and extremely consequential both for individual health and even, in some cases, for the survival of humans. The question then becomes one of why IQ researchers continue to define the problem of intelligence in terms of solving trivial problems on trivial tests when people's survival and the survival of the world are at stake. Like the corporate titans who sold sugar, they too have a stake in it all – their careers, their self-esteem (most are pretty high IQ), their adherence to accepted paradigms. But scholars are at least as susceptible as anyone else to trends, sucking in paradigms and then believing that they represent "truth."[26]

More importantly, these presumably high-IQ industrialists, politicians, or whoever, may have been misdefining problems. Such misdefinition is a sign of lower intelligence, whether viewed from a componential (computational/information-processing) standpoint or from the standpoint of adaptive intelligence. One could say they are deliberately misdefining the problems. But if one deliberately gets items wrong on an intelligence test, one still is marked down. Indeed, one might wish to mark someone down even further for being so stupid as to purposely get items wrong. In the case of purposely misdefined problems of world significance, powerful people sometimes act in ways that deliberately harm people, society, and in some cases, the future of humanity. Are we so inured to the theory of general intelligence that we nevertheless say that, despite their extremely serious misdefinition of important world problems, we should call them intelligent because they can solve number-series or vocabulary problems correctly on an IQ test? Are we, as a society, really so out of touch with what is important that good solution of trivial problems counts more in our evaluation than truly awful solution of highly consequential problems? What is sad is that traditional standardized tests skip the definition-of-problem step completely. The tests define problems for the test-takers. So, one of the most important aspects even of intelligence in a traditional information-processing sense is ignored.

Setting up a strategy for solving the problem. Once you define the nature of a problem, you still have to figure out how to solve it. What steps can you take in order to get to a solution? For example, you may define the problem facing your country as one of corruption. But then what do you do? Malaysia recently voted out a prime minister who was corrupt. But for every corrupt politician voted out, there are others who maneuver around accusations of corruption to stay in power.

Right now, the world needs strategies to fight many problems – global climate change, poverty, hunger, terrorism, poisoning of food and water supplies, and on and on. Problems such as these often get less attention than problems such as of how to use social media to manipulate people into voting against their own interests. As an example, those fighting global climate change tend to list human actions that raise carbon dioxide emissions and ask how those actions can be modified so that people and nations reduce their carbon footprint. Those doing nothing may simply ignore climate change, or falsely claim that it is part of a normal cycle, a point of view that has been debunked scientifically but that skeptics maintain simply because they have no scientific argument to fall back on.[27]

Representing the problem information mentally. How are you going to represent information about the problem? In terms of propositions? Or perhaps some kind of mental multidimensional space? Or as a mental diagram? For example, were one representing information about how to slow down global climate change, one might create, mentally or on paper or on a screen, a table of actions that could be taken. The table might include their cost, and other resources needed to effect the change, their predicted effect, and so on.

Monitoring problem-solving. As you solve the problem, do you sense that you are getting closer to a solution? Is problem-solving going as it should? Or has it somehow gone off course? In the case of global climate change, the monitoring for overall change can happen only over a very long period of time. But effects of changes such as reducing emissions can be measured in the very short term just by monitoring air quality, visits to emergency rooms for respiratory problems, sales of asthma and other related medications, and so on.

Evaluating problem-solving. After you have solved the problem, do you believe that the solution makes sense? Is it correct? Is there anything that should have been done differently, or that now should be done differently? For example, in the case of climate change, evaluation would have to consider whether, in the long term, climate change is indeed slowed down.

These steps, applied to the solution of a problem, can help arrive at a solution and then ensure that the solution is the correct one. So, componential analysis appeared to be a useful way not only of analyzing intelligence in general, but of analyzing particular levels of intelligence. In one set of articles, my colleagues and I analyzed intellectual disabilities in terms of deficits in metacomponential functioning. We compared these deficits to those in specific learning disabilities. Here, the deficits appeared more to be in the functioning of performance components and knowledge-acquisition components in specific domains. Componential analysis, at the time, also seemed to provide the kind of cognitive-causal explanation of intelligence that was lacking in factorial theories. The idea was that factors were in fact composed of components. Any factor could be understood in terms of its constituent components.

Janet Davidson and I did work on insightful problem-solving that helped to illuminate the role knowledge-acquisition components played in insightful thinking. We gave participants insight problems such as "You have black and blue socks in a drawer, mixed in a ratio of 4:5. How many socks do you have to take out of the drawer in order to be assured of having two socks of the same color?" The correct answer is three.

We analyzed performance on these problems in terms of three knowledge-acquisition components. *Selective encoding* involves distinguishing information presented in the problem that is relevant to problem solution from information presented that is not relevant. *Selective comparison* involves distinguishing between relevant and irrelevant information in long-term memory. And *selective combination* involves putting together information from the problem and from long-term memory in order to reach a solution. In the socks problem, for example, the ratio of 4:5, while appearing important, is actually irrelevant to problem solution (selective encoding). What is relevant is the realization that the worst that can happen in this situation is that you first take out a sock of one color, then a sock of another color. The third sock must match in color one or the other of the socks you have taken out (selective combination).

5.3   Competence versus Performance

One generally assumes, in the world of standardized (and other) testing, that test-takers are motivated to show their highest level of competence. Most students, for example, would rather get a higher grade than a lower grade or receive a standardized test score that will get them into a better rather than a worse university. Most potential employees would rather get a score on an employment test that will get them hired rather than not hired, or at least, hired into a better rather than a worse job. Interpreters of test scores therefore often assume that, say, the score one receives on an intelligence test represents one's IQ, plus or minus error of measurement.

The assumption that the test score represents a person's best effort may well be true most of the time although it certainly is not true all the time. For example, during the time of the military draft in the United States, some potential recruits were believed to "fake low" so as to be found mentally incompetent and thereby avoid the draft. As far back as 1863, before the era of mental testing, the US military exempted people from the draft for "manifest imbecility."[28] It also turns out that one can score too high on an IQ test for some jobs – for example, a potential police recruit was rejected in New London, Connecticut, for having too high an IQ.[29] One also could imagine students faking low who are afraid of going to highly competitive universities, or who just do not want to go and perhaps want to stay local to be with their friends; or perhaps a student who is a member of a minority group simply expects to be treated badly at an elite university.[30]

These conditions are all exceptional. In general, one would expect people to perform their best on a psychometric test of intelligence. But what about a real-life test? Then the situation becomes utterly different. There are a lot of reasons why someone's performance might not reflect his or her competence.

The stakes for being adaptively intelligent in the real world are far higher than on a typical IQ test or IQ-test proxy. One's job, one's income, indeed, one's life, may depend on how one performs. In most cases, one would expect higher adaptive intelligence to be associated with greater success, whether on the job or in life-threatening situations. But, unfortunately, in real life, what constitutes "adaptation" biologically can diverge considerably from what constitutes adaptation economically or sociologically.

Since being installed in office, as of June 25, 2019, the current president and associates have fired, otherwise let go, or seen the resignations of over fifty top officials. (The total number of firings, dismissals, and resignations as of August 7, 2020, is close to five hundred.) This is record-breaking territory.[31] Under such circumstances, the lesson a future appointee might learn is that what is "adaptive" is what the boss wants. Such a situation, although exaggerated under the current administration, is far from unique. In many cases, hanging onto a job means doing what is adaptive to stay in the job but what is maladaptive at some higher level. For example, someone likely will not retain a high-level position in a job in the tobacco industry or the coal industry if he or she publicly trashes the value of the product being sold.

Thus, for any life challenge, from taking a test to reaching decisions that may affect thousands or millions of lives, one's decisions made using one's intelligence may be compromised by external factors, some of them out of one's control. Where does adaptive intelligence come in when competing interests leave one uncertain as to how to move forward, or at least questioning actions that one may find ethically objectionable?

Componential analysis, I came to believe, was not so much "wrong" as limited, much in the way factor analysis was. It was limited in three key respects.

First, and most superficially, many tasks just did not lend themselves well to componential analysis. Sure, I could do componential analyses of inductive and deductive-reasoning tasks. Others had done similarly for spatial tasks. But how does one do a componential analysis of a job choice, a marital choice? How does one componentially analyze the decision to have children, or the decision to buy a house? How does one componentially analyze people's decision to help or rather to harm others? Componential analysis just was too limited to deal with most of the kinds of problems we solve. It did not apply well to the judgments and decisions we make in everyday life.

Second, I originally had conceived of the components as somehow "causal." But by the early to mid-1980s, it had become clear to me that they were not. Like factors, they were descriptive, although descriptive at another level. Researchers on intelligence always seem to have harbored the illusion that they somehow could generate the basic causal elements of intelligence. They have tried different units of analysis. These have included stimulus-response pairings, factors, information-processing components, speed of neuronal conduction, accuracy of neuronal conduction, and so forth. But none of these units really has "cut it." Each has been a speculative attempt to say, finally, "this is it." There is, and has been, no good evidence whatsoever that any of them is causal in any meaningful sense. They all are correlationally based and validated, usually against intelligence tests. These tests hardly constitute any ultimate criterion.

Third, and most important, I came to realize that componential analysis was not the breakthrough I had thought it was. In one sense, it was a breakthrough: Instead of primarily analyzing person variance, I was analyzing stimulus variance. That was a step forward, although others, such as John Carroll and Earl Hunt, were on the same trail. But the problem was that we were all taking the same pie and just dividing it in different ways. The pie, here, consisted of the different kinds of problems found on conventional psychometric tests of intelligence. Our universe of analysis basically was psychometric tests. But were psychometric tests broad enough to encompass all of the abilities people needed in their lives to act intelligent? I came to doubt it. We were validating our analyses by correlations with intelligence tests. But who was to say that those tests were any satisfactory ultimate criterion for what constitutes intelligence? I had criticized Boring for arguing that intelligence was nothing more than what intelligence tests test. But my colleagues in cognitive psychology and I essentially were doing the same thing. We just were slightly masking what we were doing.

Carroll and Hunt as well as Jensen and many others who did cognitive analyses ended up, in the end, accepting intelligence test scores as some kind of ultimate criterion for the validity of cognitive models. But I was not satisfied the tests were anything close to an ultimate criterion. I needed to move on. But to what? That question led me to the next phase of my journey toward understanding intelligence.

5.4   The Triarchic Theory

It was clear to me that the componential theory was inadequate. But what was missing and what did it need to come closer to accounting for adaptation to the environment? For a while, it was not obvious, at least to me. Then something changed.

At the time, I was Director of Graduate Studies in psychology at Yale. Three students applied for our graduate program. They were notably different.

One, whom I have called "Alice," was an academic superstar. She had incredible credentials that would be the envy of almost any applicant. Her test scores were sky-high. Her grades were superb. She had very strong letters of recommendation. In other words, she had the kinds of credentials that would lead many and probably most graduate programs in psychology to accept her. Our program was no exception. The faculty was all thrilled when she decided to matriculate at Yale.

In Alice's first year in graduate school, Alice performed superbly in courses. In her academic work, she was one of the two top students in the entering class. She showed all of the memory and analytical abilities that the GRE assured the faculty that she would have. Expectations for her were very high.

Yet, there was one problem. The problem was that she had more than the typical trouble coming up with research ideas. Sometimes it was that she just could not generate any ideas, and other times it was that she could not generate any ideas that were clearly meritorious. But it became evident after a while that, for whatever great skills she might have analytically, she was not a creative genius.

Alice was and is not exceptional. Tests like the SAT, ACT, GRE, and so forth do not, and never have claimed, to measure creative thinking. This would not be a problem in a profession for which creative thinking is unimportant. But for academia, in general, and science and even everyday life, in particular, creativity is generally considered to be very important. Scientists' reputations are built largely, although certainly not exclusively, on their creative thinking. The further along Alice got in graduate school, the more apparent it became that she was going to have trouble in a scientific career, unless she worked for a company's research unit in which she had supervisors who told her exactly what to do.

In contrast to Alice, Barbara, another applicant, was much less impressive on paper. She had reasonably good but not truly impressive grades. Her test scores, at least by Yale standards, were terrible. But she had terrific letters of recommendation written by eminent psychologists that emphasized her creativity in research. I was enthusiastic about her but no one else was. In the end, she received only one vote for admission from the graduate admissions committee - my own. One member commented that all the students who succeeded in the graduate program had GREs over 650 and her scores were both under that. I pointed out that the reason that successful students had GREs over 650 was that the program did not accept students with scores below 650. But my argument fell on deaf ears: She was rejected from the program and from other programs to which she applied.

I decided to do something unusual. I hired her as a research associate. I wanted to see whether someone with her profile – who would be rejected as a result of her GRE scores – actually could succeed in a demanding job as a research associate. After a couple of years, the answer was clear: She was a huge success. Thus, two years later, she applied to the graduate program and was admitted as the top pick.

The problem is that for every Barbara who gets a second chance at success, there probably are hundreds or thousands who never get such a chance. They are essentially stuck, no matter what other accomplishments they may have in their lives. Our society has marooned people like Barbara. There is very little incentive for the system to give them a second chance, because there is always someone else with better test scores waiting in the wings.

The one way people like Barbara can have hope is to be members of targeted groups, especially underrepresented minorities. The problem is that not everyone who falters on standardized tests but who has outstanding abilities is a member of an underrepresented group or has some other means of gaining access to educational and other resources. They become shipwrecked. Barbara, in contrast, was given a chance. She came to Yale. She was very successful as a graduate student. She has gone on to have a very successful career.

A third student who applied to the graduate program in psychology at Yale in roughly the same cohort was a student whom I have come to call Celia. Celia had neither Alice's academic credentials nor her academic skills. Nor did she have Barbara's creative flair.

By the time she went on the job market, Celia was looking good but not great as a job candidate. But she had something else that worked in her favor. Celia got every single job she applied for, an almost unheard-of feat. It was really hard to understand because her research was good but not outstanding and her teaching skills also, while good, were far from off the scale. I asked myself, and imagine other faculty members also asked themselves, what it was that she did so well. It took me a while, but I figured it out. Celia could go into a job interview, figure out what the audience wanted to hear, and give it to them. She had a knack for the practical – for getting the job done and, in this case, just for getting the job!

The development of the triarchic theory suggested that adaptation to the environment involved more than the memory and analytical skills involved in the original componential theory. In particular, people need creative skills to generate novel and potentially useful ideas; analytical skills to ascertain whether their ideas are good ideas; and practical skills to implement their ideas and to convince others of the value of those ideas. For example, adaptation to the environment, today, requires us as a world to lower carbon emissions so that oceans do not overrun coastal cities any more than they already have and to stop polluting the environment so that people in industrialized areas of the world can breathe. People need creative skills to figure out methods that might achieve these goals, analytical skills to ascertain whether the methods would work, and practical skills to convince people to follow the methods sufficiently so that the goals will be attained.

Much of what motivated the triarchic theory is that students like Alice are given many opportunities in schooling; students like Barbara are given hardly any at all. Instruction, assessment, and the atmosphere of the school encourage memory and analytical thinking, not creative thinking. If anything, creative thinking may be penalized, as when my oldest daughter once suggested to one of her elementary school teachers that the reason that space probes had not detected Martians was because they lived beneath the surface of the planet; Sara was dutifully admonished and informed that any Martians would in fact live on the surface of the planet, not in its interior. Well, maybe. But how would the teacher have known?

Multiple-choice test items obviously are tailor-made for Alice-type thinkers. But world problems are not tailor-made for Alice-type thinkers. The result is that we end up with Alice-type thinkers in positions for which they likely are not so much underqualified as misqualified. For example, leaders are expected to find wisely creative ways to solve problems. But how many such leaders are to be found in any domain, ranging from politics to business to law to pretty much anything? Almost none, which is predictable because the funnel of opportunity in society is so much directed to selecting leaders who are strong in analyzing highly structured problems, but not in creatively solving poorly structured ones.

The triarchic theory of intelligence served for a while and even generated some tests, discussed in Chapter 6, but it had a problem not unrelated to the problem of practically all existing tests of intelligence. Once one has a series of scores – in this case, for creative, analytical, and practical skills – how does one combine the scores, or should one even combine them? Does one average them, and if so, use unweighted scores? Are there any best weights for the scores, or does it depend on the task and situation one confronts? If that is the case, and one needs a different set of weights for every task and situation, how could one ever process the information in a way that would render it effective? The enterprise suggested by the triarchic theory reached something of a grinding halt because it was not clear what to do with scores, even if one had them.

The triarchic theory solved one problem – it got my group's research away from our use of IQ-test-like problems as the basis for measuring intelligence. But it created another problem – how can one put together information about creative, analytical, and practical abilities? The theory of successful intelligence helped to address this issue.

5.5   The Theory of Successful Intelligence

The theory of successful intelligence was intended to answer the question of how scores, and more generally, characteristics, should be combined.[32] But the answer it posed was not an arithmetical one. Rather, it suggested that there is no one formula for combining scores on ability tests, or any measures of successful intelligence. Rather, successful intelligence is largely individualized. Successful intelligence is one's skill in creating, implementing, and at times, reevaluating and recreating a life path that makes sense for one's prosocial goals in life, given one's sociocultural context. Successfully intelligent people create and then follow a path that they construct and that makes sense for them. Over time, they may recreate that path, finding different life goals and pursuits that make sense to them as time goes by. In other words, what is successfully intelligent differs for each person, so there is no one magic formula for success.[33] Everyone seeks different goals and thus needs a somewhat different path in order to be successfully intelligent.

It might seem that paths might differ by occupation but be similar within occupation. However, that is far from the case. One lawyer might seek to make a lot of money representing polluters, feeling that they too deserve the best representation possible; another lawyer might never even consider representing the polluters, even though the money would be better if he or she did. Oddly, even as a psychologist, such a question has touched on my life. I recently was asked whether I would be willing to testify in a legal case involving alleged developmental damage done by lead exposure in childhood. I was asked only to talk about IQ – what it measures and does not measure. I was not asked to talk about effects of lead exposure. But I was being asked by a representative of the lead industry. I could have used the money: I declined. Similarly, doctors, police officers, builders, and musicians can go into their fields with very different goals. I recently mentioned to a violin teacher the name of a violinist whose playing I greatly admired. But the violinist is a popularizer – she plays a very contemporary repertoire and obviously plays to the tastes of audiences who like her popularized style. I received no reply from the violin teacher, who I believe found the violinist's style distasteful.

In particular, in the theory of successful intelligence, what is at least as important as the levels of skills one has in creative, analytical, and practical pursuits is whether one recognizes one's own pattern of skills and then capitalizes on one's strengths and compensates for or corrects one's weaknesses. We might think that knowing a pattern of people's skills would help direct them toward one career or another. But within a career, very different skill patterns can lead to success – or failure. For example, one teacher may succeed in teaching in large lecture halls filled with many students but falter in small classrooms with small groups of students; another teacher might be only average in either teaching setting but stand out in one-on-one mentoring of individual students; yet another teacher might be excellent for gifted students but impatient with average students, whereas a colleague might direct her teaching toward the average student but have little idea of how to handle students who are gifted or who have learning challenges.

Similarly, two professional musicians can play exactly the same piece in very different ways, each capitalizing on a different set of strengths. For example, the first Bach Cello Suite is one of the most famous pieces of repertory for cello players. If one listens to the late Mstislav Rostropovich play the piece on recording, one hears a somewhat florid and romantic interpretation of it. If one listens to the late Janos Starker play it on recording, one hears what almost seems like a mathematically precise but much less romantic interpretation of it. Both cellists were considered to be among the best of their era. But they capitalized on different strengths and, predictably, often appealed to different audiences.

The same principles apply in people's personal lives. One person may make an excellent parent, another a relatively poor one; but even with excellent versus poor parents, there is great variation in how people would become one way or another. For example, two parents might be excellent in raising their children but do so in very different ways, with one, perhaps, emphasizing development of formal knowledge such as that learned in school and the other emphasizing the development of tacit knowledge such as that one picks up through life experiences.

The general point is that when one looks at the full range of skills one can bring to any task in any given situation, there often is not one "right" way to do the task. How one does it will depend on how one defines the task, but also on how one leverages one's strengths and weaknesses so as to optimize one's performance. The theory of successful intelligence recognizes that there is no one mathematical formula for success.

That said, the theory does not specify, except in principle, how scores from any kind of test of intelligence could be combined. Any combination would have to be idiographic – relevant to a particular individual – requiring a holistic and individualistic approach to assessing intellectual abilities. Such an approach might not seem efficient to some, but that is perhaps why society is stuck in a one-size-fits-all factory-production model for the understanding and measurement of intelligence.

The theory of successful intelligence suggests that intelligence is a slightly different thing across individuals and also that it may be different, in some respects, across cultures. In particular, one needs to distinguish between two aspects of intelligence – the underlying information-processing components of intelligence, on the one hand, and, on the other hand, how those information-processing components manifest themselves in behavior. According to the theory, the basic building blocks of intelligence – the information-processing components – are the same in all cultures. What may differ is how they are manifested in behavior.

People in all societies need to think in certain ways in order to be characterized as thinking "intelligently." These certain ways involve meta-components, as mentioned earlier – their recognizing the existence of problems; their defining the problems in a realistic way; their allocating resources to problem-solving; their mentally representing information about how to solve the problems; their formulating strategies for solving the problems; their monitoring their problem-solving as they are doing it; and their evaluating their problem-solving after they are done with problem solution. But the kinds of problems they have to solve differ widely across cultures. For example, the problems people need to solve in hunting and gathering cultures are very different from the problems they have to solve in cultures where knowledge about technology or how to manage money may be important. Even within a given culture, what one needs to do to be intelligent in the performance of a job varies widely from one job to another. A smart musician, a smart manager in business, and a smart scientist all need to think intelligently in their jobs – but that smartness manifests itself in almost entirely different ways.

We need to think of intelligence culturally, both across cultures of the world and across cultures of regions of a given country or occupations or whatever. The concept sometimes used to characterize this ability to navigate cultural differences is *cultural intelligence*. "Cultural intelligence refers to an individual's capability to function effectively in situations characterized by cultural diversity . . .."[34] Cultural intelligence is viewed by Soon Ang and her and associates as involving four components: metacognitive, cognitive, motivational, and behavioral.[35]. I would view cultural intelligence is a special case of *practical intelligence*, which is one's skill in successfully navigating one's everyday environment.[36] Practical intelligence, as described earlier, calls upon skills that are different from those of general intelligence.[37] People can score highly on tasks requiring practical intelligence but at the same time show relatively low scores on tests of general intelligence, or vice versa.

Practical intelligence derives in large part from *tacit knowledge*, mentioned earlier. This is the knowledge one requires to adapt effectively to one's environment. It is knowledge one acquires from experience – on the job, in a family, in various social settings with friends, and the like. Tacit knowledge usually is not taught and often is not even verbalized. It is the informal, or implicit, as opposed to formal, explicit knowledge that leads to success in a variety of kinds of practical situations. It can, in principle, be taught indirectly and through reflective practice, but usually is not.[38]

Practical intelligence underlies much of our success in our daily interactions with other people and on the job. Practical intelligence involves individuals' abilities in managing (a) the self, (b) others, and (c) tasks. In cultural situations, interactions with other people are especially important, as the tacit knowledge that leads to success in one cultural situation can lead to failure in another. For example, whether, upon meeting someone new, one should bow or shake hands depends on the cultural setting and whom one is meeting within it. It also depends on the times, as the era of COVID-19 has shown us – today, almost no one shakes hands!

Practical intelligence and its special case, cultural intelligence, are *not* the same as general intelligence (*g*) or general mental ability (GMA).[39] On the one hand, *g* predicts many kinds of real-world success.[40]. General intelligence is a useful attribute for success in many activities of life.[41] On the other hand, as mentioned above, the prediction from *g* of life success of any kind is far from complete. And this prediction has not improved much since the early days of intelligence testing in the beginning of the twentieth century, when Alfred Binet and Theodore Simon as well as David Wechsler were inventing their first intelligence tests. Put another way, whatever knowledge and skills went unmeasured and thus unindexed by tests of general intelligence in the past remain unmeasured and unindexed by tests of general intelligence in the present.[42] If the goal of psychologists, or society in general, is to improve prediction to real-life outcomes, especially in multicultural situations that are uncertain, potentially risky, and even possibly dangerous, psychologists or others will need to devise measures that go beyond tests of g and subsidiary knowledge deriving largely from g. Such tests constitute the large majority of standardized tests available and in use today, including IQ tests, the Armed Services Vocational Aptitude Battery (ASVAB), the SAT, the ACT and related tests, as well as the Stanford–Binet and Wechsler Intelligence Scales.[43]

My colleagues and I have developed a range of assessments to measure practical intelligence, which is key to adaptive intelligence in that practical intelligence is necessary for adaptation to, shaping of, and selection of environments in daily life. In particular, we have used tacit-knowledge tests to study students in high school and college, academic psychologists, salespersons, civilian managers, and military leaders at the platoon, company, and battalion level, as well as workers in other occupations.

People often find it challenging, if not impossible, to articulate their tacit knowledge. As a result, my colleagues and I have found it essentially useless to ask people to verbalize their tacit knowledge directly. Instead, we have measured tacit knowledge in participants' patterns of responses to challenging practical situations or problems they encounter in the course of their work. In particular, we have investigated those situations in which tacit knowledge is expected to provide an advantage. The measurement instruments used to assess relevant tacit knowledge usually consist of situations and a variety of response options geared to those situations. Such assessments have been referred to in the literature as situational-judgment tests (SJTs).[44] These kinds of SJTs typically are used to measure problem-solving in the interpersonal domain[45] or behavioral intentions of various kinds.[46] In an SJT or tacit-knowledge (TK) test, problems take a particular form. Each question presents a problem relevant to performance in the domain being assessed. Examples would be a manager who seeks to intervene in a dispute between two subordinates regarding work responsibilities, perhaps proceeded by a set of possible strategies for solving the problem. For example, the manager might choose to meet first with each of the two subordinates individually to find out their individual perspectives on the problem. She then might hold a meeting with both subordinates together and have them state their respective points of view.

Test respondents would be asked one of several things. First, they might be asked to choose both the best and the worst alternatives from among a few response options. Alternatively, they might be asked to rate, using a Likert-type scale, the quality, usefulness, or appropriateness of several potential responses to the given situation. Alternatively, participants simply might be asked to provide what they saw as the optimal solution. They also might be asked to say why they viewed the solution as optimal.

The formulation and development of tests of tacit knowledge, like of many SJTs, best starts with the identification and understanding of critical incidents that occur in the workplace.[47] Individuals in the workplace are invited to furnish accounts of workplace incidents from which they learned a meaningful and important lesson about how to perform their job. However, they are asked that the lesson they learned *not* be something that had been learned through school instruction or about which they had read in a textbook or training manual of some kind. In other words, those situations in which tacit knowledge is most pertinent are ones for which the optimal response cannot be elicited from knowledge of explicit declarative knowledge or procedural rules. In practice, the optimal response even may contradict formal, explicit knowledge of the type learned in school or in other kinds of formal training.

The lessons that are learned from the critical incidents provided by respondents then are utilized to write relevant descriptions of situations, possibly along with a set of alternative responses. A test of tacit knowledge may consist of several descriptions of work-related situations, each followed by multiple alternative response options. These options are designed to vary in their appropriateness and quality. Alternatively, the test-takers might receive no response options but rather blank lines in which they then can write in their best solution.

Such tests of tacit knowledge, when response options are used, have been scored in one of four ways. A first possibility is to correlate participants' ratings with an "index variable" reflecting group membership (e.g., a value of three is assigned to experts, a value of two to intermediates, and a value of one to novices). A second possibility is to evaluate the degree to which participants' responses are consistent with consensually agreed upon professional "rules of thumb," or accepted ways of doing things. A third possibility is to compute a profile match (e.g., using a squared difference score between participants' ratings and an expert prototype). A fourth possibility is to score on a theory-determined basis, whereby certain responses are judged to be better than others according to the specifications of the theory. Scores on TK tests then have been compared to scores on various indicators of job performance as well as measures of Big-Five personality traits.

What are some of the psychometric properties of practical intelligence?[48] First, practical intelligence can be measured in a reliable manner. In other words, scores on tests taken one day predict scores on tests taken another day. Second, measures of practical intelligence tend to show relatively weak correlations with measures of general intelligence. In one case, the correlation was negative.[49] Thus, practical intelligence is largely distinct from general intelligence, although it draws on the same mental processes, such as defining problems, formulating strategies for solving problems, and so on. The processes are the same – the contexts in which the processes are implemented are very different. Third, measures of practical intelligence provide significant incremental validity over tests of general intelligence in predicting both academic and extracurricular performance as well as job performance.[50] In other words, these tests could serve a useful function in practical predictive situations. Fourth, practical intelligence can be statistically differentiated not only from academic aspects of intelligence but also from personality. It is not the same as Big-Five personality traits – openness to experience, conscientiousness, extraversion, agreeableness, and neuroticism. Fifth, measures of practical intelligence can predict success in leadership independently of g.[51] At least in the military situations we studied, measures of practical intelligence in platoon, company, and battalion leadership situations provided prediction of success that standard measures of general intelligence did not provide. Sixth, practical-intelligence measures, at least within a given domain, tend to be moderately to highly correlated with each other.[52] We found that measures of practical intelligence for managing oneself, managing others, and managing tasks all tend to intercorrelate moderately with each other. Finally, factor analyses reveal practical intelligence to be a separate factor from general intelligence, just as long as practical intelligence is not measured through a multiple-choice format.[53]

Tacit knowledge generally increases with amount of experience. Richard Wagner and I found a significant correlation between scores on a test of tacit knowledge for business managers and the managers' level within their company. In a follow-up study with business professionals, Wagner found significant correlations between scores on a TK test for management and years of management experience. He also found mean differences in tacit-knowledge scores for groups of business managers, business graduate students, and general undergraduates. The managers showed the highest average score. Similar results were found for a test of tacit knowledge targeting academic psychologists compared with psychology professors, psychology graduate students, and undergraduates (see Note 57).

As noted earlier, the construct of general intelligence may be the best of the available standardized single predictors of job performance, at least as job performance is usually defined.[54] The relation between level of general intelligence and quality of job performance usually is viewed as due to the influence of general intelligence on the acquisition of job-related knowledge.[55] Many job-knowledge tests, however, assess primarily or even exclusively declarative knowledge of facts, rules, and predefined procedures.[56] They consist of relatively abstract and well-defined problems – problems with a single best answer and that directly address what one could learn in a book or technical manual or on the Internet. The problems on these tests are similar in many respects to the kinds of problems found on traditional tests of general intelligence, thus explaining, at least in part, the observed correlations between tests of job knowledge and tests of cognitive abilities.

Tests of tacit knowledge, however, consist of problems that are poorly defined – it sometimes is not even clear what they are asking – and that are context-rich – it matters a lot under what circumstances knowledge has to be used and a particular problem solved. For example, whether to ask your boss for a raise has no "right" or "wrong" answer – it depends on the circumstances, both of time and place. Performance on these TK tests, therefore, is a function of practical rather than just of abstract, general intelligence.

Tests of tacit knowledge usually exhibit small to moderate correlations with measures of general intelligence. In my research with Richard Wagner, as mentioned earlier, in a sample of undergraduate students, scores on a test of verbal reasoning correlated nonsignificantly with scores on tests of tacit knowledge for academic psychologists and managers. Similarly, for a sample of business executives, scores on a test of tacit knowledge for managers exhibited a nonsignificant correlation with scores on a test of verbal reasoning. Scores on the verbal-reasoning test also did not correlate significantly with scores on a test of tacit knowledge for sales in samples of both undergraduates and salespeople.[57] Further support comes from a study in which the ASVAB was given along with a test of tacit knowledge for managers to a sample of Air Force recruits.[58] Scores on the test of tacit knowledge showed trivial correlations with four scores on the ASVAB (in particular, verbal ability, mathematics, vocational–technical information, and clerical speed).

Some studies have found significant correlations between general intelligence and tacit knowledge, but these relations are not always in the positive direction. In our research with military leaders, leaders at three levels of command completed Terman's *Concept Mastery Test*, a test of general intelligence, along with a test of tacit knowledge for their respective level of command in the military. Tacit-knowledge scores exhibited correlations ranging from trivial and nonsignificant to moderate and significant. However, in one study conducted in Kenya, tacit-knowledge scores actually correlated negatively with scores on tests of general intelligence (see Note 49). Thus, in certain environments, development of practical skills may be emphasized and valued at the expense of development of more abstract, analytical, and academic skills. Such environments emphasizing practical skills are not limited to rural Kenya or even to Africa. Painters, sculptors, musicians, athletes, tailors, cooks, and craftsmen, among many others, all may view the development of skills other than those taught in conventional schooling to hold more value to them than do the more academic skills.

Practical intelligence, however, goes only so far. Societies, for the most part, follow their leaders, no matter how ridiculous they are. It may be practically intelligent to follow your leader, at least if you value your own life and the life of your family – Adolph Hitler had widespread support in Germany. The point is that no matter how utterly absurd the leaders are, those leaders will have a large following unless they are seen as betraying their followers, regardless of what they may do to everyone else (e.g., Jews and Roma in the case of Hitler). If we do not find leaders with more creative and commonsensical skills, we are in trouble.

But what is it exactly that toxic leaders like, say, Vladimir Putin or Nicolás Maduro lack? Is it just creative and practical skill? I eventually reached the conclusion that something else was missing; and that something was wisdom.

5.6   The Augmented Theory of Successful Intelligence

People can be creatively, analytically, and practically intelligent without being wise. I previously had proposed a balance theory of wisdom, believing wisdom to be related to intelligence but not an integral part of it.[59]

According to the balance theory, wisdom is the application of one's knowledge and skills to the attainment of a common good; achieved through balancing one's own, others, and higher order interests over the long as well as the short term, through the application of positive ethical values. If we unpack this definition, we see that wisdom is different from most other skills in that it is necessarily contextually defined and that although the definition might be the same across cultural groups, almost certainly how wisdom is instantiated will not be.

The greatest temptation in defining the common good is to define it narrowly in terms of one's own reference group. That is, the common good applies to people like oneself. That is what individuals of long ago (and some still today) have done when they owned slaves but nevertheless felt good about themselves. Some of them believed that the common good applied only to white people, and perhaps white Southerners, or white self-identified Christians, or white males, or whatever. Others believed that, somehow, slavery benefited not only members of their group and but also even benefited the slaves. Of course, this logic is a gross rationalization. But it is the kind of logic in which people engage when they have a vested interest in the outcome. People twist logic to suit their vested interests: They always have and probably always will. So, in thinking about the common good, one needs to take off blinders, rose-colored glasses, or any other hoped-for visual aids that will lead one to see things the way one wishes to see things rather than the way things are.

5.7   Adaptive Intelligence

The augmented theory of successful intelligence seemed to me, and continues to seem to me, to be on the right track, but it is flawed, I believe, in one major way. Wisdom, as a set of thinking skills, is not quite like creative, analytical, and practical thinking skills. To think wisely, one needs to be able to think creatively, analytically, and practically – and then apply the thinking to attain a common good. In other words, wisdom, viewed in this way, is not a separate entity but rather a way to use creative, analytical, and practical thinking. It is more of an orientation. Thus, I see adaptive intelligence as the wise application of creative, analytical, and practical thinking skills to the solution of life problems of diverse kinds but with consequences for adaptivity. Someone can be practically intelligent, for example, in looking out themselves and their family but unwise in failing to take into consideration others, or actually in harming others who are seen as somehow getting in the way of the individual's success.

On this view, tests such as IQ tests and their proxies do not measure roughly one-fourth of the skills required for adaptive intelligence (i.e., analytical skills, but not creative, practical, or wisdom-based skills). Rather, they measure *none* of the full skills required for adaptive intelligence. Rather, they measure skill subsets. But the problem with analytical skills, as measured by tests, is that they can be used for nonadaptive or maladaptive purposes, as so many bad CEOs, presidents, lawyers, doctors, academics, and others have demonstrated.

The need for wise thinking has never been greater but it is ever more difficult to find. Indeed, many of the politicians being elected in current times seem to be distinctly lacking in wisdom, whatever their analytical intelligence may be. What are the characteristics of people lacking in the wisdom needed to apply to their creative, analytical, and practical thinking?

I have suggested that people who lack wisdom – who are foolish – show at least six common characteristics in their thinking.[60] These characteristics usually go together – that is, people who show one tend to show many, if not most of the others.

Unrealistic optimism. Foolish people are unrealistically optimistic. They believe that if they have an idea, it is almost certain to be a good, if not great, idea. Their excessive confidence in their own thinking undermines their disposition even to ask if an idea they have is actually worth pursuing or continuing with. People who are unrealistically optimistic, in this sense, are extremely uncritical regarding their own ideas but may be extremely critical regarding the ideas of others, as they cannot imagine any others having ideas anywhere nearly as good as theirs are. People who are unrealistically optimistic in this sense are not wise because they fail to ask what the limitations of their own knowledge and thinking are.

Egocentrism. Foolish people are egocentric. For them, what happens does, or at least, should, center on their own desires and needs. Their self-centeredness leads them to have a world view that places them at the center and others at varying points in the periphery, depending on the extent to which those others can do things that benefit them. Egocentric people do not see themselves as egocentric. For them, the problem is others who do not realize how important they are and how their own needs can and should take precedence over the needs of others.

False omniscience. Foolish people are falsely omniscient. They believe they know everything – or everything they need to know for the decisions they make. It matters not how ignorant they are, because they do not know what they do not know, and they do not care. Because they believe themselves all-knowing, they do not seek the information they need to make informed and wise decisions. Rather, they make decisions that they feel are right, given the superior knowledge base upon which they imagine that they draw.

False omnipotence. Foolish people are falsely omnipotent. They believe they are, or at least should be, all-powerful, because they are uniquely in a position to act in optimal ways (for their own interests, that is). They do not acknowledge or approve of limits on their power, and when such limits exist, they work actively to undermine and, if possible, overthrow the limits.

False sense of invulnerability. Foolish people feel falsely invulnerable. They recognize that other people may be trying to bring them down but feel that the others will not and cannot succeed. They often work actively and even cleverly to sidetrack efforts to bring them down. Because they feel invulnerable, they often are reckless and as well as feckless in their actions.

Moral disengagement. Foolish people are morally disengaged.[61] They believe that moral thinking and behavior may be important for others but is not important for them. On the contrary, they see themselves as having somehow surpassed the need for moral constraints on their behavior. It is, in part, for this reason, that clergy can be as immoral as anyone else, and sometimes, more so. They believe that the rules that apply to others do not also apply to them.

Sunk-cost fallacy. Foolish people fall into the sunk-cost fallacy. Even when they make a mistake, they are loath to admit it, so they keep making the same mistake over and over again. Metaphorically they throw good money after bad, pursuing ideas that have proven themselves not to work out. But they are unwilling even to admit that they might make a mistake.

One would like to think that people, in general, would recognize foolishness when they see it and avoid acting foolishly, to the extent possible. But that is not the case. People often are attracted to foolish behavior, possibly more than in the past. In politics, theatrics work. Ask any politician, especially in current times. More and more elected officials are, literally, actors.

Notes

1. Carroll, J. B. (1976). Psychometric tests as cognitive tasks: A new "Structure of Intellect." In L. Resnick (Ed.), *The nature of intelligence* (pp. 27–56). Hillsdale, NJ: Lawrence Erlbaum Associates.
2. Hunt, E., Frost, N., & Lunneborg, C. (1973). Individual differences in cognition: A new approach to cognition. In G. Bower (Ed.), *The psychology of*

learning and motivation: Advances in research and theory (Vol.7, pp. 87–122). New York: Academic Press.

3. Murdoch, S. (2007). *IQ: A smart history of a failed idea.* New York: Wiley.

4. Spearman, C. (1923). *The nature of "intelligence" and the principles of cognition.* London: Macmillan.

5. Sternberg, R. J. (1977). *Intelligence, information processing, and analogical reasoning: The componential analysis of human abilities.* Hillsdale, NJ: Erlbaum.

6. Jensen, A. R. (1982). The chronometry of intelligence. In R. Sternberg (Ed.), *Advances in the psychology of human intelligence* (Vol.1, pp. 255–310). Hillsdale, NJ: Lawrence Erlbaum.

7. Nettelbeck, T. Zwalf, O., & Stough, C. (2020). Basic processes of intelligence. In R. J. Sternberg (Ed.), *Cambridge handbook of intelligence* (2nd ed., pp. 471–503). New York: Cambridge University Press.

8. Sternberg, R. J., & Gardner, M. K. (1983). Unities in inductive reasoning. *Journal of Experimental Psychology: General,* 112, 80–116.

9. Sternberg, R. J. (1980). Representation and process in linear syllogistic reasoning. *Journal of Experimental Psychology: General,* 109, 119–59.

10. Clark, H. H. (1969). Linguistic processes in deductive reasoning. *Psychological Review,* 76, 387–404.

11. Huttenlocher, J. (1968). Constructing spatial images: a strategy in reasoning. *Psychological Review,* 75, 550–60.

12. Sternberg, R. J., & Weil, E. M. (1980). An aptitude–strategy interaction in linear syllogistic reasoning. *Journal of Educational Psychology,* 72, 226–34.

13. Sternberg, R. J., & Ketron, J. L. (1982). Selection and implementation of strategies in reasoning by analogy. *Journal of Educational Psychology,* 74, 399–413.

14. Siegler, R. (1987). The perils of averaging data over strategies: An example from children's addition. *Journal of Experimental Psychology: General,* 116(3), 250–64.

15. Sternberg, R. J. (1980). Sketch of a componential subtheory of human intelligence. *Behavioral and Brain Sciences,* 3, 573–84.

16. World Health Organization (WHO). (2019). Lead poisoning and health. https://bit.ly/3ksOHPs

17. Needleman, H (2004). Lead poisoning. *Annual Review of Medicine,* 55, 209–22. doi: 10.1146/annurev.med.55.091902.103653

18. Roberts, D. (2019). With impeachment, America's epistemic crisis has arrived. *Vox,* November 16. https://bit.ly/2Dqhaoi

19. Kendall-Taylor, A., & Shullman, D. (2018). How Russia and China undermine democracy. *Foreign Affairs,* October 2. https://fam.ag/3fPJspr

20. Proctor, R. N. (2013). The history of the discovery of the cigarette–lung cancer link: evidentiary traditions, corporate denial, global toll. *BMJ,* 21(2), 87–91. https://tobaccocontrol.bmj.com/content/21/2/87

21. Kearns, C. E., Schmidt, L. A., & Glantz, S. A. (2016). Sugar industry and coronary heart disease research: A historical analysis of internal industry

documents. *JAMA Internal Medicine.* https://www.ncbi.nlm.nih.gov/pmc/a rticles/PMC5099084/; Hosie, R. (2017). Sugar industry accused of hiding evidence of sucrose's negative health effects 50 years go. *The Independent,* November 22. https://bit.ly/2EXP3gE

22. Ornish, D. (1990). *Dr. Dean Ornish's program for reversing heart disease.* New York: Random House.

23. Aubrey, A. (2017). What the industry knew about sugar's health effects, but didn't tell us. *NPR,* November 21. https://n.pr/3khmpr1

24. Davenport, C., & Landler, M. (2019). Trump administration hardens its attack on climate science. *New York Times,* May 27. https://nyti.ms/2D CrY2k; Rosza, M. (2019). How the Trump administration is attacking the science behind global warming. *Salon,* May 28. https://bit.ly/3fyfw1o

25. Linden, E. (2019). How scientists got climate change so wrong. *New York Times,* November 8. https://nyti.ms/31skDdU

26. Kuhn, T. S. (1970). *The structure of scientific revolutions* (2nd ed.). Chicago, IL: University of Chicago Press; Sternberg, R. J. (1997). Fads in psychology: What we can do. *APA Monitor,* 28(7), 19; Sternberg, R. J. (2017). We can do better than fads. In S. O. Lilienfeld, & I. D. Waldman (Eds.), *Psychological science under scrutiny: Recent challenges and proposed solutions* (pp. 340–8). New York: Wiley; Fleming, C. (2019). The tyranny of trendy ideas: Academics pretend to be above cheap and trivial fads: We aren't. *Chronicle of Higher Education,* July 1. https://bit.ly/31tU5ct

27. Haustein, K., Otto, F., Hausfather, Z., & Jacobs, P. (2019). Guest post: Why natural cycles only play small role in rate of global warming. *CarbonBrief,* May 24. https://bit.ly/33y2XjS

28. The diseases and infirmities exempting from the draft (1863). *New York Times,* November 15. https://nyti.ms/3gzcoVl

29. Dykes, M. (2018). US court ruling: You can be "too smart" to be a cop. *Global Research,* May 11. https://bit.ly/3a39GDK

30. Smith, C. (2019). Elite colleges constantly tell low-income students that they do not belong. *The Atlantic,* March 18. https://bit.ly/3ki7bSz

31. Lu, D., & Yourish, K. (2019). The turnover at the top of the Trump administration. *New York Times,* June 25. https://nyti.ms/33t4mrU

32. Sternberg, R. J. (1997). *Successful intelligence.* New York: Plume; Sternberg, R. J. (1999). The theory of successful intelligence. *Review of General Psychology,* 3, 292–316.

33. Sternberg, R. J. (2018). The triarchic theory of successful intelligence. In D. P. Flanagan, & P. L. Harrison (Eds.), *Contemporary intellectual assessment: Theories, tests, and issues* (4th ed., pp. 174–94). New York: Guilford Press.

34. Earley, P. C., & Ang, S. (2003). *Cultural intelligence: Individual interactions across cultures.* Palo Alto, CA: Stanford University Press; Ang, S., & Van Dyne, L. (2008). Conceptualization of cultural intelligence: Definition, distinctiveness, and nomological network. In S. Ang, & L. Van Dyne (Eds.), *Handbook of cultural intelligence* (pp. 3–15). New York: M. E. Sharpe; Ang, S.,

Ng, K. Y., & Rockstuhl, T. (2020). Cultural intelligence. In R. J. Sternberg (Ed.), *Cambridge handbook of intelligence* (2nd ed., pp. 820–45). New York: Cambridge University Press

35. Ang, S., Van Dyne, L., & Tan, M. L. (2011). Cultural intelligence. In R. J. Sternberg, & S. B. Kaufman (Eds.), *Cambridge handbook of intelligence* (pp. 582–602). New York: Cambridge University Press.

36. Sternberg, R. J., Forsythe, G. B., Hedlund, J. et al. (2000). *Practical intelligence in everyday life*. New York: Cambridge University Press.

37. Carraher, T. N., Carraher, D., & Schliemann, A. D. (1985). Mathematics in the streets and in schools. *British Journal of Developmental Psychology*, 3, 21–9; Ceci, S. J., & Liker, J. (1986). Academic and nonacademic intelligence: An experimental separation. In R. J. Sternberg, & R. K. Wagner (Eds.), *Practical intelligence: Nature and origins of competence in the everyday world* (pp. 119–42). New York: Cambridge University Press; Ceci, S. J., & Ruiz, A. (1992). The role of general ability in cognitive complexity: A case study of expertise. In R. Hoffman (Ed.), *The psychology of expertise: Cognitive research and empirical AI* (pp. 218–30). New York: Springer-Verlag.

38. Matthew, C. T., & Sternberg, R. J. (2009). Developing experience-based (tacit) knowledge through reflection. *Learning & Individual Differences*, 19, 530–40; Khan, A. A., & Khader, S. A. (2014). An approach for externalization of expert tacit knowledge using a query management system in an e-learning environment. *International Review of Research in Open and Distance Learning*, 15, 257–74.

39. Sternberg, R. J., & Hedlund, J. (2002). Practical intelligence, g, and work psychology. *Human Performance*, 15(1/2), 143–60.

40. Deary, I. J., Whalley, L. J., & Starr, J. M. (2009). *A lifetime of intelligence: Follow-up studies of the Scottish mental surveys of 1932 and 1947*. Washington, DC: American Psychological Association.

41. Sackett, P. R., Shewach, O. R., & Dahlke, J. A. (2020). The predictive value of general intelligence. In R. J. Sternberg (Ed.), *Human intelligence: An introduction* (pp. 381–414). New York: Cambridge University Press.

42. Sternberg, R. J. (2020). The augmented theory of successful intelligence. In R. J. Sternberg (Ed.), *Cambridge handbook of intelligence (2nd ed., pp. 679–708)*. New York: Cambridge University Press.

43. Frey, M. C., & Detterman, D. K. (2004). Scholastic assessment or g? The relationship between the Scholastic Assessment Test and general cognitive ability. *Psychological Science*, 15, 373–8; Koenig, K. A., Frey, M. C., & Detterman, D. K. (2008). ACT and general cognitive ability. *Intelligence*, 36, 153–60.

44. Frederiksen, N. (1966). Validation of a simulation technique. *Organizational Behavior and Human Performance*, 1, 87–109; Frederiksen, N. (1986). Toward a broader conception of human intelligence. In R. J. Sternberg, & R. K. Wagner (Eds.), *Practical intelligence: Nature and origins of competence in the everyday world* (pp. 84–116). New York: Cambridge University Press; Motowidlo, S. J., Dunnette, M. D., & Carter, G. W. (1990). An alternative selection procedure: The low-fidelity simulation. *Journal of Applied*

Psychology, 75, 640–7; Chan, D., & Schmitt, N. (1998). Video-based versus paper-and-pencil method of assessment in situational judgment tests: Subgroup differences in test performance and face validity perceptions. *Journal of Applied Psychology*, 82, 143–59; McDaniel, M. A., & Whetzel, D. L. (2005). Situational judgment test research: Informing the debate on practical intelligence theory. *Intelligence*, 33, 515–25.

45. Hanson, M. A., & Ramos, R. A. (1996). Situational judgment tests. In R. S. Barrett (Ed.), *Fair employment strategies in human resource management* (pp. 119–24). Westport, CT: Greenwood.

46. Weekley, J. A., & Jones, C. (1997). Video-based situational testing. *Personnel Psychology*, 50, 25–49.

47. Flanagan, J. C. (1954). The critical incident technique. *Psychological Bulletin*, 51, 327–58.

48. Hedlund, J. (2020). Practical intelligence. In R. J. Sternberg (Ed.), *Cambridge handbook of intelligence* (pp. 736–55). New York: Cambridge University Press.

49. Sternberg, R. J., Nokes, K., Geissler, P. W. et al. (2001). The relationship between academic and practical intelligence: A case study in Kenya. *Intelligence*, 29, 401–18.

50. Sternberg, R. J. (2010). *College admissions for the 21st century*. Cambridge, MA: Harvard University Press.

51. Hedlund, J., Forsythe, G. B., Horvath, J. A. et al. (2003). Identifying and assessing tacit knowledge: Understanding the practical intelligence of military leaders. *Leadership Quarterly*, 14, 117–40.

52. Wagner, R. K. (1987). Tacit knowledge in everyday intelligent behavior. *Journal of Personality and Social Psychology*, 52(6), 1236–47. http://dx.doi.org/10.1037/0 022-3514.52.6.1236; Wagner, R. K., & Sternberg, R. K. (1987). Tacit knowledge in managerial success. *Journal of Business and Psychology*, 1, 301–12.

53. Sternberg, R. J., Castejón, J. L., Prieto, M. D., Hautamäki, J., & Grigorenko, E. L. (2001). Confirmatory factor analysis of the Sternberg triarchic abilities test in three international samples: An empirical test of the triarchic theory of intelligence. *European Journal of Psychological Assessment*, 17(1), 1–16.

54. Hunter, J. E. (1986). Cognitive ability, cognitive aptitudes, job knowledge, and job performance. *Journal of Vocational Behavior*, 29, 340–62; Ree, M. J., Earle, J. A., & Teachout, M. S. (1994). Predicting job performance: Not much more than g. *Journal of Applied Psychology*, 79, 518–24.

55. Schmidt, F. L., Hunter, J. E., & Outerbridge, A. N. (1986). The impact of job experience and ability on job knowledge, work sample performance, and supervisory ratings of job performance. *Journal of Applied Psychology*, 71, 432–9; Borman, W. C., Hanson, M. A., Oppler, S. H., & Pulakos, E. D. (1993). Role of supervisory experience in supervisory performance. *Journal of Applied Psychology*, 78, 443–9.

56. McCloy, R. A., Campbell, J. P., & Cudneck, R. (1994). A confirmatory test of a model of performance determinants. *Journal of Applied Psychology*, 79, 493–505.

57. Wagner, R. K., Sujan, H., Sujan, M., Rashotte, C. A., & Sternberg, R. J. (1999). Tacit knowledge in sales. In R. J. Sternberg, & J. A. Horvath (Eds.),

Tacit knowledge in professional practice (pp. 155–82). Mahwah, NJ: Lawrence Erlbaum Associates, Inc.

58. Eddy, A. S. (1988). The relationship between the Tacit Knowledge Inventory for Managers and the Armed Services Vocational Aptitude Battery. Unpublished Master's thesis, St. Mary's University, San Antonio, TX.

59. Sternberg, R. J. (1998) A *balance theory of wisdom. Review of General Psychology*, 2, 347–65; Sternberg, R. J. (2003). *Wisdom, intelligence, and creativity synthesized.* New York: Cambridge University Press.

60. Sternberg, R. J. (2002). Smart people are not stupid, but they sure can be foolish: The imbalance theory of foolishness. In R. J. Sternberg (Ed.), *Why smart people can be so stupid* (pp. 232–42). New Haven, CT: Yale University Press; Sternberg, R. J. (2004). Why smart people can be so foolish. *European Psychologist*, 9(3), 145–50; Sternberg, R. J. (2005). Foolishness. In R. J. Sternberg, & J. Jordan (Eds.), *Handbook of wisdom: Psychological perspectives* (pp. 331–52). New York: Cambridge University Press.

61. Bandura, A. (2016). *Moral disengagement.* New York: Worth Publishers.

Measurement and Teaching of Adaptive Intelligence

How does one operationalize the theory of adaptive intelligence in school or work settings? The answers to these questions form the topic of this chapter.

6.1 Measurement of Adaptive Intelligence

How does one measure adaptive intelligence? At the time I am writing this book, we are only beginning to address this question, although the work we are doing builds on the work described in Chapter 4 on measurement and teaching of successful intelligence. Given the nature of adaptive intelligence as I have described it in this book, measures of adaptive intelligence would have to have several properties that are similar to previous tests but also several properties that are different.

Any test of adaptive intelligence needs to be reliable and construct valid. Reliability means that the tests of adaptive intelligence measure a clearly defined construct and that they can do so consistently over time; construct validity mean that the items measure what they are supposed to measure. A test can be reliable but not valid, that is, it measures a clear construct, just not the one that it is intended to measure. To be valid, however, the items must have enough reliability so that it is clear that the measure is of a clear-cut construct.

The differences are perhaps more notable:

First, the problems need to reflect serious issues in the real world, not trivial issues that only would appear on a standardized test.

Second, the problems need to be contextualized. They need to occur in an explained context rather than be decontextualized or placed in contexts irrelevant to test-takers' lives, as is the case with most standardized test problems.

Third, the test cannot be multiple-choice or have trivial (e.g., one-word) answers. Real, complex problems in life are not presented in multiple-choice format and typically do not have one-word answers.

Fourth, much of the problem needs to require the test-taker to define exactly what the problem is, rather than a test's clearly defining the problem for the test-taker, with the presented definition being the only one that is allowed.

Fifth, the problems cannot have so-called objectively "right" and "wrong" answers. Problems in everyday life rarely have answers that easily can be classified as right or wrong. Rather, answers are better or worse, and either are more thoughtful and reflective or less so.

Finally, the problems have to be ones that draw on the knowledge and skills of the individuals taking the test. For example, most of our test-takers would not know how to solve a complex econometric problem, no matter how important it may be to everyday life.

Scoring of problems on a test of adaptive intelligence obviously cannot be in terms of right and wrong answers. Rather, it is in terms of the quality and quantity of answers given. Quality of answers reflects the elements of the theory as described earlier in Chapter 5, namely, (a) *analytical strength* – does the answer reflect a reasonable understanding of the problem?; (b) *creative strength* – is the answer novel and high in quality?; (c) *practical strength* – is the answer practical and presented in a persuasive way?; and most importantly, (d) *wisdom* – might the answer help to achieve a common good, over the long as well as the short term, by balancing the interests of diverse stakeholders, through the infusion of positive ethical values? Because answers, in our experience, tend to be relatively brief, we score holistically, with a scoring system such that a one represents a weak answer; a two represents a borderline answer; a three represents a somewhat thoughtful, fairly typical answer; a four represents a thoughtful answer that shows good understanding of the problem and how to approach it; and a five represents an excellent answer that shows deep understanding of the problem and how to solve it. Scores of five, in our experience to date, are relatively rare. Typical scores are threes and twos are more common than fours.

We have several different current projects on adaptive intelligence. The first one, in collaboration with Siying Li, Caiwei Zhu, Deeksha Sharma, and Anastasia Kreisel, deals with issues identified in an informal study as serious world problems. Examples of topics are water pollution, air pollution, food shortages, mental health, health care, and global climate change. In each case, the respondent is told to imagine that he is a hypothetical individual facing a problem that affects not only him or her, but also many others. These topics are shown in Table 6.1.

Table 6.1 *Abbreviated test of adaptive intelligence*

Water pollution

You live in Collier County, Florida, in the United State of America. The water bodies nearby are polluted with red tide organism – harmful algae blooms (*Karenia brevis*) – due to dumping of chemicals (nitrogen- and phosphorus-based) and nutrients. The sources of red tide are commercial agriculture and industries near the county. This condition makes the water unfit for healthy living conditions. Many respiratory irritations, liver conditions, and skin problems have been observed due to airborne toxins from the bloom. In 2016, the Government of Florida announced a state of emergency due to loss of aquatic life and public health risk. In 2017 and 2018, the area suffered through an unusual persistent, toxic red tide for a long period. Now, in October 2019, there is an abrupt increase in red tide, *Karenia brevis* >1,000,000 (cells/liter), which has caused an emergency red alert.

Food adulteration

You live in New Delhi, the capital of India, on the bank of river Yamuna. The river Yamuna at present is critically suffering from serious water pollution. In July 2019, the National Environmental Engineering Research Institute (NEERI) took samples from east Delhi and found dangerous metal concentrations (lead, nickel, cadmium, and mercury) in seven vegetables – cabbage, cauliflower, radish, eggplant, coriander, spinach, and fenugreek. The metal content was in the range of 2.8 mg/Kg to 13.8 mg/Kg, which is quite a bit higher than the safe limit of 2.5 mg/Kg. The prolonged unsafe concentrations of these metals in the food can lead to disruption of biochemical and biological processes in the human body. This contamination also can lead to damage to the human organs and blood composition. It was found that possible sources of this condition are due to soil and water irrigated from river Yamuna for these vegetables.

Mental health

You live in Tokyo, Japan, and you find the issue of mental health a daunting challenge. A 2016 study of 4,000 people by the Department of Mental Health at the University of Tokyo suggested that the issue of mental health is still unsolvable in Japan due to the cultural approach of not considering it a problem at all. Even with good mental-health facilities, the suicide rates are high in your country, which is a grave issue. In 2019, the world population review by the World Health Organization (WHO) commented that the leading cause of deaths was suicides in Japan among men in the age range 20–44 years and women in the age range 15–34 years. Also, the WHO estimated that more than 300 million people were affected worldwide with depression in the year 2015, which is equivalent to 4.4 percent of the world's population.

Air pollution

You live in the city of Beijing, China. Recently, due to a surge in coal consumption and the relaxation on industrial output over the winter of 2018–19, problems of serious smog increased. Also, air pollution by PM2.5 (airborne particulate matter) read at an average of 81 micrograms per cubic meter in the first four months of 2019. PM2.5 is one of the most dangerous types of pollutants, as it can penetrate deep into human lungs, causing respiratory illnesses.

Healthcare

Your friend is suffering from cancer and is under a huge financial debt due to costly treatments to treat the disease. Cancer turns out to be a financial killer. The Fred Hutchinson Cancer Center in Seattle found that cancer patients are 2.5 times more likely to go bankrupt as compared with healthy people, but also that the patient who goes bankrupt has an 80 percent likelihood of dying from this disease. Average cost for the treatment is in the range of $150,000. Even with insurance, cancer treatments are still a costly affair for the afflicted individuals.

Wealth inequality

Wealth means the sum total of one's assets minus liabilities. In 2018, the combined wealth of Amazon founder Jeff Bezos, Microsoft founder Bill Gates, and investor Warren Buffet was worth more than the combination of the wealth of the bottom 50 percent of Americans. Over the past decades, the richest 1 percent in the United States have doubled their net worth, while the poor bottom 40 percent are trapped in negative wealth – their debts exceeding their assets. The wealth of the rich comes from a variety of sources, such as stocks and mutual funds. The bottom 90 percent, however, have their residences as the major component of their wealth and a large number of them are prone to debts.

Poverty

As reported by the Children's Defense Fund, about 13 million American children are living in homes with income levels below the poverty line. Children in poverty often are continuously lacking proper nutrition and education and are at risk for homelessness and violence. The Children's Defense Fund suggested that, compared with those who have not experienced poverty, people who have experienced poverty during childhood are three times more likely to be in poverty at age thirty. Therefore, child poverty is critical to the intergenerational cycle of poverty.

Gun violence

On May 7, 2019, a school shooting occurred at the STEM School Highland Ranch. One student died and eight others were injured in a school shooting. The youngest of them was fifteen years old. The two suspects were an eighteen-year-old male and a sixteen-year-old transgender boy. The shooters were charged with murder and attempted murder. The transgender boy told the police that they wanted to target the classmates who had bullied him. As of July 2019, there have been a total of 329 mass shootings in the United States with a total of 370 people killed and 1,339 people injured.

Racism

Black farmers make up only about 1.3 percent of the farming population in the United States today. After slavery was abolished, African Americans were not redressed properly. Essential tools of wealth creation such as land and jobs are still relatively inaccessible to many African Americans. Systemic discrimination and prejudice make the farming industry inhospitable for African Americans. Often unable to receive loans from the US Department of Agriculture and lacking access to legal protection, black farmers have experienced enormous land loss.

Illegal migrants

In September 2019, a twenty-six-year-old mother and her toddler drowned crossing the Rio Grande River from Matamoros, Mexico. They were the second parent and child to die there since June 2019. Legal entry is becoming nearly impossible for most migrants. And after being denied asylum or refugee status, some have considered life-threatening ways of crossing the border, such as crossing the Rio Grande River, to get across the border. According to the Border Patrol, the number of migrants caught hiding in tractor-trailers to cross the border has gone up by 40 percent in 2019. Agents at the border crossing also have reported a significant increase in numbers of migrants caught hidden in tiny rooms in homes and hotels. Smugglers become the last hope for many migrants.

Table 6.1 (*cont.*)

Migrants know that their months of waiting for American asylum requests are usually pointless and hopeless.

Gender inequality

A 2019 study found that women earn seventy-nine cents for every dollar earned by men. This means that the median salary for men is about 21 percent higher than the median salary for women. When the qualifications and kinds of jobs are controlled, which means men and women with similar employment characteristics working on jobs of the same kind and level, women earn $0.98 for every dollar earned by men. Even when a woman who is as well qualified as a man does the exact same job as the man, she is still paid 2 percent less. This gender wage gap has only decreased by a tiny amount of $0.008 from 2015 to 2019.

Climate change

According to an analysis by NASA, Earth's surface temperature in 2018 was 1.5 degrees Fahrenheit warmer than the average temperature between 1951 and 1980. Increases in temperature can lead to extreme weather events, agriculture and food security issues, extinction of animal and plant species, challenges to human health and well-being, and risks in almost every aspect of our life. It is estimated that if our carbon emissions continue to increase at the current rate, we can expect a 10-degree Fahrenheit increase in the hottest daily temperatures by the end of the twenty-first century as compared with that in the twentieth century.

In each case, respondents were asked the following questions:

1 What could you do personally about the problem?
2 What is wrong with what is being done (or not done) about it now?
3 What would you recommend those in authority do about it?
4 What are the obstacles to doing what needs to be done about it?

A second study, in collaboration with Chak (Vina) Haang Wong, specifically addresses adaptive intelligence in a *scientific context*. Participants are presented with problems of a scientific nature and are asked to address them. The motivation for this study is that many of the problems in the world today are scientific in nature and failure to address them can lead to bad or even disastrous consequences. But many people understand science so poorly that they cannot even understand the problems, much less contribute to solving them. Moreover, politicians, including the current president of the United States, deliberately belittle and discourage scientific thinking so as to support an economic and political agenda that is strongly contraindicated by science (e.g., actions that will severely worsen global climate change without significant compensating economic or other benefits).

Examples of items are shown in Table 6.2.

Table 6.2 *Test of adaptive intelligence in the context of scientific pursuits*

For each of the following items, you will be reading about some innovative products and novel scientific ideas. As with any innovation, there are potential pluses and minuses to each idea. Thus, despite their benefits, there might be drawbacks.

You will be asked to examine the costs and benefits of the studies by generating as many questions and/or comments as you can. (Please keep in mind that the studies described are hypothetical. None has actually been done or is being planned to be done.)

You will be scored based on (1) The number, (2) Analytical validity, (3) Usefulness and practicality, (4) Creativity, and (5) Wisdom toward serving a common good, of your questions/ comments.

Here is an example with possible answers:

Nutritional supplementation. A scientific entrepreneur has developed a nutritional supplement that he believes offers great promise for helping people to lose weight. Because it is a supplement to be sold over the counter, it is not subject to FDA (Food and Drug Administration) approval. He has tested the nutritional supplement on 200 people, half of whom were randomly assigned to the supplement condition and half to a placebo condition. People, of course, did not know to which condition they were assigned. After 3 months in which members of each group took their respective daily pills, the experimental (supplement) group had lost an average of 21 pounds whereas the placebo group had lost an average of 1 pound. A venture-capital firm is considering offering the entrepreneur $5.5 million to start producing, marketing, and selling the product. You have been asked to advise the venture-capital firm as to whether to fund the production, marketing, and sales of the supplement. What would you want to ask and/or tell them?

1. Have potential side effects of the weight-reducing supplement been adequately studied, or studied at all? "Are there any undesirable consequences of using the drug, such as physical or psychological addiction?

2. For what population or populations is the supplement safe? Children, and if so, of what ages? Older people? People with weakened immune systems?

3. Does the supplement interact with pharmaceutical drugs, such that there might be unexpected side effects for people taking those drugs, including weight-loss drugs?"

4. Maybe 3 months was not long enough to assess the supplement's effectiveness. The supplement's effect might decrease over time.

5. Can the supplement safely be used by people with unusual weight-related conditions, such as morbid obesity or anorexia (i.e., people taking the supplement to lose weight that they do not need to lose)?

6. "Can the supplement be priced so that it is available to all who really would benefit from it, or will it 'price out' many people who potentially could use it but who could not afford it?"

1. **Salicylates in foods**. A twenty-year study found a negative correlation between the use of salicylates and the number of headaches reported by the study participants. As a result, researchers concluded that salicylates, which are members of the same chemical family as aspirin (a medicine used to treat headaches), have a possible therapeutic effect that eases patients' headaches. On the other hand, however, nausea, vomiting, and abdominal pain are common with mild salicylates ingestions (levels 40 to 80 mg/dL). Commercially, although many foods are naturally rich in salicylates, salicylates are also used as preservatives and flavor additives for foods by food-processing companies. Now that the study has been published, more food-processing companies are thinking about increasing

Table 6.2 (*cont.*)

the usage of salicylates and proclaiming their effect of easing headaches. You have been asked to advise the food-processing companies as to whether to increase the usage of salicylates in foods. What would you want to ask and/or tell them?

2. **Landfills and recycling.** A garbage-disposal company wants to purchase more land because its landfill will be completely filled within five years. During the past two years, however, residents in town have been recycling and reusing twice as much material as they did previously. Consultants predicted that the amount of recycled and reused material, including paper, plastic, metal, and glass, should further increase because of the residents' strong commitment to protecting the environment. Thus, consultants believed that there is no need for the company to purchase more land. The company's CEO, however, wants to make the purchase because more land creates more economic benefits, more places for garbage disposal, and a higher rate of employment. You have been asked to advise the company as to whether to purchase more landfills for garbage disposal. What would you want to ask and/or tell them?

3. **Birds' extinction.** In 1995, a wildlife census reported that there were over 200 species of birds in Yellowstone National Park, and each species had an abundant number of members. However, in 2019, tourists could observe a maximum of only fifty species in the park, and the numbers of each species were seemingly drastically reduced. Besides obvious factors, such as global warming and air pollution, ornithologists believed that the main reason as to why bird species in Yellowstone National Park were going extinct was because of the trash tourists left behind. A bird-conservation program is planning on applying for funding in order to properly deal with the trash. The participants in the program plan to put up "no littering" signs, have more convenient places for garbage disposal, separate recyclable and nonrecyclable trash, and so on. The board, however, thinks the plan will cost too much money and will not be effective. You have been asked to advise on the program and as to whether the board should fund the conservation program. What would you want to ask and/or tell them?

4. **Copper mining.** Scientists have found that copper is not only a highly utilized metal for electrical and household objects but also an effective antimicrobial surface. Bacteria, such as Salmonellae and Cronobacter sakazakii, often found in food contamination, can be rapidly killed with copper alloys. Scientists then suggested that copper-containing solutions could be used in the healthcare environment (such as hospitals and clinics) and could be applied to prevent/kill bacterial and fungal infections. A copper company has been contacted by scientists and is interested in purchasing over 10,000 square miles of land for copper mining and making more copper-containing solutions. However, copper mining negatively impacts the environment and creates sources of pollution. You have been asked to advise the company as to whether to purchase the land. What would you want to ask and/or tell them?

5. **Air pollution.** The NYC Department of Public Health received an energy-efficiency program proposal designed to reduce air pollution exposure. The program researchers have shown that, in many urban areas, significant disparities in urban air pollution exposures often are associated with significant health consequences. For example, low-income and vulnerable populations often live in places with unhealthful exposures to environmental factors that lead to higher risks of heart diseases. The proposed program aimed to minimize the health impact of urban air pollution by mainly targeting indoor air quality. The program proposed to perform energy upgrades (e.g., adding an indoor filtered mechanical ventilation system) that would improve energy efficiency in

Table 6.2 (*cont.*)

residential homes. The upgrade would cost up to $11,000 per home, to be paid for by the homeowners; however, this price could be prohibitive for low-income families. You have been asked to advise the Department of Public Health as to whether the proposal is valid and effective, and whether they should endorse the program. What would you want to ask and/or tell them?

6. **Power station.** Data indicated that residents who are living close to a coal-fired power station showed a higher rate of asthma, heart disease, and low birth weight; air pollution apparently caused by the power station is a risk factor for all these conditions. Because of this, the coal company plans to retire the power station. After assessing multiple factors, such as employment levels and air/water quality, researchers found that retirement of the power station would create the greatest reduction in negative environmental effects on health; however, it would also greatly negatively impact the employment and local economy. Moreover, losing jobs could affect health through increased risk of heart attack, alcohol or drug abuse, and decreased mental health status and physical activity. You have been asked to advise the power company as to how to proceed. What would you want to ask and/or tell them?

7. **Bicycling safety.** A ten-year nationwide study showed that the percentage of teenagers wearing a helmet while bicycling increased from 35 percent to 80 percent over the ten years. On the other hand, during the same time period, the number of bicycle-related accidents increased by 200 percent. These results demonstrated that the teenage bicyclists might have felt safer because they were wearing helmets; as a result, they became careless and performed riskier actions. The researchers suggested to bicycle companies that instead of making more advanced, high-tech, or fashion-conscious helmets that attract and encourage the teenagers to wear helmets while bicycling, the companies should stop making helmets and concentrate more on teenage-safety education. You have been asked to advise the helmet company as to what they should do about the suggestion. What would you want to ask and/or tell them?

8. **Diet supplementation.** A scientific entrepreneur has invented a diet supplement to help people lose weight and have a balanced diet. The entrepreneur recruited sixty participants and asked them to drink the supplement of three bottles (10 ml per bottle) per day before meals. In addition, he randomly assigned the participants into three groups: people in Group 1 were asked to exercise thirty minutes per day; people in Group 2 were asked to exercise one hour per day; and people in Group 3 were asked to exercise one-and-a-half hours per day. The experiment lasted for one month, and the results showed that people in Group 3 lost the most weight, on average. However, five out of the sixty participants showed signs of mood swing and diarrhea. A pharmaceutical company would like to sponsor the entrepreneur for his invention. You have been asked to advise the company as to whether to sponsor the invention. What would you want to ask and/or tell them?

9. **Late teething.** A scientist believes that late teething in babies could be solved by having the infants consume at least 300 mg of calcium every day. She randomly selected and assigned 100 twelve-month-old infants, who were experiencing late teething, into four groups. Group 1 consumed 100 mg of calcium per day; Group 2 consumed 200 mg of calcium per day; Group 3 consumed 300 mg of calcium per day; and Group 4 did not consume any calcium. The scientist observed and measured the participants' teeth-growing status and found that both Group 2 and Group 3 showed significant teeth-growing results compared to the control. Based on this study, a company that makes

Table 6.2 (*cont.*)

infant food decided to increase the amount of calcium in their powdered milk. However, they are not sure how many grams of calcium they should increase by, and moreover, they are worried that too much calcium might interfere with the body's ability to absorb iron and zinc, which are also important for a baby's development. You have been asked to advise the company. What would you want to ask and/or tell them?

10. **Genetic alteration.** A genetic engineer has recently invented a type of chemical fertilizer to grow more "advanced" agricultural products, such as sweeter tomatoes, bigger watermelons, and herbicide-resistant crops. Successful utilization of his invention produced food and crops that were bigger and grew faster, that were more resistant to disease, and that thrived in different environments. More importantly, this invention could reduce levels of hunger throughout the world. Even though the scientist assured potential investors that the products provided only an extension of the "natural" way in which plants breed, there are potential side effects caused by the chemicals. For example, chemical fertilizers may lead to fewer or poorer quality crops in the long term because of the intricacies of soil health; excessive use of chemicals in the soil can kill off fish in nearby bodies of water; and so on. The scientist asked for a company to fund his invention. You have been asked to advise the company as to whether to fund the invention. What do you want to ask and/or tell them?

11. **Hydroelectric dams.** A hydroelectric company proposed to build a hydroelectric dam in the South, a region that has abundant water resources but not much electricity. The company has done research regarding the benefits of building this hydroelectric power station, such as providing more jobs for the surrounding residents, saving and generating electricity, providing backup power during major electricity outages or disruptions, and controlling flood and irrigation. On the other hand, a group of environmentalists and scientists argued that the dam could cause significant seismic changes that could act as an earthquake trigger. Moreover, the hydroelectric station and reservoirs can affect people's land use, homes, and natural habitats in the dam area. You have been asked to advise the company as to whether to build the hydroelectric dam. What do you want to ask and/or tell them?

12. **Antibiotic resistance.** Scientists in a pharmaceutical firm have developed a new antibiotic that treats a range of respiratory illnesses of bacterial origin. In clinical tests, the drug has shown itself to be effective and to be superior to alternative medications in that bacteria have not developed resistance to it. After a long process, the drug has won FDA approval, which is hard to get. At the same time, the firm realizes that doctors and patients alike are often reluctant to be among the first to try out a new antibiotic drug. The company has received a large order from a country that it knows routinely allows antibiotics to be sold without a doctor's prescription. The company recognizes that selling antibiotics in this way has disadvantages, such as patients excessively buying/taking the drug without knowing whether they are allergic to it or whether the particular antibiotic is right for the particular infection. However, this way of selling would allow the company to recover the tremendous cost of developing the medication, as well as the need to show domestic markets that the drug is being used effectively. You have been asked to advise the pharmaceutical firm as to whether to fulfill the order. What would you want to ask and/or tell them?

A third study in collaboration with Anastasia Kreisel and Chak Haang Wong investigates what is sometimes called *cultural intelligence*. The concept sometimes used to characterize this ability to navigate cultural differences is *cultural intelligence*. "Cultural intelligence refers to an individual's capability to function effectively in situations characterized by cultural diversity (Earley & Ang, 2003; Ang & Van Dyne, 2008)."[1] Cultural intelligence is viewed by Ang and collaborators as having four components: metacognitive, cognitive, motivational and behavioral.[2] Cultural intelligence is a part of practical intelligence, which itself is related to adaptive intelligence.

Often, educators look at instruction and assessment as very different. However, those such as myself, who believe in a more dynamic assessment model, see instruction and assessment as closely interrelated.[3] One can use the same problems for instruction that one uses for assessment, and vice versa. Thus, the test problems, as described below in Table 6.3, also form a basis for developing adaptive intelligence. One can use them in class discussions to encourage students to think in adaptive ways in their everyday lives.

6.2   How Does One Teach for Adaptive Intelligence?

Adaptive intelligence is obviously not something people are born with. When people are born, they do not know yet the problems they or their family, neighbors, friends, and communities will face. Here is a set of principles for teaching for adaptive intelligence. These principles expand upon teaching for successful intelligence.[4] All of these principles have as their core the importance of understanding intelligence as it applies in the real world.

6.2.1   Relate What You Teach to Issues That Matter to Individuals and to the World

In our assessments, as shown in the previous tables and especially Table 6.1, we try to choose issues that matter to individuals and to the world. The world is at a crossroads, and we have to ask ourselves why we would be spending so much time teaching about things that, once school is over, students never will think about again. Interestingly, the humanities, which are in decline in colleges and universities with respect to both course-taking and majors, probably most clearly of all sets of disciplines deal with issues that matter not just now, but also over the centuries. But there are current pressing issues, as discussed in this book, and especially Chapters 1 and 3, that get nowhere near the attention they deserve in schools.

Table 6.3 *Cultural intelligence test*

You have just arrived on your current confidential assignment in a foreign country with which you are largely unfamiliar. Your assignment is to negotiate a memorandum of agreement between your organization and a large organization in the foreign country. You were told that you were expected to return to the US with a signed agreement. Before leaving the US, you were given very little information about your destination country, and most of that was basic information on the political system, imports and exports, and the general economy. You do not know the language and you know that relations with the country are tense. You realize that your room in the hotel in which you are staying has no access to the World Wide Web. Moreover, your cell phone does not work in this country.

1. As you get off the train, a well-dressed man comes to greet you. He obviously was waiting for you. You smile and hold out your hand. His face is serious and he raises his hand up in the air with his palm facing toward you. You do not know what his gesture means. What would you do?

2. You need some food, so you go to a restaurant in the train station. You cannot read and understand the menu. You want to order food, but you also want to convey your likes and dislikes to the waiter, who seems not to speak any English. Hoping for the best, you ask for "fish." He smiles and writes down nothing. What would you do?

3. After dinner, you begin to have a stomachache. You are worried that, somehow, you might have eaten something to which you are allergic or even have gotten food poisoning. You think you better go to a hospital. But none of the signs on the street are in English nor have a picture that looks like a hospital. What would you do?

4. You eventually arrive at a hospital. You quickly realize that no one there speaks English, or at least, lets on that they do. You explain your symptoms to a woman who appears to be checking you in. She points to your head and writes something down on a piece of paper. What would you do?

5. A few days later, you are now recovered, and you are walking down a street toward the American embassy. After a while, you realize both that you are lost and that people are giving you strange looks. The neighborhood you are in seems sketchy to you. A group of young, rough-looking men approaches you and one of the members of the group says something to you. He looks and sounds angry. What would you do?

6. You finally are ready to conduct your business. You go to the office to which you were told to report. You announce yourself to an assistant. He leads you through a door to what looks like a high-level administrator. She says "Hello" to you in perfect English. You explain why you are there. To your astonishment, she laughs in your face. What would you do?

7. You have important sensitive and confidential information to convey back to your superiors. When you go down to the receptionist, you are told that there is no problem. You can use a hotel computer, which is connected to the World Wide Web. Or, she says, you can use the phone in your room and she can connect you to wherever you need to be connected. She then leads you to a computer in the business center. What would you do?

8. That night, you go to a dinner in your honor at the organization with which you are negotiating. You sit down to eat, and, after a bunch of speeches, a waiter comes and puts down in front of you what might be the most disgusting food you ever have seen. It looks like it comprises wriggly worms that might even be alive. Whatever they are, they smell no better than they look. Others at your table begin eating the food with gusto. You feel slightly nauseated. You notice other people casually looking at you. What would you do?

9. Some of the people at the dinner speak English; others don't. After the meal, there is a lot of drinking as people socialize. You try your best to control your drinking. But you let a joke slip out about the leader of the country. You realize you should not have made the joke and that you would not have made it if you had not had a few too many drinks. You can tell by people's faces that you have committed a faux pas, maybe a serious one. What would you do?

10. One of the organizational executives with whom you are supposed to negotiate a deal hands you another a glass of the national drink, which is very strong. He smiles and obviously expects you to drink it. Other people from the organization are standing by, watching, and nodding approvingly. You know you already have drunk way too much. What would you do?

11. Two nights later, at an organizational party, you are introduced to a very attractive individual. It is pretty obvious to you that the introduction was not incidental but rather was planned. The individual shows great interest in you, perhaps, you think, too great an interest, given that you are strangers. The introducer smiles and puts a finger over his lips. He seems to you to be saying that "What happens at the party stays at the party," but you really can't be sure. What would you do?

12. You are negotiating with a high-level official in the organization with which you need to sign an agreement. No matter what you say, she seems to disagree. You feel that the negotiation is not going well and that it really doesn't matter what you say, she will disagree. You really want and need for this negotiation to succeed. What would you do?

13. During your last day on the assignment, the organization with which you are negotiating asks you to sign a form. They explain to you that the form is simply an acknowledgment that you negotiated with them. But the document is in the language of the country, which you do not know, and no one seems willing to explain it in any detail. You really need this negotiation to work out. What would you do?

14. On your last night on assignment, there is a knock on your hotel door. You open the door and two men, in what appear to be military or police uniforms, are standing facing you. They explain to you in perfect English that they need to search your room, as is standard procedure before someone leaves the country. No one ever told you about any standard room searches. You have highly confidential documents in the room but no contraband or anything that, to your knowledge, would cause legal problems. What would you do?

15. The next day you arrive at the airport for your flight home. You are waiting to go through a customs inspection, which you believe should be nonproblematic because you bought nothing during the trip that you are taking home. You then see a sign, which comes as a total surprise, that says that you are allowed to take only a small amount of the local currency out of the country. You have at least ten times the specified amount, as you

Table 6.3 (*cont.*)

had planned to change the currency when you got home. You now have passed all the money-changing booths. You really cannot easily afford to throw the money away. What would you do?

16. As you get ready to approach customs, a woman seems to come out of nowhere and approaches you. You think you recognize her from your trip. You can't quite place her but believe she was one of the employees of the organization with which you negotiated. She says that the organization forgot to give you a farewell gift and that she was instructed to give it to you before you departed. She has only now caught up with you. She shoves a gift box into your hands. It is packed in gift wrap with a gold ribbon but otherwise has no identifying marks. On the one hand, you don't want to insult the organization but, on the other hand, you have no idea what is in the box. What would you do?

There may be reasons why: Issues like global climate change may be seen as politically charged, or as beyond the grasp of many students, or as hopelessly complicated, or (God forbid!) as not having right and wrong answers, or as not fitting neatly into existing curricula (except, perhaps, in courses related to ecological issues). Yet, the issues with which this book has dealt are ones that future generations *must* confront, even though past generations have taken a pass in seriously dealing with many of them. When the issues are not dealt with, there are consequences, as shown by recent rioting in Chile, Hong Kong, Iraq, and other places. People want an opportunity to live their lives with dignity, respect, and at least a reasonable degree of comfort. Many governments have made these goals impossible to achieve for many of their citizens. Governments have to do better. But if we do not educate the next generation to deal with the serious problems the world is confronting, how are the youth of today going to deal with the problems of tomorrow?

Here is an example:

"We have been studying the importance of good nutrition. Sometimes, foods become contaminated with unwanted substances. For example, there is evidence that sometimes rice can be contaminated with arsenic, a deadly poison.[5] We will divide into small groups. Your task is to report back to us on how what we know about arsenic contamination should affect nutritional recommendations, if at all."

All of these tasks require some level of creative thinking, as described next.

6.2.2   Teach in Ways That Encourage Creative Thinking

Creative thinking involves creating, discovering, inventing, designing, imagining, and supposing. The multiple-choice and short-answer mentality that prevails in so many schools enlivens the testing industry but kills the minds of our youth. Whoever originated the idea that solving trivial multiple-choice problems would teach students to think in the divergent ways that current world problems require made a mistake. Real-world problems do not have multiple-choice answer options or even single correct answers. The problem is that we have raised generations of people to be leaders who do well solving these problems, so they continue to engage in, and to promote in their children, the kinds of thinking into which they have been socialized.[6]

We need to teach students to think creatively. For the most part, this means developing in the students a creative attitude toward their work and their live.[7] These attitudes include, among others:

- *Willingness to defy the crowd* – the realization that creative people go their own way and, by the nature of their originality, inevitably generate opposition.
- *Willingness to defy oneself* – the realization that sometimes one has to let go of one's past beliefs and opinions and move on, even if it is uncomfortable.
- *Willingness to defy the Zeitgeist* – the realization that one may have to let go of unconscious biases that almost everyone shares (in my view, such as the view that intelligence is what IQ tests test; many people in my field just accept it and the evidence for it as sufficient, end of story, period).
- *Willingness to redefine problems* – the realization that often the way problems are framed for us is wrong and that it is up to us to frame the problems properly. For example, framing the concept of intelligence as about the ability to have a prestigious title, or to make a lot of money, or to work in a prestigious company, misses the point that one could do all of those things while moving the world downhill. Such anachronistic framing provides a platform to people who are seeking their own gain by covertly undermining humanity for their personal gain.
- *Willingness to persuade others of one's creative ideas* – the realization that, because one is defying the crowd, many others will be reluctant to accept what one suggests and will oppose one's efforts.
- *Willingness to surmount obstacles* – resilience in the face of sometimes severe critiques is a necessity for creative people. They will be

continually attacked and if they cannot handle the attacks, almost certainly they either will conform or find something else to do.

- *Self-efficacy* – to be creative, one has to believe in one's ability to get done the job one has set out for oneself. There almost always will be times when others will not believe in one; if one loses confidence in oneself, then there is no hope of continuing to do creative work.
- *Realization that knowledge can hurt creativity as well as help it* – knowledge can both help and hurt creativity. It can help because to go beyond past work, one has to know what the past work is. It can hurt because knowledge can lead to entrenchment – one becomes so used to seeing things in a certain way that one no longer can see them in any other way. That is what has happened in the field of intelligence.
- *Intellectual humility* – people who believe they have found "the answer" to a problem are at risk of stopping being creative, because they fail to realize that once one thinks one has a final answer, one has little or no incentive to continue to pursue a problem – one already has solved it, or so one thinks.
- *Willingness to take risks* – creativity always involves intellectual risk-taking. One has to be willing to try out new things and ideas, realizing they may fail. There can be no creativity without prior failure, or at least the distinct possibility of it.

Here is an example emphasizing creative thinking:

> "We have been studying various kinds of ocean life. Water pollution is killing off ocean life and threatens human life as well. In your small groups, figure out creative ways to reduce water pollution. What could we do better than we are doing now and how could we do it in a feasible way? Report back to the class. You will need to get a handle first on what the problem is and what has been done to address the problem."

Adaptively intelligent thinking requires divergence – thinking in new ways. But it also is important to use analytical thinking to ensure that the ideas are not only novel, but also conceptually and, where relevant, logically sound.

6.2.3   Teach in Ways That Encourage Analytical Thinking

Analytical thinking involves analyzing, evaluating, critiquing, comparing and contrasting, and judging. Once, people thought they could trust others to do their analytical thinking for them. Essentially, "critical thinking" could be outsourced to newspaper editors and television reports. When I was young, television viewers had three major choices of newscasters from whom they could hear the early-evening news: Walter Cronkite on CBS, Chet Huntley and David Brinkley on NBC, and Howard K. Smith on ABC. The newscasters had different styles and different emphases, but the content they conveyed was pretty much the same. One came away knowing, or thinking one was knowing, what was going on. The reports may not always have been accurate but they were consistent. Today, people who watched no news at all answered 1.22 questions correctly about domestic affairs and 1.28 questions about international affairs. Unsurprisingly, many news watchers did better. For example, those who listened to news on NPR (National Public Radio) answered, on average, 1.51 domestic questions and 1.97 international questions. At the bottom of the list were Fox News watchers: They answered correctly 1.04 domestic questions and 1.08 international questions.[8] That is, Fox News watchers knew less about what was going on in their country and in the world than those who watched no news! That is quite an extraordinary, if negative, accomplishment, reminiscent of what one might expect in the Soviet Union of old. But the results for MSNBC News, which some would regard as a left-wing counterpart to Fox News, were definitely better but not a whole lot better. The average MSNBC watcher answered 1.26 domestic questions correctly and 1.23 international questions correctly. Thus, they did slightly better than the non-watchers on the domestic questions but slightly worse on the international questions.

These results remind us how, in the absence of serious critical thinking, the future of any democracy is in jeopardy. If people merely believe whatever propaganda they are handed, what hope is there for citizens to make informed, rational choices in elections?

The examples of lack of critical thinking are legion. The large anti-vaxxer movement, mentioned earlier in Chapter 1, seems immune to evidence, but seems satisfied to rely on the refuted and retracted studies of the discredited and disgraced ex-physician Andrew Wakefield, who continues to peddle anti-vaxxer hype.

Sometimes, critical thinking is difficult or impossible for lack of knowledge. In the lead-up to the War in Iraq, Colin Powell, Secretary of State under George W. Bush, gave an address to the United Nations in February of 2003 in which Powell set out to prove that the Iraqis harbored weapons of mass destruction. The whole talk proved to be based on data that charitably could be called "flimsy."[9] The purpose of the talk was to gin up support for the War in Iraq, which it did. Unfortunately, the support was based on false information. False information, of course, is not limited to Republicans, as many of us remember from former President Bill

Clinton's assurance that "I did not have sexual relations with that woman, Miss Lewinsky" (*Washington Post*, 2018).[10]

Here is an example emphasizing analytical thinking:

> "We have been studying social mobility in our country. Research suggests that in the last several decades, social mobility in our country and in many other economically developed countries has decreased. As a result, people, on average, are less able to rise economically than was true in the past. How does one even measure social mobility? How much has social mobility decreased? What are some of the causes of this decrease in social mobility and how have they brought us to where we are today?"

Analytical thinking is important in life, but at some point, it needs to be put into practice. This is where practical thinking comes in.

6.2.4 Teach in Ways That Emphasize Practical Thinking

Practical thinking is the application of creative and analytical thinking to everyday, contextually rich situations that an individual is likely to encounter in his or her life, either at present or in the near future. Practical thinking involves putting ideas into practice, implementing ideas, contextualizing ideas, using ideas, and persuading people of ideas.

The view of *g* (general intelligence) theory is that practical intelligence is merely general intelligence put into practice – that practical intelligence is nothing different from general intelligence. Our evidence, provided in Chapter 4, is that practical intelligence is largely distinct from general intelligence – that someone could be strong in abstract analytical thinking but not in practical thinking, and vice versa. Teaching for practical thinking in schools could help all students of any level of general intelligence better apply their thinking skills to everyday life.

Students often become bored in school. They cannot see any connection between what they are learning in the classroom and what they need to know to flourish in their everyday lives. In our own work, we have striven to make these connections.

For example, I teach a course on leadership. Part of the course involves learning about psychological and other theories of leadership, because leaders ought to understand what leadership is and how, at least in theory, it is best achieved. But without connections to real-world leadership, the lessons would fall flat. I therefore purposefully build into the course activities to strengthen the connection.

1 *Drawing on my own past practical experiences.* I have held a number of
somewhat major leadership positions in my career – as a university
dean, provost, and (briefly) president; as president of the American
Psychological Association and also four of its divisions; as president of
the Federation of Associations in Brain and Behavioral Sciences; and as
treasurer of the Association of American Colleges and Universities.
Although these positions were all somewhat academic, the politics were
real – sometimes, I felt, all too real. I relate concepts from the course to
these leadership experiences so students can see how what they learn in
the classroom has applied in my life and could apply in theirs.

2 *Outside speakers' series.* I bring in leaders from many different pursuits
in life – business, nonprofits, arts, sciences, and beyond. In the past,
I've tried to bring in one outside leader per week. The leaders each
speak for fifteen minutes about their leadership experience – what they
have done well, what they have not done so well and how they might
have done it better, what they have found to be major ethical or
practical challenges, how they got to the leadership position.
Students then ask questions for forty-five minutes. Students are
encouraged to contact the leaders by email beyond the class, and
some have gone on to internships. Students have identified the outside
talks as the best part of the course (and that, despite my super-
outstanding teaching!). The students see how the concepts in the
course can be applied in diverse kinds of leadership.

3 *Analysis of real-world leaders.* Students work in small groups to prepare
and then give presentations to the class on the careers of well-known
leaders in the world. The only constraint is that the leaders be alive (so
that students can see that the analysis applies to the present day, not just
to past days). Students talk about the leaders' backgrounds, their
accomplishments, their strengths and weaknesses as leaders, what
they could and should have done better.

4 *Analysis of one's own leadership or that of a community leader whom they
interview.* Students have a choice of either applying principles of the
course to their own leadership or to the leadership of a leader they
choose to interview. The idea is for them individually to apply the
course concepts to their own leadership or to that of someone whose
leadership they analyze in-depth.

5 *Group analysis of contemporary leadership challenges.* Almost
every day, at least in the last several years, the media portray major
leadership challenges faced by leaders in the past twenty-four hours.
I use the reports of major media – *CNN*, the *New York Times*, the

Washington Post, and others – to describe contemporary leadership challenges and ask students how they think the leaders should address them.

Here is an example emphasizing practical thinking:

> "The rain forest in the Amazon is burning up at an increasing and record rate. For example, there have been 74,000 fires this year, compared with 40,000 at this time last year. Why is the forest burning at a record rate – what are the reasons? What are practical solutions that the government might impose to deal with the problem? What are the obstacles to implementing these solutions? Is it even important to deal with the problem? Why or why not?"

Ideas that are practical are not necessarily wise. For example, dictators and would-be dictators have practically useful ways of rigging elections. Does anyone seriously think Vladimir Putin will ever lose an "election"? Adaptively intelligent thinking also needs to be wise.

6.2.5 Teach in Ways That Emphasize Wise Thinking

Wisdom, as discussed previously, involves the application of one's creative, analytical, and practical skills as well as one's knowledge to the common good, by balancing one's own, with others', and with larger interests, over the long as well as the short term, through the infusion of positive ethical values. If there ever has been a time in human history when wisdom has been important, this is it. The basic idea is simply to reflect upon how what one has been learning can be turned toward achieving a common good that transcends just one's own interests and the interests of those one perceives as belonging to one's in-groups.

Here is an example emphasizing wise thinking:

> "Vora and Tamlin, two countries in the Far North, are having a serious clash. The Taron River flows in the direction from Vora to Tamlin. Tamlin claims that Vora is diverting more than its fair share of the water from the river. It is getting ready to go to war over this precious water resource. What should the two countries do?"

Participants taking a wisdom assessment can then present a solution to the problem of distributing water between Vora and Tamlin. Consider an example of a possible solution:

> "Vora and Tamlin need outside help to resolve their difference regarding the river water. They should each appoint a commission of people who are water experts from their own country. This commission should be

responsible for choosing top experts to form a five-person panel. One expert should be from Vora, one from Tamlin, and three from outside with no allegiance to either country. Vora and Tamlin should agree in advance to abide by their recommendation. The deliberations of the panel should be secret, and the panel should be provided with any resources they need to make a decision. They should propose a solution and vote on it, with a majority decision accepted as their final solution to the problem. There should be no right of appeal of their decision."

Wisdom-based problems such as this one have no one "correct" answer. There are many possible answers, some of which would show wise reasoning, at least in accord with my balance theory of wisdom, through which one balances all interests in search of a common good. In this case, the essay seems to represent wise use of creative, analytical, and practical reasoning. First, the two countries decide jointly to resolve their difference through reasoned negotiation. Second, the decision will be made by a third party (the commission). Third, the commission will consist of representatives of both Vora and Tamlin and will also have representatives from outside the countries who have no personal stake in the decision. Fourth, the countries agree in advance to abide by the recommendations of the commission, so that the commission is not just a "showpiece" whose recommendations will be thrown out when, most likely, neither country is entirely satisfied with the outcome of the commission's deliberations. Fifth, the deliberations are secret so that public or private pressure is not applied when the negotiations do not seem to be going the way some parties would like. Sixth, the final decision is made by a majority vote of the commission members. Finally, the decision is final with no right of appeal so that action is not held up indefinitely while there is one appeal after another.

There are, without doubt, other decision-making processes that would have been as wise or wiser. Again, there is no one "right" way to decide. But the decision process shows how two parties can reach a decision without entering into a long-term conflict or going to war. Some years ago, my colleagues and I did a series of studies on styles of conflict resolution – on which the problem above is based – and found that the better resolvers of difficult conflicts were ones as in this example – they sought to mitigate and reasonably resolve their conflicts rather than resorting to physical, economic, social, or other pressures.[11]

Every wisdom-based problem has different parameters, and there is no magic formula that will enable one to solve them. But the principles of the balance theory provide guidelines for the formal properties of wise solutions, regardless of the particulars of any given problem. The problems of the real world look much more like the Vora/Tamlin problem than they do like problems on standardized tests. They also require, for their solution, skills that include but go well beyond general intelligence. If, in schools, we only emphasize the academic skills that lead to success on standardized tests, where are young people supposed to acquire the skills they need to solve problems in the real world? They need to acquire these real-world skills, not only as individuals, but to work together effectively in groups.

6.2.6 Emphasize Small-Group Problem-Solving

Most serious problem-solving in the world is done in small groups. Students therefore need to learn to collaborate in their problem-solving and decision-making. Such group problem-solving is often a challenge for students, especially given that they are used to working individually and to getting credit for individual work. Sometimes, teacher-intervention is needed to make small-group problem-solving work. Nevertheless, students need to learn how to do it because this will be the way they solve problems for most of their lives – at work, in personal relationships, and in the variety of kinds of endeavors in which they engage.

6.2.7 To the Extent Possible, Let Students Recognize and Define Their Own Problems

Teachers are used to giving students problems and asking the students to solve them. But in life, there often is no one to say exactly what the problem is or exactly how it should be solved. Students are told what the problem is and sometimes graded not only on whether they provide a correct answer, but also on the basis of whether they solve the problem they were told to solve. This practice is nonoptimal. Students need to figure out problems for themselves and then need to find their own ways of solving those problems. Teachers should provide guidance, not fixed protocols, for how things should get done.

6.3   Conclusion

People are not born with adaptive intelligence; they develop it over the course of their lifetime. Teachers could do a lot to help them develop adaptive intelligence. The greatest obstacle is that standardized tests do not generally test for adaptive intelligence. There is one question educators therefore need to answer. Which is more important – hanging on to instruction and assessment that often reflects a world long gone by or adopting new methods to face contemporary challenges? It is time for them to choose the latter. If they do not, eventually, there will be no teachers and no students to teach. So, the choice is a stark one and one we need to face now, not at some time we keep putting off until it is too late.

Notes

1. Ang, S., Ng, K. Y., & Rockstuhl, T. (in press). Cultural intelligence. In R. J. Sternberg (Ed.), *Cambridge handbook of intelligence* (2nd ed.). New York: Cambridge University Press.
2. Ang, S., Van Dyne, L., Koh, C. et al. (2007). Cultural intelligence: Its measurement and effects on cultural judgment and decision making, *Management and Organization Review*, 3(3), 335–71; Ang, S., & Van Dyne, L. (2008). Conceptualization of cultural intelligence: Definition, distinctiveness, and nomological network. In S. Ang, & L. Van Dyne (Eds.), *Handbook of cultural intelligence* (pp. 3–15). New York: M.E. Sharpe; Ang, S., Van Dyne, L., & Tan, M. L. (2011). Cultural intelligence. In R. J. Sternberg, & S. B. Kaufman (Eds.), *Cambridge handbook of intelligence* (pp. 582–602). New York: Cambridge University Press.
3. Sternberg, R. J., & Grigorenko, E. L. (2002). *Dynamic testing*. New York: Cambridge University Press.
4. Sternberg, R. J. (2002). Raising the achievement of all students: Teaching for successful intelligence. *Educational Psychology Review*, 14, 383–93; Sternberg, R. J., & Grigorenko, E. L. (2007). *Teaching for successful intelligence* (2nd ed.). Thousand Oaks, CA: Corwin Press; Sternberg, R. J., Jarvin, L., & Grigorenko, E. L. (2009). *Teaching for wisdom, intelligence, creativity, and success*. Thousand Oaks, CA: Corwin.
5. Food and Drug Administration. (2016). Arsenic in rice and rice products: Risk assessment report. *FDA*, March. https://bit.ly/31q5l9B
6. Sternberg, R. J. (2016). *What universities can be: A new model for preparing students for active concerned citizenship and ethical leadership*. Ithaca, NY: Cornell University Press; Sternberg, R. J. (2019). Creativity is not enough: The WICS model of leadership. In B. Mainemelis, Epitropaki, O., & Kark, R. (Eds.), *Creative leadership: Contexts and prospects* (pp. 139–55). New York: Routledge.
7. Sternberg, R. J. (2010). Teaching for creativity. In R. A. Beghetto, & J. C. Kaufman (Eds.), *Nurturing creativity in the classroom* (pp. 394–414). New York: Cambridge University Press; Sternberg, R. J. (2015). Teaching for creativity: The sounds of silence. *Psychology of Aesthetics, Creativity, and the Arts*, 9(2), 115–17; Sternberg, R. J. (2018). A triangular theory of creativity. *Psychology of Aesthetics, Creativity, and the Arts*, 12, 50–67.
8. Kelley, M. B. (2012). Study: Watching only Fox News makes you less informed than watching no news at all. *Business Insider*, May 22. https://bit.ly/3ijbhrQ
9. Breslow, J. M. (2016). Colin Powell: U.N. speech "was a great intelligence failure." *Frontline*, May 17. https://to.pbs.org/30JRQ5i

10. Washington Post (2018). "I did not have sexual relations with that woman, Miss Lewinsky." *Washington Post*, January 25. https://wapo.st/3oGQPLm
11. Sternberg, R. J., & Soriano, L. J. (1984). Styles of conflict resolution. *Journal of Personality and Social Psychology*, 47, 115–26; Sternberg, R. J., & Dobson, D. M. (1987). Resolving interpersonal conflicts: An analysis of stylistic consistency. *Journal of Personality and Social Psychology*, 52, 794–812.

CHAPTER 7

Why Do People Persist in Species-Suicidal Beliefs and Practices and What's to Be Done?

Two-thirds of smokers will die early from smoking-related illness.[1] Tobacco smoke has been linked to at least thirteen different types of cancers. Smoking a half-pack a day doubles one's risk of death and smoking a pack a day quadruples it. Two-thirds of smokers will die of smoking-related causes.[2] A close relative of mine, anytime she sees someone smoking, does not hesitate to point out how stupid they are. Really, how could anyone be stupid enough to engage in behavior that is more likely than not to kill them, probably in what will prove to be a slow and painful death? Although fewer and fewer people smoke, at least in the United States, one in five deaths is smoking-related.

Some smokers have switched to vaping. Vaping is a new habit, with a very brief history. Already, though, as of when I am writing these words, almost 2,000 serious cases of illness have been linked to vaping, with thirty-seven deaths.[3] That is impressive for a habit that hardly existed a couple of years ago. Even smoking has not been linked to such a rapid decline in health.

Of course, there are plenty of other habits that kill people – excessive drinking, hard-drug use, drag racing in the streets, and on and on. There are always people who believe that, whereas other people will fall victims to the ills of their bad habits, they will not. The last time I heard about this – "My husband finally died of COPD; he believed it wouldn't happen to him" – was only a few weeks ago. The husband had been a heavy smoker until it was too late.

Of course, there was a time when people did not realize just how bad smoking was, or overeating, for that matter. Now they do: People still smoke, overeat, over-drink, and whatever. And many of them die as a result of their maladaptive habits. But what if there were an extremely bad habit that was not limited to just a minority but that was extremely highly prevalent, even in the face of overwhelming evidence of where it was leading?

As I am writing, wildfires are engulfing California, droughts are prevalent in many parts of the world, including much of Australia and major parts of the United States. Glaciers are continuing to break up in the arctic and coastlines are disappearing. As I am reading copyediting on this book, COVID-19 is ravaging the United States and many other countries. We know that these conditions are partly, probably largely, due to human behavior. The virus can be stopped or at least greatly slowed down by straightforward health measures – masks, avoiding crowds, social distancing, handwashing. But what is the most common human solution, even for many immediately pressing problems? Do nothing or, as in the case of the President of the United States, do what you can to make thing worse. Say that the virus will disappear on its own, and watch as it does anything but that.

However much IQs may have risen in the twentieth century, adaptive intelligence today is at a low level, at least among the older generation. Fortunately, many of the younger generation seem to have gotten the message that earlier generations have betrayed them, leaving them a world that will become increasingly hostile to human habitation. Yet we continue, through our system of education, to value students who, whatever their test scores and grades, are willing to leave for their children a world even more degraded than the one the previous generations left them. What school or university values students on the basis of the positive, meaningful, and potentially enduring change they may make to the world?[4]

When I was a mentee of my professor, Endel Tulving, and I told him of my hope to change the way instruction and assessment are done, his laconic answer was simply that "It is extremely hard to effect change." He was right.

In order to address this question, I recently did an informal, but I think, informative survey of elementary-school reading primers from contemporary times (the early twenty-first century), modern times (the mid-twentieth century), and early modern times (the early twentieth century).[5] I chose basal reading texts at the second-grade level. The children using the books would be roughly seven to eight years old, a time when schools might start thinking about teaching wisdom, ethical behavior, good citizenship, civic duty, and related topics. At the time I did the survey, less than a year ago, my triplets – Samuel, Brittany, and Melody – were in second grade. I was curious as to what they were learning about civic behavior and related topics, compared with what I had learned in the mid-1950s, when I was in second grade. In particular, I looked for lessons that were somehow wisdom-based. I defined a lesson as at least partially wisdom-based if it would help students develop positive ethical values or related values. These would be the kinds of values that ultimately could be used to resolve the kinds of intrapersonal (self-related), interpersonal (other-related), and extrapersonal (world-related) problems that all people face during the course of their lives.[6] The result was simple: There was a steep, monotone decrease in the absolute and the relative proportion of material devoted to wisdom-related content as the years went by. By contemporary times, wisdom-related content was almost gone, replaced by increasingly abstract, academic content relating only minimally to students' current citizenship, civic, and related human responsibilities.

I view the decreasing wisdom-related content in reading primers as at least partially causal of the low levels of the wisdom aspect of adaptive intelligence that we see in the world today for children brought up with contemporary texts. But I believe the problem is more systemic, and that the content of the textbooks as well as of tests is merely symptomatic of a larger problem. I have discussed some of these problems elsewhere,[7] and others I am discussing here for the first time.

7.1   Why Extremely Suboptimal Testing Practices Continue to Exist

Why, at this point in the evolution of teaching and testing, are we still doing what we did a century ago when we assess students' abilities and achievements? One reason pertains to preservation of the existence of the extant social order.

7.1.1   Preservation of the Social Order

In the beginning, standardized testing was about creating a new merito-cratic social order.[8] But as with any new system, those in power often look to mold it to serve their purposes, and this particular system of assessing merit did not need a lot of molding. It benefits now, as it has in the past, those students who go to better schools. It further benefits those whose parents can afford to send them for test preparation (in school or outside) and whose parents are highly educated and thus can transmit to them the skills and values that are embedded in doing well on standardized tests (as opposed to, for example, "Why should I care since I don't have the money for a competitive college anyway?"). But "standardized tests are a very poor measurement of human worth and potential," a point made, refreshingly, by Andrew Yang, a primary candidate for the 2020 election for President of the United States.[9]

Testing launders socioeconomic status (SES) but does not do a thorough job, in that research repeatedly has shown a substantial although certainly not perfect correlation between test scores and SES.[10] That correlation is not going to go away so long as educational systems give more opportunities to some than to others. That is to say, the difference is not going to go away.

What is to be done? There is a partial solution. Use tests that are at least as valid as those now in use but that at the same time reduce rather than increase inequalities. We have designed such tests, both for measuring aptitudes and for measuring achievements.[11] These tests assess creative as well as analytical, practical, and in some cases, wisdom-based skills. They increase prediction of various criteria while reducing the effects of ethnic-group differences and the socioeconomic differences that accompany them. But for reasons discussed below, society has been slow to adopt tests that would serve it and its members better. Part of the reason is that tests offer a false sense of accountability.

7.1.2   Pseudo-Accountability

The field of education is enchanted, or perhaps the word is "obsessed," with accountability.[12] The success of the standardized-testing movement is due, in large part, to the strident clarion calls for accountability. And really, who could be against accountability? We want doctors to be accountable for the services they provide to their patients. Certainly, we do not want quacks with inadequate medical training prescribing placebos or even harmful medicines that will make a medical condition worse. Similarly, we want accountability from lawyers (who wants a lawyer who does not even try to win a case?), accountants (who wants to hear from the tax services that they really owe a whole lot more money?), and clergymen entrusted with our youth (who wants children to be abused by clergymen or anyone else?). Why would we not want accountability from teachers if we want it from all other professionals?

Of course, schools and the teachers in them should be accountable. I would not question that assertion and do not know anyone who would. The problem is not with accountability, per se, but rather with what is meant by accountability. Are narrow tests of academic achievements that measure factual recall and, at best, some analysis of those facts, adequate measures of accountability? From the standpoint of the theory of adaptive intelligence, they obviously are not. If the tests are truly to assess account-ability, they need to assess not only memory for factual knowledge and analytical skills but also creative, practical, and wisdom-based knowledge and skills. That they measure none of these speaks to why the graduates who excel on these tests and thus become eligible to be leaders of our countries have proven, in so many cases, to be such an unmitigated disaster. How many politicians – especially ones who appeal to ignorance and the worst aspects of human nature, such as racism, xenophobia, and sexism – have shown any meaningful critical thinking, creativity, common sense, or wisdom whatsoever? Not a whole lot, despite many having degrees from highly prestigious schools and universities. It is beyond me why the public does not realize the failure is not just in the individuals but in the individuals that, in the name of accountability, have failed these individuals and society as a whole.

What is to be done? I believe the answer is straightforward. Accountability is good; narrow accountability is not. Accountability should be broadened to include not only recollection of facts and basic analysis of ideas but also creative, practical, and wisdom-based utilization of what one has learned. In other words, accountability should be about not just whether a student has learned material but also about whether the student can use the material beyond school and in life. I have written in various places about how educators can teach for and evaluate students for these broader skills.[13] In a nutshell, teaching and assessing for analytical skills involves questions that engage analyzing, critiquing, judging, comparing and contrasting, and evaluating. Teaching and assessing for creative skills involve questions that engage creating, discovering, inventing, imagining, designing, and suppos-ing. Teaching and assessing for practical skills involve questions that engage applying, putting into practice, using, implementing, and persuading. Finally, teaching and assessing for wisdom-based skills involve questions that engage seeking a common good; by balancing one's own, others', and larger interests; over the long as well as the short term; through the infusion of positive ethical values. Measuring these skills is complex. It cannot be done in ways that are pseudo-quantitative, as is much of psychological and educational measurement today.

7.1.3   Pseudo-Quantitative Precision

Pseudo-quantitative precision refers to our tendency to put faith in numbers far beyond the faith those numbers deserve. Psychologists, with their claims of understanding something about human nature, should know better, but they sometimes are among the worst. For example, some of them have apotheosized IQ and related constructs.

IQ predicts a lot of things, but it predicts them no better now than it did a century ago. Every other field advances – medical research, physical research, biological research – yet psychometric research remains with its morbid fascination fixated upon a construct that has scarcely evolved in well over a century. If that is not a sorry testament to a science, I do not know what is.

There are always many papers to be written with new explanations of *g* and new phenomena that *g* predicts, but the lack of theoretical innovation in the field has been breathtaking. The work is still in the stage of an expansion upon a theory first proposed in 1904 that never worked all so well and still does not.[14] In 1904, syphilis was treated with mercury. Imagine if, in medicine, researchers and practitioners were as self-satisfied as they seem to be in the field of intelligence and we were still using ideas from the beginning of the twentieth century to treat medical problems. Of course, one could argue that, in 1904, Charles Spearman discovered some kind of inherent "truth" with his discovery of *g*. But of course, scientists could have said the same about fire, air, water, and earth as the basic elements of which everything once was believed to be composed. Science is never "done" – there is always much more to be learned.

The problem with numbers is that they give a feeling of precision and confidence, even if their validity is meager or nonexistent. In the case of testing, the result is truly frightening. Whether a prisoner who has been convicted of a capital crime is put to death may depend on whether his intelligence, as measured by IQ, falls above or below an IQ of seventy (the borderline for "intellectual deficiency"). Such numbers never meant much but now mean even less, given that we have become aware of the Flynn effect, according to which IQs in the twentieth century increased roughly thirty points.[15] So, what norms should a courtroom even use to assess the IQ of the offender? The current norms? The norms that were current when the offender was growing up – and if then, at what stage of growing up? And now that IQs are decreasing again in some places, how do we factor in that IQs are going down in some places, up in others, and in still others, remaining relatively flat? Should we really be making literally "life-or-death" decisions on the basis of tests that in turn depend on numbers that do not even have stable meanings?

In the same way, IQs have been used as a primary, sometimes sole basis for identification of children as gifted, really since the times of Lewis Terman.[16] Again, we are using century-old technology to solve a current problem. Is being gifted even the same thing today it was in 1925? Is it the same in a preliterate society as in a literate one, and similarly, in a particular Eastern culture as in a particular Western culture? Does IQ tell us who will be technologically literate but who also will show creativity, common sense, and wisdom? Does it tell us who will be able to work effectively in a team to solve the kinds of pressing problems the world faces today – climate change, poverty, nuclear weapons, pollution, and so forth?

In the days of Alfred Binet – the first decades of the twentieth century – as today, it made sense to have a test that would distinguish those who would have learning difficulties from those who would adjust normally to school. But that was the extent of the problem Binet's test was invented to solve. Because people were so entranced with the precise-sounding numbers of the tests, they extended the use of the tests far beyond the intentions for which the tests were created.

The pseudo-quantitative precision fallacy extends way beyond just the testing industry. The credit banks and other agencies are willing to extend to consumers is determined in large part by credit ratings that are, at best, on a par with IQ tests. My daughter, Sara Sternberg Greene, is a law professor who studies poverty law. Both of us were impressed with the extent to which credit ratings accomplish, for adults, the same societally tainted task that standardized tests accomplish for younger people: They ensure that those who come into the world with few resources will stay with few resources. Moreover, once one is locked into a low credit rating, it is hard to get out of it, because the credit rating (like the low SAT, or ACT, or other test scores) prevents one from attaining the kind of financial support one might need to bootstrap one's way out of financial duress.

In academia, my field, I have noticed that members of tenure and promotion committees seem less likely to read candidates' work than in the past, because they so much have they come to rely on quantitative indices of citations in the professional literature. Yet, these indices are confounded by many factors, such as whether the field in which one works has a lot of people or few people and whether the work one is doing fits in well with what others are doing or is, God forbid, highly creative and outside mainstream paradigms, often leading to lower rates of citation.

What is to be done? The first thing is for experts to put quantitative indices into perspective and to realize that they are limited in what they can tell us. That applies to all quantitative indices, including my own. Experts should stop embarrassing themselves by pretending that the numbers have some kind of magic associated with them. The second thing is to teach laypersons to think critically, in this case, more critically than experts have, about the limitations of the quantitative indices we use to assess people. In particular, people need to learn about construct validity (the extent to which a test measures what it is supposed to measure) and reliability (the extent to which a test measures whatever it measures consistently). Third, we need tests that, at least, measure constructs more broadly than do our current tests. Finally, if we use tests, we need valid ways to extend their social mission. Our society has not done that. The US College Board attempted to do so by introducing, in the spring of 2019, a kind of "adversity index" that would spot test-takers for whom the tests would present challenges beyond those presented for other students. But the Board did such a spectacularly bad job of operationalizing the index that it had to embarrass itself within just a few months by publicly withdrawing its plans to use the index. To its credit, it realized just how awful its own plan was, which is more than can be said for what many of the companies in the US and elsewhere do. The adversity index was yet another attempt to appear to be objective about things that do not easily lend themselves to traditional notions of objectivity.

7.1.3 Pseudo-Objectivity

A common selling point of standardized testing, at least as it is done in the United States, is that it is "objective." For most tests, the large majority of items, if not all the items, have "right" and "wrong" answers.

There are multiple problems with the mindset that so-called "objective tests" are better tests. First, the use of multiple-choice tests squashes creativity. We have found in our research that multiple-choice and related short-answer tests are a really bad way of measuring creativity, and as well, common sense and wisdom.[17]

Second, even the analytical skills measured by multiple-choice tests are very limited. We have found, for example, that when we wanted to measure scientific reasoning, making our tests multiple-choice increased the correlation of the tests with various standardized tests but reduced the effectiveness of the tests as measures of scientific reasoning.[18] In other words, one gained the appearance of "objectivity" at the expense of measuring the construct of interest (scientific reasoning). Meaningful skills typically do not easily lend themselves to multiple-choice.

Third, the tests send students a terrible message – namely, that serious problems have objectively "right" and "wrong" answers. No wonder that so many of today's leaders are so incompetent at solving real-world problems.

And no wonder they so often oversimplify the problems and seek easy solutions that do not exist.

Fourth, even so-called objective problems are decontextualized. In order to make the problems fit in a testing session, one is asked to make decisions that can be made fairly quickly. Most real-life decisions of any consequence cannot be made in a matter of seconds, or at most, a few minutes. And the decisions have to take into account the context in which they occur. For example, whether taxes should be raised or lowered depends on a whole host of economic conditions. Similarly, who decides on serious financial investments in a few minutes? And what might work for healthcare in one country might not work in another country.

Fifth, the supposed objectivity of the tests hides the fact that they may be appropriate for some cultural groups but not for others. There is no such thing as a culture-free or even a culture-fair test. All tests are culturally loaded.[19] Even what we think is worth testing as part of intelligence or achievement is culturally loaded. There is no test that is objective, or truly fair, for every group that might take it.

What can be done? Throw away the illusion that standardized tests are objective. Rather, realize that they convey the illusion of objectivity but in solving some problems, such as the appearance of objectivity, the tests create other problems, such as the attainment of true objectivity. In everyday life, assessments of achievements of various kinds are subjective. What is a great work of art? A great work of literature? A major scientific contribution? A compelling musical composition or performance? No contribution of any importance lends itself to so-called "objective assessment." Even a contribution in business, which might be evaluated by whether it increases the bottom line of the business, may be compromised if it does so at the expense of people's health and well-being. There are always multiple ways in which contributions can be assessed, none of which is perfect and none of which is truly objective. The solution is not to attain some kind of objectivity but rather to acknowledge that such a standard does not exist. But we keep seeking a false sense of objectivity, because we are so entrenched in our thinking that the appearance of objectivity is what creates a good test.

7.1.4   Entrenchment

Schools, colleges, and universities get used to doing things in a certain way and then they have difficulty changing. When they do change, it often is for reasons that have nothing to do with providing a better education and much to do with political pressure. For example, the *No Child Left Behind* and *Race to the Top* efforts were excellent examples of ill-conceived programs initiated for political reasons that had little to do with providing a first-rate education to the students who were supposed to be served. *No Child Left Behind* resulted in massive spending supposed to be directed toward students in need, but the spending was not targeted toward interventions proven to work and left behind bright students whose needs may have been as great as or greater than those of the children who were supposedly served. *Race to the Top* was an ill-conceived effort by a failed former superintendent of schools whose ideas almost always seemed to revolve around test scores. Programs such as these catered to political interests of the times without genuinely serving students in need. It is sad that much progress has been made on understanding the psychology and sociology of learning but almost none of this understanding translates into practice. In current times, the COVID-19 pandemic may have done more to change standardized-testing practices than any well thought through effort on the part of schools to improve the ways they assess their students.

I was a Special Assistant to the Dean of Undergraduate Admissions at Yale after I graduated from college in 1972. What has changed in college admissions since then? First, the system of admissions is now largely automated rather than being paper-based. That, however, is a cosmetic change. Second, many colleges rely on the Common Application, or a similar shared application, rather than just on their own individual applications, saving time and money for applicants but also greatly increasing the number of schools to which students apply and to which they pay application fees. But in terms of innovation in what schools are actually looking for, there has been hardly any change at all.

I am partial to my own theory of adaptive intelligence as a basis for admission. But there are other theories, such as Howard Gardner's and David Perkins's that could be used in admissions.[20] The theories, educational practices, and technology exist to change. Only the will is absent, in large part because of entrenchment. Entrenchment is understandable because of a system whereby teachers learn a certain way, then are taught to teach in that way, and then starting teaching in that way. To break the cycle, education schools need to get involved, but often, unfortunately, they are stuck in the past as well.

Related to entrenchment is intellectual laziness – people who stick with the existing ways because they do not want to be bothered to think in new ways. Sometimes, the intellectual laziness is simply lack of desire to think at all about what one is doing. Often, however, especially in the admissions business, the difficulty people encounter is in thinking creatively when they are pressed for time. Most admissions offices, at any level of schooling, are extremely busy places. There often are more applications to handle than there are admissions officers who can process them comfortably. Admissions officers frequently have to travel to market their schools and, when they are at home, they may be busy conducting interviews. So, if they are intellectually lazy in thinking about why they are doing what they are doing, it may be because they just do not want to devote time that they feel they do not have to the task of asking why they are doing what they are doing in the first place. For the most part, their job is simply to find people like themselves.

7.1.5   Similarity

It is old news in the field of relationships theory that we are most attracted to those who are similar to us.[21] If the members of a couple have different interests, different values, different religions, different preferred activities, different views on having children, and so on, it just is much harder for them to make a relationship work than if they are more similar on these and other dimensions.

The desire for similarity extends beyond close relationships. When people hire others for jobs, they look for people similar to themselves. And when admissions officers look to admit students, whether they will admit it or not, they look for students who are similar to them, at least in ways that are meaningful to them. To get to be an admissions officer, especially at a prestigious college or university, they probably had to do reasonably well on standardized tests throughout their careers. The admissions officers then often look for applicants who, like themselves, have tested reasonably well. After all, it must have worked for the admissions officers, as they are now in positions of power. So high test scores should work for the applicants too.

Test scores are not all that will matter. Most admissions officers either grew up or have become middle-class or perhaps upper middle-class. Upper middle-class individuals, especially, often present themselves differently from lower middle-class individuals – the way they speak, the way they dress, their expectations for social interactions, their expectations for outcomes in the college-admissions process. The admissions officers, therefore, are likely to be more comfortable with the students whose backgrounds are more similar to their own.

Nothing, of course, is totally simple. It is not just admissions officers who are, for the most part, looking for students who are fundamentally like themselves. Professors want students who are easy to teach. Students who test well on standardized tests are likely to be among the easier students to teach because they understand the educational system. Professors, too, therefore, like to teach students who are like themselves, and all things equal, would rather have the students whose academic preparation, as shown by standardized tests, best prepares them to do well in the professors' courses.

The bottom line is that similarity can perniciously keep the same forces operating in society that have operated before. If the current generation advances to the top people like themselves (those who succeeded by whatever standard the current generation viewed itself as succeeding in – wealth, religion, skin color, test scores, or whatever), then the next generation in power will look much like the last generation, because those in power made it so. Correlationally, though, it will look like they found the holy grail, as they will have created a correlation between what led to success in previous generations and what leads to success in future generations.

A great deal of research purports to show the correlation between some variable in the past and some other variable in the future, presenting this correlation as both causal and important. It is not causal, however, and it may not even be important. In the education business, many of the correlations are created by our own failing educational systems. We then blame the children. So, if children go to poor schools, it is reasonable to expect that they will not do well on educational tests, either at one time in the past or at another time in the future. But if an earlier test is offered as a test of "ability" and another later test is offered as a test of "achievement," and the correlation is moderately high, then people can be deceived into believing that the ability test results are somehow causal of the later achievement-test results. In fact, all ability tests are, at some level, achievement tests – they measure what test-takers know, such as reading skills, the vocabulary test-takers bring to their reading, test-takers' understanding of how to follow directions, and so forth.[22]

What is to be done? The first thing is to have admissions officers who are diverse and who do not just seek people who look like or think as they do. We need admissions officers who want diversity not only in the features that mark most current diversity efforts – What color is your skin? What state are you from? What is your ethnicity? – but also in the latent ability patterns of matriculating students. Schools need to seek students who represent the best the applicant pool has to offer in terms of creative, practical, and wisdom-based skills, not just knowledge and analytical skills. The admitted students may not be all so similar to the admissions officers in how they think, but the attitude of those making decisions should be, "All the better . . .." Choosing applicants for a broad set of abilities is risky, however.

7.1.6   Risk

Changing any system entails risk. For example, it has taken colleges and universities that have gone *test-optional* some courage to do so because professors and administrators worry about whether the new students admitted will be able to do the academic work. The schools worry about their academic reputations. In schools that use tests, it is risky for an individual admissions officer or an admissions committee to recommend admission of someone who has strong credentials but weak standardized-test scores. If the student does well, no one will notice. But if the student has academic problems, then someone might go back to the admissions credentials and wonder why a student was admitted with such low scores. In particular, they might wonder why the admissions officer would bring forward an application with such weak scores.

At a larger level, there was a time earlier when colleges and universities were afraid to stop requiring SAT and ACT scores because, basically, everyone else was requiring them. To be in a very small group of schools taking a risk seemed to be more than many schools would bear. That seems to be changing. More and more schools, including prestigious ones, are at least going test-optional, with success.

Going test-optional, in itself, is not an ideal solution. The reason is that it takes away information without providing any incremental information in return. The kinds of assessments described in this book provide that incremental information. Schools could adopt such measures. Few have, for the reasons described here. But if we want to select adaptively intelligent students who will go on to be positive, constructive leaders who make a positive, meaningful, and possibly enduring difference to the world, we will not get the information either from standardized tests, or from grades, or from participation in extracurricular activities, many of which are arranged by parents and schools. Put another way, schools need to be willing to take more risk than they have taken.

The solution to the problem, I believe, is to mitigate risk by experimenting with new measures on a trial basis, which is what we did at Tufts and at

Oklahoma State. Rather than announcing a permanent change in admissions policies, we introduced our admissions projects (Kaleidoscope at Tufts, Panorama at Oklahoma State) on a trial basis. The idea was to try the new measures for up to three years and see how they worked. Both schools went way beyond the three-year trial. Oklahoma State is still implementing Panorama; I do not know what Tufts is doing, as they have a different admissions dean from the one that implemented Kaleidoscope.

Also, we did not admit our whole classes based on the new programs. Much of each new entering class was admitted in a standard way. The students with the top credentials were admitted as before; the students with the worst credentials were not admitted, as before; where the new measures were particularly useful was for students whose credentials were more ambiguous – who would have been on the borderlines under the old system. In this way, it was possible better to select among borderline students. Such a group of students, if admitted, can increase enrollments.

7.1.7 Desire to Increase Enrollments

Selective schools turn down very large numbers of applicants. I look back at my deanship at Tufts University and wonder how I, as a dean, was so proud of all the applicants we turned down – the more the better. The more selective schools take pride in turning down as many students as possible so that they can claim to be highly selective and also get better ratings from *US News* and *World Report* and other ratings of colleges and universities.

What, in retrospect, seems odd is that very pride I and others took in turning people down – in telling them, in essence, "No opportunities for you here!" That is a statement to be proud of? After my time as dean at Tufts, I went to Oklahoma State as provost and senior vice-president and our attitude was the opposite: "We want to provide opportunities for higher education to as many students as possible." The mindset was focused on getting people in, not on keeping them out.

Today, most colleges are not like Harvard, Yale, and other highly selective schools that turn down almost everyone. Rather, the colleges, especially small liberal-arts colleges and state campuses (other than the flagship campuses) are actively seeking to increase their enrollments. That is, colleges are fighting declining enrollments and they need to keep those enrollments up to stay financially stable. So, they are not looking for measures that might rock the boat – that might in any way decrease their enrollments. These colleges and universities are already fairly liberal in their standards for standardized-test scores – where they want to invest is in how to recruit more students, not in how to make sure they only get the true best of the best.

What is the solution? For colleges and universities that are somewhat desperate for tuition dollars, the problem is filling the class. Using new measures such as of creativity, practical skills, and wisdom may enable colleges and universities to accept students, in good conscience, whom they previously believed it was incumbent on them to reject. These would be students whose grades and/or standardized-test scores might be below what the schools previously would have viewed as minimal but who show such creative, practical, or wisdom-based skills that can serve as a basis for admission. And our previous data show that such incremental skills can lead to both academic and extracurricular success in college as well as success in life after college.[23]

The other advantage to the new approach for schools that are hungry for students is the added advantage one gains in marketing. One now can advertise oneself, as a university, as seeking not just traditionally bright students but also as seeking the students who are going to make a positive, meaningful, and enduring difference to the world of the future. Of course, any college or university can claim they do this. But using measures of adaptive intelligence, one actually can show concretely what the college does to make it so.

In the ideal, for any college, whether desperate to accept students or eager to reject them, one could adapt the framework I have discussed within teaching and assessment as well as admissions.[24] This means not only teaching students knowledge, but also how to use their knowledge for a common good that will help preserve the world. This is a very special mission. It is also not an automatic sell. Green Mountain College in Vermont adopted an environmental mission; it also closed down in 2019. The mission has to be accompanied by the general academic strength to make the college or university viable. This means, I believe, going beyond the environmental mission to a broader mission of doing what it takes to teach students how they can make the world a better place. Often, however, a sense of new mission loses out to an old sense of superstition about what "must" be true.

7.1.8 Superstition

When I was a teenager, my parents gave me a religious locket that I was led to believe would bring me good luck in the future. Inside the locket are supposed to be some Biblical verses, but the locket is sealed, so I cannot even confirm that those passages, or any passages, are in there. Now, many years later, I still wear that locket. Why?

When I look back on my life, it has been a mixed one. Sometimes I have had great luck, sometimes good luck, sometimes bad luck, and a few times, what I, at least, considered to be terrible luck. I suppose my luck has been above average. I have never wanted for food on the table, never gone bankrupt, never been seriously injured to the point of needing a hospital stay. My five children are all healthy and my wife is happily engaged in a variety of pursuits. So, I still wear the locket because just maybe it has brought me good luck. The only time I take it off is for chest X-rays, which, of course, in sufficient doses can cause cancer. So, taking off the locket reminds me of . . . cancer.

Has the locket brought me good luck? I really do not know. Yet I am reluctant even now to take it off for fear that, if I do, my luck will turn really seriously bad. I have even promised the locket to my older son upon my death, although I believe he views it more as a curiosity than as anything that will bring him good luck.

Maybe the locket *is* bringing me good luck, or at least better luck than I would have had otherwise. But it's not just about a locket that I or someone else wears. A good place to look for superstitious behavior is in front of . . . an elevator. Someone in a hurry approaches the elevator. They really need to get up or down, fast. The light on the button is already lit, indicating that someone already has pushed the button. That does not stop them from pushing it again, and perhaps again, and again. Why do they keep pushing an elevator button that is already lit? I cannot say for sure, of course, but the truth is that when they push it, the elevator always comes. So maybe the repeated pushes helped, because they are on a 100 percent reinforcement schedule. They always get rewarded for pushing the button, whether it helps or not. They probably also keep pushing the "walk" button at pedestrian traffic lights.

When I was Director of Graduate Studies in Psychology at Yale, I got into an argument with a very well-known and highly esteemed professor. He seemed to me much higher in IQ than I was and should have been less susceptible to superstition. The argument was over the value of the Graduate Record Examination (GRE). I argued that it was not particularly useful for graduate admissions, at least in psychology at Yale, and that a colleague and I even had published a paper demonstrating of just how little use the test was.[25] As the colleague was a scientist and as the scientific study had been done at Yale with Yale students, I expected him to be impressed. He was not impressed. Rather he responded that, whatever results we might have obtained, the fact of the matter was that virtually everyone who had succeeded in our graduate program in psychology had GREs over 650 (a high score). I thought about it for a moment, and then agreed. Basically, I pointed out that our unwritten admission practice had been only to accept students with GREs over 650, so the statement he made had to be true. I did not mention it, but his statement was the equivalent of my arguing that my locket had brought me good luck. If you do not give a hypothesis a chance to be shown to be wrong, you have no chance of showing the hypothesis to be wrong. By only accepting students with GREs over 650, we were stuck in a loop where we could only confirm but not disconfirm our belief (or, at least, the belief of others in my department) in the validity of the GRE.

A first problem with superstitions is that they create self-fulfilling prophecies. If, say, teachers believe that students with lower scores cannot succeed, then the teachers will act toward those students in ways that tend to produce confirmation of the belief.[26] I experienced such a phenomenon in my own life, as have at least four of my five children. As a child, I was test-anxious and performed poorly on IQ tests. My poor test scores led teachers to believe I was stupid. The teachers treated me as though I was stupid. I got the message. I started to act like I was stupid. The teachers thereby received confirmation of their beliefs. But was their belief based on a superstition? It was not until I was in fourth grade that I had a teacher who believed that there is more to a student than his IQ scores. I was able to turn around my academic performance, and I did. Yes, it was a superstition.

When my son Seth was in first grade, he moved to a new school. He was also living in a new house in a new neighborhood. As soon as he got to his new school, he was given a reading test. Predictably, he bombed out. He had too many other things on his mind. The school put him in the bottom reading group. Eventually, he showed that he could read at a level above that of the bottom group. One might think that Seth then would be moved to a better reading group. But the school was so in love with tests that instead of trusting his actual reading performance, they gave him the reading test again. This time Seth scored at the level of the middle reading group. Seth then was moved to the middle group because the test said he should be moved.

Soon Seth was reading at the level of the top reading group. They gave him the reading test yet again. He scored at the level of the top group. One would think that now, given the school's reliance on tests, they would move him to the top group. They did not. Seth's mother and I went to the school and had a fancy conference with people with fancy titles at the school to ask why. We were told that he was not moved because he was now a full year behind the children in the top reading group. This was a self-fulfilling prophecy if ever I saw one. He was a full year behind because they held him back.

We offered to help Seth at home in his reading. I was doing research on reading and Seth's mother had a PhD from Stanford in curriculum and was Associate Commissioner for Education in the State of Connecticut. (She later became Commissioner.) No dice. They did not allow the reading books to go home. We wanted to argue but were afraid that, if we did, the school would take out their anger at us on Seth. Years later, Seth's reading apparently miraculously improved – he graduated from Yale with a major in political science, was admitted to Stanford Business School, and is now a CEO.

More recently, one of our then eight-year-old triplet daughters took a reading test and bombed it. It all was so familiar. We went to see the teacher. I told her that my daughter Melody, like I, was test-anxious. She told us that she, the teacher, normally would have conducted the reading test, which she knew would have helped because Melody knew her. But she had other testing to do so they had someone whom our child did not know conduct the test. The teacher was great – she was sympathetic and under-standing. But soon Melody was placed in a special-help group in reading, even though, in the classroom and at home, her reading was totally fine. Today, she is reading well above grade level. The more things change, the more they stay the same. Schools are treating children today pretty much the way they did in my day. And testing is taken as somehow telling the "truth." Superstitions die hard.

Oddly, my triplet-son Samuel also has trouble with tests, or at least current statewide math tests, but for a different reason that shows even more how inane the current testing movement has become and how it can lead us to value the wrong students. Our son is something of a math whiz. We, his parents, give him math problems, which he then proceeds to do in his head, quickly and correctly. We have to check his work by writing out the mathematical equations and then determining, as is almost always the case, that he got the correct answer though we have no idea what mental processes he used. But there was a problem.

On the mathematics tests he was receiving, children were expected to show their work. Our son solved the math problems, even hard ones, automatically, with no effort. His teachers would no more be able to do what he did than we were able to do so. We are pretty good in math, although not as good as our son. But our son lost credit because he did not show his work, or when he did, the method in his written work did not correspond to the one that the school taught.

Effectively, Samuel was being penalized for being smarter than the test-constructors. Rather, full credit was being given, as usual, to those who did what they were told exactly as they were told to do it. Are those the children, who, in the future, are going to make the world a better place? Perhaps not. They will be too busy doing exactly what they are being told what to do, namely, what has been done before or, in some cases, what makes money for a company that is exploiting the Earth's natural resources.

The irony of testing extends beyond those who are test-anxious or who are particularly bright at what the tests test. There are all sorts of reasons that students do poorly on standardized tests. They may have been socialized to be smart in ways that simply do not correspond to what test-world demands. Many Yup'ik Native American children in isolated fishing villages in Alaska learn many adaptive skills for coping with their environments – how to do ice fishing, how to hunt game, how to gather wild-grown berries – but the academic skills tested on standardized tests are not the highest on their list of skills for survival.[27] They can survive and find remote villages in the frozen tundra – you, the reader, perhaps would find these tasks more challenging, just as they find abstract geometric problems challenging. But teach and present those problems with content more familiar to them, such as fish racks, and they do just fine.[28] Nevertheless, we superstitiously continue to believe that our tests measure skills in a way that is valid for all those who take the tests.

If superstitions can influence the behavior of eminent Yale professors, presumably with high IQs, who is immune? For some superstitions, really, who cares? Who cares whether I wear a medallion around my neck? No one, except maybe me. But if our societies are depriving millions of students of opportunities because of scores on tests or other assessments that are only marginally valid for some students and invalid for others, what is our defense? What we need are children who later will become stewards of a world we are rapidly destroying, not students who do what they are told, even if it is to defend people or policies that contribute to the destruction of the Earth and those live on it. Destruction is costly for everyone, but most of us focus on costs in a narrower sense.

7.1.9   Cost

There are not a lot of schools that believe they are drowning in money, even if they are. Every year, I receive multiple requests from my alma maters – Yale and Stanford – for funds, even though they are two of the wealthiest universities in the world. Neither is exactly hard up for cash. But huge numbers of universities are, indeed, hard up for cash. They are not looking for extra expenses, as they might assume would be incurred if they were to add new tests to their battery of admissions tests.

Moreover, using the available tests, the SAT and the ACT in the United States, the A-levels in England and some other parts of the UK, and other tests in other countries, very much benefits the colleges and universities because it is essentially cost-free to them. The students (or the government, in some countries) are the ones who pay. So, the colleges get a valuable service performed for them, at little or no expense. Moreover, the testing companies create incentives for the students to pay more and more money. In the US, each time the applicant sends scores to another school, that costs more. Every time they retake the test, that costs more. The testing companies, for an extra fee, can send highest scores or at least those from a chosen date, which provides further incentive to applicants to keep retaking the test in the hope of getting higher scores.

If colleges and universities had to pay like students do to receive scores – which, after all, is a service to the institutions – they would have more incentive to think carefully about how much they really gain from the tests. But when the students pay, the institutions have little to lose.

Some admissions offices, especially in selective schools, use "holistic admissions," meaning that test scores are considered only in the context of a wide range of variables, such as students' backgrounds and educational opportunities. But such holistic admissions seem repeatedly to work in favor of certain targeted groups – especially "under-represented minorities" – and help other groups equally in need of help, less, if at all. Moreover, how holistic admissions are conducted depends a lot on who is reading an application and when they are reading it. As a former admissions officer and a faculty member who has read thousands of dossiers, I think it fair to say that early in the evening when I am reading dossiers, I have tried to be as holistic as possible. But as the hours of the evening have passed by and I have gotten more and more tired, the test scores have started to jump out at me. It becomes harder and harder to focus on lengthy essays and easier and easier to focus on hard numbers, even though I know how lacking in meaning they can be. If it is hard for me, I can imagine how hard it is for others.

I would argue, therefore, that the solution to the freeloader problem of colleges and universities is to make them pay. If they want information, they should pay for it. At worst, students and colleges should share the costs. This would make both parties more cautious about what kinds of funds they are willing to put into test scores. More importantly, they should insist on much more value than they are getting. Many schools lack resources or knowledge regarding how to validate the tests in their own settings. They should insist that the testing companies provide such "synthetic" validity information – that is, information regarding how valid the tests are in their own setting for the criteria they care about (hopefully, more than GPAs and graduation rates). They might be in for an unpleasant surprise.

These deep questions about tests and their roles in universities are not often asked, because they are not the questions that lead to quick publications. Rather, shallower questions and answers are the ones that more quickly get into journals.

7.1.10   Publication and Promotion

There is a potent reason why colleges and universities, among other institutions, use standardized tests and thereby end up selecting students for a narrow band of skills that are mostly irrelevant to how they will act when they get out in the world. That reason is publication about, and promotion of the institutions.

Universities at all levels of quality and prestige are locked in a battle against each other for students, faculty, staff, and funds. In this respect, they are no different from other organizations that compete in their own respective marketplaces. There are things that it is important to compete for. Would it not be great, for example, if universities competed by showing that their students have made powerful, unique, and transformative changes in the world that have made the world a better place in which to live? Sure, it would be. But that is so hard to do. How do they get the information for even a few students, much less, their entire student body in any one year or over multiple years?

How much easier and cheaper it is to market one's school by the level of the students' test scores. Not only is the information easily available. It also seems to be, in the public's mind, easy to understand and valid, given that the public does not know just how limited the tests really are. Not only do colleges and universities take the easy marketing route; so do the magazines, newspapers, and websites that hope to increase their sales by marketing average test scores for a range of schools.

Media that seek to make money off test scores make it hard for colleges and universities to stop using such scores. They lead parents and applicants to suspect that schools with lower scores are lesser schools, or that schools that go test-optional do so because they have something to hide, such as that their scores never were very high in the first place. The media sites may even downgrade schools that are test-optional or that provide incomplete information about test scores. Because many applicants and their parents use these media to make decisions about which colleges to apply to and which to matriculate in, there is tremendous pressure on colleges and universities to enter the test-score demolition derby. And they do so, falsely believing the tests they are using are valid.

7.1.11 The Illusion of Validity

I have saved for last what I believe to be the most important factor that preserves the existing suboptimal system of choosing the leaders of the future. This is the illusion that, in the end and for whatever faults they may have, test scores are valid and about the best we have.

I have discussed in this book any number of studies that cast doubt on this claim. But before talking about research, we need to review exactly what we mean by "validity."

The usual method of validating tests is to look at their correlation with other tests or with school grades. There is an old saw in the field of psychology that the best predictor of any kind of behavior in the present is past behavior of the same kind. It therefore is scarcely surprising that test scores would predict test scores. When Alfred Binet and Theodore Simon developed the first of the modern IQ tests, their main goal was to predict performances similar to those on the test.[29] Test scores also predict other outcomes in life associated with success, such as health and income.[30] The behaviors they predict tend to be those that benefit the individual with the high test scores. What they are not designed to predict, and given the current state of the world, what they seem not to predict, is positive contribution to making the world a better place. Test publishers purposely use trivial criteria to evaluate tests because such data are easy to collect and because they are what colleges and universities seem most to care about. The main preoccupation of the colleges and universities often is not what positive difference students will make, but rather whether the students will be able to stay in school (and hence keep paying tuition fees) and, ideally, future income that might be donated to the institution. People busy doing good for the world are not necessarily those with the incomes that will enable them to become major donors to their alma maters.

Some years back, we did the Rainbow and Kaleidoscope Projects to show that tests of creative, practical, and wisdom-based skills would improve prediction of academic performance in college and also decrease ethnic-group differences. In other words, the tests would enhance prediction of who could succeed academically in college at the same time that the tests would reduce the differences between ethnicities, such as African-American, Latino-American, European-American, Asian-American, Native American, and so forth. We succeeded in showing this (see Note 11). The assumption in this work, however, was that traditional standardized tests are pretty good measures of analytical abilities. What our tests added were measures of creative, practical, and wisdom-based abilities. Since coming to Cornell University, I have turned my attention to the question of whether the standardized tests are even particularly good measures of analytical abilities, at least as they apply in specific domains.

The domain we chose was science/technology/engineering/mathematics (STEM). STEM careers are important to modern societies, in part because of the technological innovations they bring us, such as cell phones, but also because in the same way that science, engineering, and technology have brought us innovations, they have brought us the costs of such innovations, such as air and water pollution and global climate change. The solution of these problems, like their origins, will have to be at least in part in STEM.

If we want to find the students who will be best prepared to take advantage of educational opportunities and to help create a better world, then we need some way of assessing which students will be the best STEM reasoners – who will, given the opportunity, best be able to excel not only in STEM courses but in the kinds of thinking required to turn STEM thinking into a positive rather than the very mixed bag it currently is.

At present, many selection committees for admission in STEM disciplines rely primarily on a combination of somewhat diverse measures. The problem is that none of the measures directly assesses scientific reasoning. The measures include (a) high school (for undergraduate admissions) or undergraduate (for graduate admissions) grades, (b) standardized-test scores, typically ACTs or SATs for undergraduate admission, and GREs for graduate admission, (c) letters of recommendation from professors who are presumed to know the students' work and to have some basis for predicting their success in a future STEM career, and (d) documented research experience, preferably experience that is relevant to the field one wishes to pursue.[31]

The conventional measures are all pretty far from perfect. For example, school grades and standardized-test scores measure how well students can solve problems that are explicitly presented to them, but they have nothing to say about whether the students can figure out what problems are worth studying in the first place. They also convey little information about how to generate alternative hypotheses, or experimental designs, or about how to draw conclusions from experimental research results. Tests like the ACT, SAT, and GRE provide reasonably good measures of general cognitive ability, as I have noted earlier in this chapter.[32] But these tests do not measure, or even come close to measuring, the research and teaching skills that are particularly relevant to success in STEM fields. The major argument in the past has been that it makes sense to use standardized tests because they measure the abilities required in STEM fields, even though the problems are not, for the most part, STEM-related. I, myself, believed that they measure pretty well the analytical component needed for success, although not the creative, practical, and wisdom-based components. I was wrong.

In collaborative research with several colleagues, I sought to discover whether these standardized tests measuring analytical skills actually predict the specific set of analytical skills needed for success in STEM fields. In other words, was I right, and were others right, in believing that the usual-suspect tests were adequate as measures of analytical reasoning for STEM? We found out. The answer, as I describe here, is no.[33]

The research we have done at Cornell has been motivated, in part, by research I did with Wendy Williams some years ago.[34] That earlier research demonstrated that the GRE was not, in fact, a particularly successful predictor of success in the graduate psychology program at Yale University, at least beyond the first year of course grades. Others, looking at a broader sampling of institutions, have come to more positive conclusions about the GRE.[35] Although Wendy Williams and I showed that the GRE was not a great predictor at Yale, we provided no alternative or even supplementary measures, and we did not show the performance of the GRE in predicting at any institution beyond Yale.

The studies we have performed at Cornell were designed further to explore whether standardized tests, once one gets into specific domains such as STEM reasoning, actually are good predictors of performance. Our studies were based on the simple notion, discussed previously, that the best predictor of future behavior of any given kind is past behavior of that same kind. So, we explored what particular skills future professionals in STEM fields need for success in school but also later, when they take jobs. Two of the main activities of STEM scientists are research and teaching. So, we focused our efforts on developing new measures designed to assess reasoning about research and teaching as well as related activities in the context of STEM disciplines.

The measures we have created require test-takers to (a) generate alternative scientific hypotheses to explain data, (b) generate scientific experiments, (c) draw scientific conclusions, (d) review scientific articles, and (e) evaluate teaching in STEM. For example, in one subtest, test-takers were confronted with situations and then presented with a hypothesis about why the results for each situation were obtained. Test-takers were asked to propose alternative hypotheses about why the outcomes were obtained. In another subtest, test-takers were presented with videos of professors teaching scientific lessons. The test-takers then were asked to specify what each teacher was doing wrong, from a pedagogical point of view, in his or her teaching of the lesson.

Consider three actual examples of problems we have used regarding reasoning about research.

7.1.11.1   Generating Hypotheses

"Marie is interested in child development. One day, she notices that whenever Laura's nanny comes in to pick up Laura from nursery school, Laura starts to cry. Marie reflects upon how sad it is that Laura has a poor relationship with her nanny.

What are some alternative hypotheses regarding why Laura starts to cry when she is picked up from nursery school by the nanny?"

7.1.11.2   Generating Experiments

"Devon is interested in making her seeds sprout faster. She hypothesizes that higher temperatures, up to a point, can make the seeds sprout faster and earlier. However, Devon is not sure how to properly design an experiment to test this hypothesis.

Please suggest an experimental design to test this hypothesis and describe the experiment in some detail. Assume you have the resources you need to be able to do the experiment (e.g., access to students and their academic records, sufficient funds to pay subjects, etc.)."

7.1.11.3   Drawing Conclusions

"Henry tested the hypothesis that sugar helps students to be alert and focus in class. Three groups of 200 participants each were asked to consume one of three pieces of chocolate: a piece of dark chocolate (~8 g sugar), or a piece of milk chocolate (~10 g sugar), or a piece of completely sugar-free chocolate. It was found that both groups that consumed sugar in their chocolate were more alert and focused in class than was the sugar-free group; moreover, the milk chocolate group performed better than the dark-chocolate group in paying attention. Henry concluded that students should eat snacks that contain more sugar in order to stay awake in class. Is this conclusion correct? Why or why not?"

We found rated performance on these and related measures to be highly reliable, meaning that on a given subtest, all the items measured more or less the same scientific-reasoning skills. We compared performance on our scientific-reasoning tests with performance on tests of fluid intelligence. In one fluid-intelligence test, *Number Series*, test-takers had to complete a series of numbers. In a second fluid-intelligence test, *Letter Sets*, test-takers had to say which of a set of letters was unlike other sets of letters with which the test-taker was presented. (For example, one letter set might have all vowels, whereas none of the other letter sets did.) We also compared performance on our tests with scores on standardized tests, including the SAT and the ACT, and where possible, with undergraduate GPAs.

The findings were straightforward.

First, the various measures of scientific reasoning generally correlated moderately with each other. In other words, they seemed to be measuring the same basic underlying construct.

Second, factor analysis, a way of assessing what underlying psychological construct is being measured, confirmed our impressions. The scientific-reasoning tests generally clustered into a single factor.

Third, the tests of reasoning about teaching (and also of reviewing the quality of scientific articles) also correlated moderately with the scientific-reasoning tests and factored together with them.

Fourth, the tests of fluid intelligence and the standardized tests (SAT, ACT) also factored together, presumably because they are all, at some level, measures of general intelligence, or *g*.

Fifth, and most critically for present purposes, our tests of scientific reasoning did NOT factor with the inductive-reasoning or standardized reading and mathematical tests, suggesting that our tests measure a different construct from whatever it is that the fluid-intelligence tests and standardized tests measure. This is not to say that the constructs measured by conventional tests have no use in scientific pursuits. Rather, it is to say that these tests measure something other than scientific reasoning.

Finally, our tests did *not* show the gender gap that is commonly found on many standardized tests of abilities and achievement. In other words, men and women did not show a significant difference in their performance on our scientific-reasoning tests. This finding is important because, on conventional tests, there often is a gender gap.

We found it interesting and, to us, somewhat surprising, that our measures of reasoning about research and about teaching clustered together factorially, suggesting that many of the same analytical, creative, and practical skills that investigators apply to research can be applied to teaching – if the researchers expend the effort to think about their teaching in the same way they do about their research.

If society wants to select and then train the best STEM researchers and teachers, society will need to move beyond standardized tests, grades, and even letters of recommendation to assess the skills that are most relevant for success in STEM disciplines. We believe our measures help get at these skills. But the issue is not just with STEM disciplines. Our results might lead one to wonder how well the standardized tests would predict success in *any* discipline. How about if we studied skills needed for contributions in history, literature, political science, economics, anthropology, the arts, or any discipline at all? Are we using tests to determine students' futures that bear only the most casual resemblance to the tests we should be using if we want to assess who will make a difference to the world, whatever the field?

The goal of research like ours is not to suggest that schools "dump" the SAT, ACT, GRE, or any related tests. Students who lack sufficient levels and quality of the kind of academic preparation as measured by standardized tests may have trouble simply meeting the academic requirements of many STEM or other kinds of programs. Such students also possibly may be challenged in their later research and teaching. But we cannot say this for sure, because our reliance on standardized testing has been so slavish that one cannot say what would happen if we utterly abandoned the tests.

Ultimately, whatever the field of endeavor, colleges, universities, and other schools have an obligation – at least, a moral one – to provide opportunities to students who can best succeed in the programs but also who can best make a positive, meaningful, and enduring difference to the world. It has become clear from the present state of the world that, in general, we are doing a poor job of selecting people who will save the world from the self-imposed catastrophes humans are bringing not only upon themselves but upon myriad other species as well. This book suggests how we can change all this – teach and assess students in ways that recognize, encourage, reward, and encourage the adaptive-intellectual skills that can save the world for future generations. It is not too late – yet. The contemporary challenges of the world – even the problem of horrible unexpected pandemics – can be solved. But they only can be solved if we all work together, collectively and adaptively, for a common good.

Notes

1. Paquette, D. (2015). The terrifying rate at which smokers die from smoking. *Washington Post*, February 26. https://wapo.st/311gY80
2. Banks, E., Joshy, G., Weber, M. F. et al. (2015). Tobacco smoking and all-cause mortality in a large Australian cohort study: findings from a mature epidemic with current low smoking prevalence. *BMC Medicine*, February 24. https://bit.ly/31azkDA
3. Abbott, B. (2019). Vaping-related cases surge to 1888, with 37 deaths. *Wall Street Journal*, October 31. https://on.wsj.com/3heESm7
4. Sternberg, R. J. (2016). *What universities can be*. Ithaca, NY: Cornell University Press.
5. Sternberg, R. J. (2019). Where have all the flowers of wisdom gone? An analysis of teaching of wisdom over the years. In R. J. Sternberg, H. Nusbaum, & J. Glueck (Eds.), *Applying wisdom to contemporary world problems* (pp. 1–20). Cham, Switzerland: Palgrave-Macmillan.
6. Sternberg, R. J. (2019). Why people often prefer wise guys to guys who are wise: An augmented balance theory of the production and reception of wisdom. In R. J. Sternberg, & J. Glueck (Eds.), *Cambridge handbook of wisdom* (pp. 162–81). New York: Cambridge University Press.
7. Sternberg, R. J. (1988). *The triarchic mind: A new theory of human intelligence*. New York: Viking; Sternberg, R. J. (1997). *Successful intelligence*. New York: Plume.
8. Lemann, N. (1999). *The big test: The secret history of the American meritocracy*. New York: Farrar, Straus, & Giroux; Kabaservice, G. (2004). *Kingman Brewster, his circle, and the rise of the liberal establishment*. New York: Henry Holt.
9. Yang, A. (2019). In C. Lane, "Math or bust." *Newsweek*, November 15, p. 22.
10. Croizet, J.-C., & Dutrevis, M. (2008). Socioeconomic status and intelligence: Why test scores do not equal merit. *Journal of Poverty*, https://doi.org/10.1300/J134v08n03_05
11. Stemler, S. E., Grigorenko, E. L., Jarvin, L., & Sternberg, R. J. (2006). Using the theory of successful intelligence as a basis for augmenting AP exams in psychology and statistics. *Contemporary Educational Psychology*, 31(2), 344–76 ; Sternberg, R.J., & The Rainbow Project Collaborators. (2006). The Rainbow Project: Enhancing the SAT through assessments of analytical, practical and creative skills. *Intelligence*, 34(4), 321–50; Stemler, S., Sternberg, R. J., Grigorenko, E. L., Jarvin, L., & Sharpes, D. K. (2009). Using the theory of successful intelligence as a framework for developing assessments in AP Physics. *Contemporary Educational Psychology*, 34, 195–209; Sternberg, R. J. (2009). The Rainbow and Kaleidoscope Projects: A new psychological approach to under-graduate admissions. *European Psychologist*, 14, 279–87.

12. Polikoff, M. S. (2017). Why accountability matters, and why it must evolve. *Education Next*, Summer. https://bit.ly/3g17XjD; Accountability (N.D.). Edu cationpost.org. https://educationpost.org/conversation/blog/accountability/

13. Sternberg, R. J., Torff, B., & Grigorenko, E. L. (1998). Teaching for success-ful intelligence raises school achievement. *Phi Delta Kappan*, 79, 667–9; Sternberg, R. J., & Grigorenko, E. L. (2007). *Teaching for successful intelligence* (2nd ed.). Thousand Oaks, CA: Corwin Press; Sternberg, R. J., Jarvin, L., & Grigorenko, E. L. (2009). *Teaching for wisdom, intelligence, creativity, and success*. Thousand Oaks, CA: Corwin.

14. Spearman, C. (1904). "General intelligence," objectively determined and measured. *American Journal of Psychology*, 15, 201–93.

15. Flynn, J. R. (1984). The mean IQ of Americans: Massive gains 1932 to 1978. *Psychological Bulletin*, 95, 29–51; Flynn, J. R. (1987). Massive IQ gains in 14 nations. *Psychological Bulletin*, 101, 171–91.

16. Terman, L. M. (1925–1959). *Genetic studies of genius* (5 vols.). Stanford, CA: Stanford University Press.

17. Sternberg, R. J. (2010). *College admissions for the 21st century*. Cambridge, MA: Harvard University Press.

18. Sternberg, R. J., Wong, C. H., & Sternberg, K. (2019). The relation of tests of scientific reasoning to each other and to tests of fluid intelligence. *Journal of Intelligence*, 7(3), 20. https://doi.org/10.3390/jintelligence7030020

19. Sternberg, R. J. (2004). Culture and intelligence. *American Psychologist*, 59(5), 325–38; Sternberg, R., J., & Grigorenko, E. L. (2004). Why we need to explore development in its cultural context. *50th Anniversary Issue of Merrill–Palmer Quarterly*, 50(3), 369–86.

20. Perkins, D. (1995). *Outsmarting IQ: The emerging science of learnable intelli-gence*. New York: The Free Press; Gardner, H. (2011). *Frames of mind: The theory of multiple intelligences*. New York: Basic Books.

21. Sternberg, R. J. (1998a). *Cupid's arrow*. New York: Cambridge University Press; Sternberg, R. J. (1998b). *Love is a story*. New York: Oxford University Press.

22. Sternberg, R. J. (1998). Abilities are forms of developing expertise. *Educational Researcher*, 27(3), 11–20.

23. Sternberg, R. J., Forsythe, G. B., Hedlund, J. et al. (2000). *Practical intelli-gence in everyday life*. New York: Cambridge University Press; Sternberg, R. J. (2010). *College admissions for the 21st century*. Cambridge, MA: Harvard University Press.

24. Sternberg, R. J. (2016). *What universities can be*. Ithaca, NY: Cornell University Press.

25. Sternberg, R. J., & Williams, W. M. (1997). Does the Graduate Record Examination predict meaningful success in the graduate training of psycholo-gists? A case study. *American Psychologist*, 52, 630–41.

26. Rosenthal, R., & Jacobson, L. (1992). *Pygmalion in the classroom* (expanded ed.). New York: Irvington.

27. Grigorenko, E. L., Meier, E., Lipka, J. et al. (2004). Academic and practical intelligence: A case study of the Yup'ik in Alaska. *Learning and Individual Differences*, 14, 183–207.
28. Sternberg, R. J., Lipka, J., Newman, T., Wildfeuer, S., & Grigorenko, E. L. (2007). Triarchically-based instruction and assessment of sixth-grade mathematics in a Yup'ik cultural setting in Alaska. *International Journal of Giftedness and Creativity*, 21(2), 6–19.
29. Binet, A., & Simon, T. (1916). *The development of intelligence in children* (E. S. Kite, trans.). Baltimore, MD: Williams & Wilkins.
30. Deary, I. J., & Whalley, L. J. (2008). *A lifetime of intelligence*. Washington, DC: American Psychological Association.
31. Posselt, J. R. (2016). *Inside graduate admissions: Merit, diversity, and faculty gatekeeping*. Cambridge, MA: Harvard University Press.
32. Frey, M. C., & Detterman, D. K. (2004). Scholastic assessment or g? The relationship between the scholastic assessment test and general g. *Psychological Science*, 15, 373–8; Sackett, P. R., Shewach, O. R., & Dahlke, J. A. (2020). The predictive value of general intelligence. In R. J. Sternberg (Ed.), *Human intelligence: An introduction* (pp. 381–414). New York: Cambridge University Press.
33. Sternberg, R. J., & Sternberg, K. (2017). Measuring scientific reasoning for graduate admissions in psychology and related disciplines. *Journal of Intelligence*. http://www.mdpi.com/2079-3200/5/3/29/pdf; Sternberg, R. J., Sternberg, K., & Todhunter, R. J. E. (2017). Measuring reasoning about teaching for graduate admissions in psychology and related disciplines. *Journal of Intelligence*. www.mdpi.com/2079-3200/5/4/34/pdf; Sternberg, R. J., Wong, C. H., & Sternberg, K. (2019). The relation of tests of scientific reasoning to each other and to tests of fluid intelligence. *Journal of Intelligence*, 7(3), 20. https://doi.org/10.3390/jintelligence7030020
34. Sternberg, R. J., & Williams, W. M. (1997). Does the Graduate Record Examination predict meaningful success in the graduate training of psychologists? A case study. *American Psychologist*, 52, 630–41.
35. Kuncel, N. R., Hezlett, S. A., & Ones, D. S. (2001). A comprehensive meta-analysis of the predictive validity of the Graduate Record Examinations: Implications for graduate student selection and performance. *Psychological Bulletin*, 127, 162–81.

CHAPTER 8

The Great Adaptive-Intelligence Test

"Wait!" my colleagues in the intelligence-testing business might say. "We have a test; you don't. And it's the intelligence test that has single-handedly created the field of intelligence research and testing as it is today." It is a stunning piece of technology. It is also being shown to be utterly useless for saving civilization as we know it.

But there already is an adaptive-intelligence test, the Great Adaptive-Intelligence Test. Like many intelligence tests, it comes in multiple forms. (The Stanford–Binet Intelligence Scale originally came in two forms, L and M, which just happened to correspond to the first and middle initials of the name of its inventor, Lewis M. Terman.) In this book, I have referred to one form of the test, the Global Climate Change form, repeatedly, but many people fail to see it as an adaptive-intelligence test because it has an extremely prolonged time limit. By the time people get to the end of the test – most likely, successors to the people living today – it will be too late for people to recognize that they failed the test. We cannot wait that long.

Fortunately, today, there is a shorter form of the test, the novel coronavirus pandemic, COVID-19. I write these words on the day that, so far, more people have died of COVID-19 than any previous day (over 200),[1] and also on the day that COVID-19 deaths topped 21,000 worldwide, with over 1,000 in the United States.[2] (By the time I am reading copyediting on August 18, 2020, the number of deaths in the US is about 170,000). Unemployment in the United States (and elsewhere) is reaching record levels.[3] By tomorrow, when I finish writing this chapter, the picture will be worse. The day after, the picture will be still worse.

Biologically, as I have emphasized throughout this book, adaptive intelligence is about survival both of individuals, in particular, and of humanity, in general. During the COVID-19 pandemic, the numbers make it clear that we are not scoring highly on this particular intelligence test. We are also scoring poorly on the global-climate-change form of the intelligence test. We just do not see it as well for the global-change form of the test because the test is being "administered" over a long period of time, and only will be finished by future generations – we hope.

By the time you read this chapter, the COVID-19 pandemic may well be over, or be tamed by the discovery of a vaccine. But this will not be the last pandemic, and the question each time will be whether anything is learned from the experience, or whether people will just go back to doing things the way they did before, hoping that this pandemic and crash of the worldwide economy will be the last. Of course, there will be other pandemics and crashes of economies. Will people learn anything from the present ones?

People are dying because even medical personnel in many instances lack inexpensive masks to protect not only patients but also themselves.[4] The United States somehow can put together 2 trillion dollars ($2,000,000,000,000) in economic aid but has not found the money for $2 masks. N-95 masks could save the lives of countless frontline medical professionals, but a search of the Internet on March 26, 2020, shows that they are widely unavailable at any price. Many medical personnel lack the masks, and even if they have the masks, are having to reuse them beyond the point that they are safe.[5]

The current central administration in the United States knew for two months about the impending pandemic and chose to do nothing about it, denying that the United States, at least, would face a major health problem; once they saw that denial was no longer possible, they chose to attempt to rewrite history by claiming they knew all along and were preparing for it.[6] But the government was not preparing for it, with the result that people began dying in record numbers. They lied; people died. It is that simple.

What hope is there for the future, in the United States, or in other nations where leaders have been asleep at the wheel while a deadly illness harms and even kills large swaths of their populations? COVID-19 will not be the end. This pandemic was long predicted, and unless the world changes what it is doing, others will follow, as they have throughout history. The difference is that now we know enough to do something about it. But will we?

The current COVID-19 crisis highlights some of the features of adaptive intelligence and how it is measured, whether we like it or not.

1 *Adaptive intelligence refers to real-world adaption to the environment, not just to a score on an artificial multiple-choice or short-answer test of general intelligence.* Adaptive intelligence is about intelligence as it exists in the real world, not about artificial constructions of psychologists. Alfred Binet and his successors invented intelligence tests as we know them today.[7] Nature

or society invents adaptive-intelligence tests. We humans discover such tests. They are not artificial constructions – they are there, whether we like them or not. They measure intelligence as adaptation, which is how intelligence was defined in the first place.[8] It is exceedingly strange that, even as people are getting sick and dying because of a pandemic for which the world had more than adequate warning, so many people continue to see intelligence not as about avoiding getting sick and dying – as about adaptation to the environment in the sense of preserving lives, including their own – but rather as about filling in bubbles on multiple-test choices. Is the general intelligence needed to fill in multiple-choice bubbles more important than the adaptive intelligence needed to save lives? The more important intelligence is the one that is for the higher stakes.

2 *The real-world stakes for adaptive intelligence are extremely high – the future of civilization as we know it.* When this book was first reviewed in early 2020, I suspect such a statement might have sounded like an over-statement. Does it still sound like an overstatement when novel corona-virus is quickly killing more people than any past pandemic in history. World War I claimed the lives of perhaps 16 million people. The Spanish flu got 50 million, more than any past pandemic. Depending on the rate of vaccine development – assuming a vaccine arrives – novel coronavirus may kill more or fewer. But people are dying, the world has entered into a global recession, people are out of work and uncertain of future prospects for an income. Is the idea that intelligence cannot be captured by a trivial mul-tiple-choice test still so overstated? How many preventable deaths does it take, whether as a result of pandemics, or global climate change, or pollution, or weapons of mass destruction, before people realize that we are glorifying the trivial at the expense of the profound? Are we that short-sighted – that trapped in our mind bubble and our bubble tests? The people most likely to die are the ones in squalid, crowded conditions, and perhaps unfortunately, they are not the ones who write the items for standardized intelligence tests. They know what the elites do not: We cannot afford to waste lives merely so that elite institutions can continue to serve primarily the elite and their children.

I am reminded of a trip I once took with a colleague to a slum in northern India. I had grown up near Newark, NJ, in a time of urban riots, and I thought I knew what bad conditions were. But they paled by comparison to the conditions I saw in the city I visited. There was one thing I knew for certain: No matter what their IQs, children growing up in that environment would never have a chance in life. They were adapting to conditions that made the idea of intelligence as predictive of adaptation . . . well, laughable. Many of us, placed in that environment, might not last in good health and safety a day, and almost certainly, not a week.[9]

The stakes are the future for our children and their children. Certainly, those stakes are higher than the so-called "high stakes" of filling in bubbles on a computer-scored answer sheet. General intelligence as measured by conventional tests tells us little about adaptive intelligence or how to support it.

3 *High IQs have apparently done relatively little to support adaptive intelligence.* Often, they have been used for undermining it. Presumably, national leaders have above-average IQs. Nevertheless, some of them have minimized the danger of the pandemic, even comparing it to a common cold.[10] These leaders are literally toxic, causing people to die because of their failing the Great Adaptive-Intelligence Test. Others have failed in other ways, such as those who knew of the danger, lied about it to the public, and sought to enrich themselves financially at others' expense.[11] Wisdom is part of adaptive intelligence, and some people not only lack it, but show that foolishness is much worse than low IQ.

Richard Burr, a senator who betrayed the public trust by selling stock trading on insider information about the coming pandemic and then lying about it to the public, not only trashed his reputation, but now is being sued for insider trading, not a great position for a senator to be in.[12] Whatever the outcome of the lawsuit, Burr showed that, whatever his IQ (which, presumably, is fairly high, given that he went to prestigious Wake Forest University for his bachelor's degree), adaptive intelligence must be applied at a collective level, not just at an individual level. In this way, it is different from both general intelligence (and the closely associated IQ) and practical intelligence, both of which can be and are applied at an individual level, sometimes to the detriment of others.[13] Or some of these narcissistic leaders pretend to consult, but surround themselves only with sycophants. Those who are not sycophants do not last long in the administrations of narcissistic leaders such as Vladimir Putin or Donald Trump. They are quickly replaced by flunkeys who do what they are told.

How much instruction in school and how much school assessment prepares children and young adults to exercise their collective intelligence, and to exercise it for a common good? If one were to assign a percentage, it certainly would be in the single digits – less than 10 percent, probably much less. So, perhaps it is no surprise, especially in individualist societies, that we are locked into the notion of intelligence as individual. Well, it certainly is in part individual. But the problem with the view of intelligence as exclusively individual is that individuals cannot solve problems of staggering complexity, such as the problem of what to do in response to COVID-19, or really, what to do in response to any major real-world challenge. Rather, we teach and test children as though maximizing individual gain is the ultimate goal of education, and perhaps then we should not be surprised that young people so often act that way. Ignoring the collective functioning of adaptive intelligence is not something we can afford.

None of this is to say that IQ does not matter. As stated throughout the book, the knowledge and abstract analytical skills measured by IQ tests matter in various aspects of life, as many investigators have shown.[14] The issue is that lots of things matter: what parents one happens to have, whether one is born into wealth or poverty, whether one goes to good schools, whether one is fed properly. All these factors contribute to the development of cognitive abilities. The problem is not with IQ, but rather with the fixation of some psychologists and educators on it and with the blinders they wear when it comes to recognizing how many other things matter at least as much, or more, for individual lives and for society as a whole. Wearing blinders is a decision – it is part of an attitude toward life.

4 *Adaptive intelligence is in large part an attitude toward life.* A large literature has evolved on intelligence as an ability.[15] No doubt the "ability" construct is highly relevant to understanding intelligence. But the response to the novel coronavirus outbreak shows that adaptive intelligence is much more an attitude toward life than it is an ability. While psychologists are mired in the mud of trying to understand some supposed "true" structure of intelligence, people are dying because of a lack of an attitude toward life, not an ability. The attitude is simply that, on a grand scale, adaptation is about using one's knowledge and skills toward a common good, balancing one's own with others' interests and larger interests, over the long as well as well as the short term, through the infusion of positive ethical values.[16] Regrettably, as the field of intelligence illustrates too well, "The saddest aspect of life right now is that science gathers knowledge faster than society gathers wisdom."[17] Many of our leaders have knowledge and skills, but do not use them for a common good, balance no one's interests other than their own, and completely ignore positive ethical values, as in the example of Senator Richard Burr. The science should help them know what to do. Instead, they do the opposite, such as, amazingly, disbanding an advisory committee on how to handle pandemics.[18] What good, exactly, did a thirty-point rise in IQs do society in the twentieth century?

Because adaptive intelligence is largely an attitude toward life, it is something that anyone can develop if they so choose. But given enough bad role models, which the world has an over-abundance of right now, children often learn to think maladaptively. How far we as a nation and a world have come since President John F. Kennedy challenged young people to ask not what their country could do for them, but rather, what they could do for their country.[19] Kennedy recognized the importance of serving the collective good.

5 *Adaptive intelligence is as much a collective phenomenon as an individual phenomenon.* As discussed earlier in this chapter, we are used to thinking of intelligence as an individual phenomenon even though intelligence in the real world mostly is manifested in a collective manner. Except for dictators and the monarchs of old, leaders are responsible to others. They may be responsible to a board of directors, or a populace that elects them, or to an immediate supervisor, or to whomever. As a result, they ideally need to take into account interests other than their own. Usually, they do so by having advisers, cabinets, consultants, boards, or whomever to consult with. Some leaders fail to do so, usually to their detriment, as no one can be an expert on everything, although some people, like the president of my own country, imagine themselves to be experts on everything. This is even more frightening than lack of expertise, because so much of wisdom is knowing what you do not know,[20] and only fools and knaves believe they are omniscient.[21] Unfortunately, often the fools and knaves are the same people, and because people are attracted to toxic leaders, they often end up being leaders of major organizations or even countries.[22]

Adaptive intelligence often is exercised collectively and it virtually always has collective effects.[23] And it can be modified, upward or downward, through education.

6 *Adaptive intelligence is modifiable.* There is a huge and stultifying literature on the heritability of intelligence, all of which deals with the wrong question.[24] General intelligence, as an ability, always certainly shows some heritability,[25] but so what? Height is also highly heritable, but heights have increased greatly over the years. Average heights have increased more than four inches (about eleven cm) since the mid-nineteenth century.[26] Weight is heritable, but average weights have increased greatly over the years. The average American man today weighs 198 pounds. In the 1960s, the average American man weighed 166.[27] Both height and weight show that heritability is not tantamount to the stability of a statistic. People change both within their lifetimes and, in the long term, over the course of many people's

lifetimes. For example, many of the older people alive today indeed weighed in the 160s in the 1960s but are struggling to stay under 200 in 2020.

Moreover, even the seemingly important question of the heritability of intelligence is far less important today than it was in the twentieth century, when researchers argued vociferously and furiously over the "true" heritability of intelligence.[28] Researchers such as Hans Eysenck and many others believed that intelligence was mostly heritable; researchers such as Leon Kamin believed that there was no good evidence for any heritability of intelligence. But they created a false dichotomy – an opposition that did not exist then and does not exist now.

Intelligence develops as an interaction between genes and environment.[29] Moreover, environment, although not affecting the genes with which we are born, greatly affects genetic expression through the mechanisms of epigenetics, which result in genes being "switched on" and "switched off" over the course of a lifetime as a result of environmental pressure. An adverse environment for the development of intelligence is not just an "environmental effect" – it also can lead to an epigenetic effect. So, the opposition between genes and environment always was a misstatement of the facts about heredity and environment. The two work together, for better or worse.

Far more important than the question of heritability is the question of modifiability. And, for sure, attitudes are modifiable. They are not inborn. One is not born with a set of attitudes; one acquires them through life. Working for the common good may draw on abilities. But to the extent that people fail to do it, it is not because they cannot, but rather because they choose not to. Similarly, balancing off one's interests with the interests of others is not an inborn ability. It is a decision that others' interests matter too, not just one's own. The bottom line is that the pathetic response to COVID-19 of some countries, such as the United States (death rate: 1.5 percent) and Italy (8.2 percent) versus Germany (death rate: 0.04 percent),[30] shows that adaptively intelligent leadership leads to adaptation in the sense of fewer deaths and longer lives.

Some of the differences in death rates can be attributed to a variety of factors, but in the end, some countries, such as Germany, quickly instituted mass testing and contract tracing; other countries, such as Italy and the United States, dithered. Should leaders' intelligence be measured by an IQ test or by their using their heads to save thousand, tens of thousands, or millions of lives? Can we seriously believe that scores on multiple-choice tests of academic skills tell us more about the leaders' intelligence than their either saving their followers' lives or mindlessly, even willfully, leaving them to die? Adaptive intelligence is more important than general intelligence.

7 *Adaptive intelligence trumps general intelligence.* It is the SAT that was called off by COVID-19, not the adaptive-intelligence test. It is ironic that major standardized proxy-intelligence tests, such as the SAT, are being postponed. Their postponement illustrates rather dramatically that these tests cannot compete with the Great Adaptive-Intelligence Test. It is they that are postponed, not the Great Adaptive-Intelligence Test. Administration of the Great Adaptive-Intelligence Test cannot be postponed because it is yet another of nature's wake-up calls that the test is mandatory, and that human society is failing it. What is frightening is that, at least in the United States, many people do not realize how badly they are failing and how badly their government is failing them.

Psychologists and educators are facing the greatest intelligence tests of their lives, and like the intentionally blinded people viewing but not seeing the elephant in the room that no one wants to see, they may lament that their precious intelligence tests are being postponed. The Great Adaptive-Intelligence Test is not being postponed, only their inconsequential ones. The problem is staring us all in the face; but do we see it?

8 *Adaptive intelligence is at least as much about problem recognition and problem definition as it is about problem solving.* We are now paying the price for an educational system, including an assessment system, that pays so much attention to having people solve problems rather than recognize and define problems. Experts were warning about an impending pandemic for years. The pandemic was totally expected, except perhaps by those, including the US president, whose hubris is so great that they view themselves, in their ignorance, as greater experts than the experts. It is for this reason that some talk of the "death of expertise."[31] Experts have known for many years that it was not a question of whether there would be another pandemic, but only a question of when. But the leaders of the world dithered, so that countries were caught unprepared.

It may sound like my speaking of political leaders is an attempt to send a political message. It is not. There are adaptively unintelligent leaders of all ideological political persuasions. The question is not what political party a leader is in, but rather, what that leader does to preserve and enrich lives rather than to let people suffer and die. Does the leader promote adaptivity, or squelch it? That is not about politics but rather about the "right to live." Those who talk about the "right to life" are sometimes the first to ignore it when it actually matters to those who are living in the world.

Adaptive-intelligence tests do not present problems and say, "Here is the problem. Which of the following five solutions will solve the problem?"

The hardest part of an adaptive-intelligence test is recognizing that a problem is on the horizon, and then figuring out exactly what it is at present and what it will be in the future.

The near-uselessness of intelligence tests for adaptive intelligence is shown by the failure of inductive-reasoning tests to generalize to the real world. Almost any reasonably intelligent adult could solve the following problem:

> "What number comes next in the following series?
> 1, 2, 4, 8, 16, . . .?"

The answer, of course, is thirty-two. But very few people and almost no world leaders have been able to translate that problem into real-world terms, such as the geometric progression of an epidemic. If one person is sick, and then spreads it to one more, and those two each spread it to one more, and those four then each spread it to one more, one has the same geometric series. Very quickly, a disease gets out of control.

A common insight problem, one I have used myself, is:

> "At the beginning of the summer, there is one water lily on a lake. The coverage of the lake in water lilies doubles every day. On the last day of the summer, the lake is completely covered with water lilies. On what day is the lake half-covered with water lilies?"

This problem is largely isomorphic to the series problem just presented. The answer is "the day before the last day of the summer." That is harder, even though it is the same problem. Here you divide by two instead of multiplying by two. What this means, though, is that for a long period of time, a pandemic can be spreading and be hardly noticeable. Then, as the geometric expansion takes hold, it will become noticeable very quickly and overwhelming even more quickly. And, of course, each person may infect more than just one person, as in the case of novel coronavirus, so that the latter days become even more challenging.

The point is that leaders cannot dally in recognizing problems of pandemics or other problems that threaten civilization. They need to recognize quickly that something is wrong and define quickly what the something is. Many leaders have failed us in doing so. So have many followers. They had much teaching and testing on solving given problems, not on figuring out what are real problems in the first place.

The same applies for global climate change. But because global warming takes hold much more slowly than a pandemic, people can be very slow even to notice that anything is wrong. If they do not notice, they ignore the facts to their own detriment and the detriment of others.

A reviewer of this book suggested that the book was alarmist. That was before the onset of the COVID-19 pandemic. And many of high IQ will come to the same conclusion. How many pandemics, how many hurricanes, how many floods, how many millions dead of pollution, does it take for people to realize that they are misdefining intelligence so as to restrict it beyond any definition that is adaptively useful? They are seeing it in a way that highly values the skills of most of the test researchers, test-constructors, and successful test-takers, but that devalues the skills the world will need to continue to have people to do important jobs, or really, any jobs. Claims for unemployment have skyrocketed and the decade-long expansion of the job market has ended[32] because leaders failed to choose to recognize and define problems that have been staring them in the face.

9   *The Great Adaptive-Intelligence Test gives people no multiple-choice options or easy fill-in-the-blanks. People have to figure out the options as well as the problems for themselves.* If one took most contemporary intelligence-test proxies seriously, one would believe that intelligence is about providing short, simple answers to highly structured, clearly defined problems. But real-world problems are neither highly structured nor clearly defined. That is not just a matter of pandemics. What do you do about a failing marriage? What about a job that is not working out? What about a child who keeps getting into trouble in school or with the law? What about bills one needs to pay but lacks the funds to pay?

These are the kinds of problems that the Great Adaptive-Intelligence Test presents, and for which students are almost totally unprepared even after twelve or sixteen or more years of education. Schooling prepares children for IQ tests and their proxies, but not for the Great Adaptive-Intelligence Test. And scores on that test can be quantified, just as can be scores on a traditional intelligence test.

10   *Adaptive intelligence can be quantified, in terms of positive outcomes such as having measurably clean air to breathe, and water to drink, and temperatures to live in, but also in negative terms such as numbers of illnesses and deaths resulting from its lack thereof.* Psychometricians are preoccupied with quantification. They provide scores that at times illustrate pseudo-quantitative precision, or the appearance of precision that the scores do not really offer. When psychometricians validate their intelligence tests, they look for criteria that often are not much more meaningful than the tests, such as grades in school, or in organizational settings, income or supervisory ratings. The problem is that not everyone who is adaptively intelligent seeks to maximize income or supervisory ratings. Greta Thunberg, the

environmental activist, for example, is a contrarian young person who is not likely to please supervisors. She, like most creative people, is at least somewhat contrarian.[33] Oddly, therefore, the criteria used to validate intelligence tests are ones whose satisfaction is maximized by people who "play the game." But the most creative people often are precisely those who do not play the societal game.[34]

Adaptive intelligence can be measured by criteria far more important than grades in school and personal income or supervisory ratings. It can be measured by how many people live, how many die, how many are able to eat at a level that enables them to be fully nourished, how many are able to provide for their families, how many are able to breathe the air without falling ill. These are not individual criteria. They are collective criteria. And it is unlikely that many psychometricians any time soon will go beyond their beloved school grades and supervisory ratings to consider collective criteria.

Some psychologists do look at more consequential criteria. For example, Ian Deary, Linda Gottfredson, and others look at individual health and life-expectancy outcomes.[35] A problem is that the correlations they find are so confounded with environmental circumstances – how one is brought up, what kinds of opportunities are available, what kind of education one receives, how much parental support one receives, one's early health, and so on. The rub is that cause and effect may be, and probably are, fully intertwined. We do not know exactly what causes high IQ, and what causes good environment.

11 *Adaptive intelligence is best measured over prolonged periods of time rather than over the course of an hour, or two, or three.* A typical intelligence test or proxy-intelligence test is administered over the course of somewhere between about an hour (for a typical intelligence test) and three hours (for an academically oriented proxy test, such as the ACT or SAT). But, in contrast, adaptive intelligence does not lend itself well to being measured over an hour, or two, or three, but rather over an extended period of time. For example, the leadership of the United States has had many opportunities over the last several months to adopt measures to mitigate the effects of coronavirus. At almost every step, some governments, including that of the United States, have either done nothing or minimized the threat of the virus. If the virus could talk, it might publicly thank those governments for creating the conditions to maximize the spread of COVID-19. Of course, the virus cannot talk, but it sends its message silently, with devastating results.

As of the day I am writing here – the day after I started writing the chapter – the United States has reached the dubious distinction of having more coronavirus cases than any other country in the world.[36] As Fareed Zakaria has pointed out, the United States retains its exceptionality – for its incompetence in the face of the virus. "The United States has shortages of everything – ventilators, masks, gloves, gowns – and no national emergency system to provide new supplies fast."[37] And the prices of many of the available supplies reflect price gouging.

The virus would also thank governments for planning to open up countries as early as possible, such as by Easter of 2020.[38] The virus only can spread if people are in close proximity to each other. So, opening up the country to commerce has allowed it to spread at full speed. So, first President Trump said the virus was nothing to worry about. Then he said he predicted a pandemic. Then he suggested, again, that we just pretty much ignore it, despite the record number of deaths in the United States.[39]

It is not just in the United States, but in other countries, such as England and Brazil, where leaders have minimized the danger of the coronavirus. Perhaps, ironically, Prime Minister Boris Johnson of the UK, who minimized the danger of the virus (perhaps on the advice of advisors), came down with the coronavirus.[40] So did Jair Bolsonaro of Brazil. The English and Brazilians, too, had many chances to set things on a better course. They waited too long.

Some theorists of intelligence and others possibly might attribute what has transpired in countries that have suffered most from coronavirus (e.g., Italy, Spain, the United States) versus those that have suffered least (e.g., Germany, Taiwan, Singapore, South Korea) to bad versus good decision making, or political calculation, or availability of resources, or any number of other factors. But in the end, adaptive intelligence deals with how we solve real-world problems, make real-world decisions, and render judgments about real-world situations. Adaptive intelligence is what you do in real life, not what you do on a piece of paper or at a computer terminal in a testing room. Of what use is what you do on the paper, or the terminal, if you cannot generalize it to the real world? Why focus on the artificial rather than the real? What matters is not what a person could do in ideal circumstances if the stakes were low, the answers were given as multiple-choice options, and the situations were emotionally neutral. What matters is what the person actually would do in real situations. Adaptive-intelligence tests are presented to us every day. We do not need to focus on trivial problems, because they are not great predictors of performance on serious ones.

When the *Titanic* was sinking, it is said, as noted earlier, that the musicians played on. One could argue that they played to calm the passengers. They did what they were good at. But the world changed suddenly, and the adaptive intelligence of the musicians was no longer a matter of how well they could please their music-loving listeners. It was a matter of what they or anyone else could do to try (even if unsuccessfully) to save the ship. They reputedly kept playing, just as we keep indulging ourselves in IQ tests as the world sinks. IQ testing is what certain psychologists have been trained to do and damn if they are going to give it up as the ship sinks.

Not only is an adaptive-intelligence test given over time; feedback also is given over time. One rarely finds out all at once whether one's solution to an adaptive problem is optimal. This is because solutions that work in the short term often fail in the long term and vice versa. Oil and gas may once have seemed like a great solution to energy problems, but they have caused their own long-term serious problems in terms of global climate change. Nuclear weapons once may have seemed the solution to a world war, but they have become a long-term threat to humanity. Antibiotics were a great solution until they were overused, allowing bacteria to acquire resistance or even immunity to them. If we could foresee all long-term consequences, feedback might be much quicker. But we cannot, and so feedback often is slow and its positivity or negativity may change over time. The important thing is that there is feedback.

12 *The Great Adaptive-Intelligence Test is a dynamic test, not a static test.* Psychologists distinguish between two kinds of tests, static and dynamic ones.[41] Static tests are given, often in one sitting, with test-takers answering questions. Then, sometime after the test-takers finish the tests, they probably get their test score. There is no feedback to the test-takers regarding their performance until after the test-takers take the test. Dynamic tests, in contrast, offer feedback as the test-takers solve problems on the tests. As test-takers move through the test, they are given feedback about whether their answers are right or wrong, and sometimes, about why their answers are right or wrong. Their score depends in large part upon their ability to profit from instruction.

The Great Adaptive-Intelligence Test is dynamic. Some test-takers, like our current US president, learn little or nothing from experience and keep making the same mistakes, at least with regard to adaptive intelligence. Others, like the leaders of Singapore, see what works and what does not, and adapt what they do to the circumstances, at least with regard to COVID-19, so their number of cases quickly goes down rather than up, as in the US.

Why would people, taking a dynamic test, not profit from experience or actually start to do worse as time goes on? This question has been answered by those who study heuristics in human thinking, such as the late Amos

Tversky, Daniel Kahneman, Gerd Gigerenzer, Keith Stanovich, and others.[42] Basically, smart people use mental shortcuts to arrive at better decisions. Not so smart people use shortcuts to short-circuit good thinking and to come, repeatedly, to suboptimal conclusions.

Heuristics are learned from experience. Thus, one has only to watch what is happening in the world and then to modify one's heuristics. But adaptively unintelligent people do not watch, do not learn, and just keep making the same mistakes, over and over again. They keep doing the same wrong things over and over again. The Great Adaptive-Intelligence Test allows people to learn from experience – it is a dynamic test. But some people have an attitude toward life that prevents them from learning much of anything.

13 *The Great Adaptive-Intelligence Test is both a maximal-performance test and a typical-performance test, in that passing it requires a great expenditure of mental effort and of motivation to succeed, but on a continual basis.* Psychologists sometimes distinguish between two kinds of tests – maximal-performance tests and typical-performance tests. Maximal-performance tests require people to expend a great deal of mental effort on the test. Ability tests, such as the SAT, the ACT, IQ tests, and school-achievement tests are maximal-performance tests. Personality tests, in contrast, usually are typical-performance tests. One simply indicates how one typically thinks or acts in particular situations or kinds of situations. The tests require relatively less effort to complete.

The Great Adaptive-Intelligence Test is both maximal- and typical-performance. Problems like COVID-19 require great effort to solve. They do not lend themselves well to the kind of lazy thinking that many leaders today are showing, simply taking whatever ideology they have and blindly applying it to the problem (e.g., Blame the members of another political party! Blame foreigners! Blame poor people! Or whatever). Lazy thinking, of which we have plenty, does not solve hard and especially novel problems. Those who are not willing to extend themselves cognitively, such as many of our world leaders, come up with failed solutions. But the Great Adaptive-Intelligence Test is also a typical-performance test. The failure of leaders to solve major problems, such as of COVID-19, or of pollution, or of global climate change, also represents lazy or rigid ideological thinking on a day-to-day, week-to-week, and month-to-month basis. Their thinking is not only placed in "park" for major crises but for many of the problems they face on a daily basis. Their typical performance does not rise to the occasion, so they are especially unprepared when they need to confront the problems that have been building up over time.

The distinction between maximal- and typical-performance tests is another of the false dichotomies that pervade psychology, much like the phony heredity-environment debate. Serious tests of adaptive intelligence always are both. Many of the crises that require maximal performance arise because the problems that require typical performance have been handled so poorly. And they arise because the people who put the leaders in place also were lazy in their thinking, falling back on ideologically based arguments that suffice only when people put their blinders in place. Adaptive intelligence requires us to think hard every day, to prevent the crises that arise when we do not.

14 *There are no uniquely correct answers on the Great Adaptive-Intelligence test.* Individuals and collectivities have to find answers that work for them and most of these answers will be in a gray zone of being neither wholly correct nor wholly incorrect. There are always, in this dynamic test, multiple answers of various degrees of correctness. Those who score well arrive at better and better answers; those who score poorly keep making the same mistakes or proceed making even bigger ones than before. The rate of COVID-19 infections and deaths in the United States has been on an exponential upswing, at least as I write these pages.[43] That is about as objective as the feedback on any standardized test – you do not get much clearer results than that. The main difference is that the stakes are much higher and that one will never know absolutely for sure how much better or worse one might have done on the test, because there is no exactly parallel control group.

The absence of strictly right or wrong answers can lead some people to throw up their hands in despair, but that is only because they have been so schooled in a culture of right and wrong answers to test problems. Almost no problems in life have a uniquely correct answer. One muddles through the best one can, accepting that one never will know for sure whether one's response was the best one could do.

15 *One cannot buy a good score on the Great Adaptive-Intelligence Test.* Many societies are deferential to the rich. But having a lot of money guarantees nothing. There is no tutoring course, no preparation book, no magic formula that will guarantee a good solution. Socioeconomic status (SES) is not enough. The richest country in the world, the United States, is approaching the problem of COVID-19 economically, again showing that it does not understand that public-health catastrophes cannot be solved just by throwing money at them. Instead of investing in public health, it disinvested in public health, and throwing money at corporations or people will not fix this disinvestment in public health that has occurred over the course of many years.

Adaptive intelligence is not about filling in bubbles on a computer or a piece of paper. It is about the future of humanity. It is not about what university one is admitted to. Adaptive intelligence is not about how much money a particular individual will make. Often, they make this money in part because a society gives many advantages to people who test well and then views their success as a result of the test scores, rather than their success as a result of the advantages society gives merely by virtue of those higher scores. But as people take the Great Adaptive-Intelligence Test, they discover that traditional notions of intelligence fall dreadfully short when it comes to preserving or possibly saving the world. The people who did reasonably or extremely well on so-called tests of general intelligence sometimes have proved to be remarkably incompetent at preserving advantage for anyone except, perhaps, themselves.

COVID-19 is one of many warnings that we cannot go on this way. Will we? I do not know. Many of the intelligence testers are blind to the problem. Years ago, a colleague and I discovered that when a strategy that has worked in the past stops working, experts are slower than novices to adapt to the change.[44]

The experts on intelligence probably will not save us. Too many of them are busy doing the same thing experts on intelligence have done for over a century. That vinyl record is broken and stuck in place. It will take others – experts in behavioral economics, decision-making, political science, sociology, perhaps social psychology, and who knows what else? And it will take a smart population that realizes that experts stuck in the past and, more to the point, demagogues are not going to save the world. COVID-19 probably will not go away so quickly. And if it does, there will be other pandemics and other world problems to replace it. We need to teach children, from an early age, that smart isn't what you do in school. It is what you do in life. And that is what adaptive intelligence is.

Notes

1. McLaughlin, E. C., Maxouris, C., & Almasy, S. (2020). Wednesday has been the deadliest day in reported coronavirus deaths in US. *CNN*, March 25. http s://cnn.it/2FuFkyx
2. Ross, J. (2020). America hits grim milestone of 1,000 coronavirus deaths. *The Daily Beast*, March 26. https://bit.ly/3iOdLIv
3. Rainey, R. (2020). Jobless claims soar to record 3.3 million. *Politico*, March 26. https://bit.ly/3iMZGS4

4. Jacobs, A., Richtel, M., & Baker, M. (2020). "At war with no ammo": Doctors say shortage of protective gear is dire. *New York Times*, March 19. https://nyti.ms/3iOhk7R

5. Hopkins, C. (2020). "We are desperate": Trump's inaction has created a crisis with protective medical gear. *Vox*, March 23. https://bit.ly/349MwKW

6. Rogers, K. (2020). Trump now claims he always knew the coronavirus would be a pandemic. *New York Times*, March 17. https://nyti.ms/2E0KL83

7. Binet, A., & Simon, T. (1916). *The development of intelligence in children*. Baltimore, MD: Williams & Wilkins. (Originally published in 1905); Wechsler, D. (1974). *The measurement and appraisal of adult intelligence*. Baltimore, MD: Williams & Wilkins.

8. "Intelligence and its measurement": A symposium (1921). *Journal of Educational Psychology*, 12, 123–47, 195–216, 271–5.

9. Sternberg, R. J., & Grigorenko, E. L. (1999). A smelly 113° in the shade, or, why we do field research. *APS Observer*, 12(1), 10–11, 20–21.

10. McCoy, T., & Traiano, H. (2020). Brazil's Bolsonaro, channeling Trump, dismisses coronavirus measures – it's just "a little cold." *Washington Post*, March 25. https://wapo.st/3iXOFxd

11. Risen, J. (2020). After 9/11, Richard Burr selfishly ignored a tip about domestic spying. Now he's betrayed Americans again. *The Intercept*, March 23. https://bit.ly/347AbXn

12. Mak, T. (2020). Sen. Richard Burr faces lawsuit over timing of stock sale. *NPR*, March 25. https://n.pr/3kMYShX

13. Sternberg, R. J. (1988). *The triarchic mind: A new theory of human intelligence*. New York: Viking; Hedlund, J. (2020). Practical intelligence. In R. J. Sternberg (Ed.), *Cambridge handbook of intelligence* (2nd ed., pp. 736–55). New York: Cambridge University Press.

14. Sackett, P. R., Shewach, O., & Dahlke, J. A. (2020). The predictive value of general intelligence. In R. J. Sternberg (Ed.), *Human intelligence: An introduction* (pp. 381–414). New York: Cambridge University Press.

15. Deary, I. J. (2020). *Intelligence: A very short introduction*. Oxford: Oxford University Press; Sternberg, R. J. (Ed.) (2020a). *Cambridge handbook of intelligence* (2nd ed.). New York: Cambridge University Press; Sternberg, R. J. (Ed.) (2020b). *Human intelligence: An introduction* (pp. 381–414). New York: Cambridge University Press.

16. Sternberg, R. J. (2019). Why people often prefer wise guys to guys who are wise: An augmented balance theory of the production and reception of wisdom. In R. J. Sternberg, & J. Glueck (Eds.), *Cambridge handbook of wisdom* (pp. 162–81). New York: Cambridge University Press.

17. Asimov, I. (1988). *Goodreads*. https://bit.ly/349F966

18. Reichmann, D. (2020). Trump disbanded NSC pandemic unit that experts had praised. *AP News*, March 14. https://apnews.com/ce014d94b64e98b7203b873e56f80e9a

19. JFK Library. (N.D.). "Ask not what your country can do for you." John F. Kennedy. https://bit.ly/2YbSA1H

20. Sternberg, R. J. (1998) A balance theory of wisdom. *Review of General Psychology*, 2, 347–65.

21. Sternberg, R. J. (2002). Smart people are not stupid, but they sure can be foolish: The imbalance theory of foolishness. In R. J. Sternberg (Ed.), *Why smart people can be so stupid* (pp. 232–42). New Haven, CT: Yale University Press; Sternberg, R. J. (2005). Foolishness. In R. J. Sternberg, & J. Jordan (Eds.), *Handbook of wisdom: Psychological perspectives* (pp. 331–52). New York: Cambridge University Press.

22. Lipman-Blumen, J. (2006). *The allure of toxic leaders.* New York: Oxford University Press.

23. Malone, T. W., & Wooley, A. W. (2020). Collective intelligence. In R. J. Sternberg (Ed.), *Cambridge handbook of intelligence* (2nd ed., pp. 780–801). New York: Cambridge University Press.

24. Sternberg, R. J. (2015). Wrong problem, wrong solution. A review of Nicholas Wade, A troublesome inheritance: Genes, race, and human history. *PsycCritiques*, 60(13). http://dx.doi.org/10.1037/a0038982

25. Plomin, R. (2018). *Blueprint: How DNA makes us who we are.* Cambridge, MA: MIT Press.

26. Parkinson, C. (2013). Men's average height "up 11 cm since 1870s." *BBC News*, September 2. www.bbc.com/news/health-23896855

27. Roland, J. (2019). *Healthline*, February 27. https://bit.ly/3120qNa

28. Eysenck, H. J., & Kamin, L. (1981). *Intelligence: The battle for the mind: Environment or heredity? The crucial debate on the shaping of intelligence.* Cham, Switzerland: Palgrave-Macmillan.

29. Flynn, J. R. (2016). *Does your family make you smarter? Nature, nurture, and human autonomy.* New York: Cambridge University Press; Grigorenko, E. L., & Burenkova, O. (2020). Genetic bases of intelligence. In R. J. Sternberg (Ed.), *Cambridge handbook of intelligence* (2nd ed., pp. 101–23). New York: Cambridge University Press.

30. Sepkowitz, K. (2020). Why is COVID-19 death rate so low in Germany? *CNN*, March 25. https://cnn.it/3iOqmSj; Worldometers. (2020a). Worldometers, March 26. www.worldometers.info/coronavirus/country/italy/; Worldometers. (2020b). Worldometers, March 26. www.worldometers.info/coronavirus/coun try/us/

31. Nichols, T. (2017). *The death of expertise: The campaign against established knowledge and why it matters.* New York: Oxford University Press.

32. Morath, E., Hilsenrath, & Chaney, S. (2020). Record rise in unemployment claims halts historic run of job growth. *Wall Street Journal*, March 26. https:// on.wsj.com/32cT2On

33. Sternberg, R. J., & Lubart, T. I. (1995). *Defying the crowd: Cultivating creativity in a culture of conformity.* New York: Free Press.

34. Sternberg, R. J. (2018). Creative giftedness is not just what creativity tests test: Implications of a triangular theory of creativity for understanding creative giftedness. *Roeper Review*, 40(3), 158–65. doi: 10.1080/ 02783193.2018.1467248

35. Deary, I. J., Whalley, L. J., & Starr, J. M. (2009). *A lifetime of intelligence.* Washington, DC: American Psychological Association.
36. Huddle, R., & Ciras, H. (2020). The US now has more confirmed cases of coronavirus than any other country. Here's how we got there. *Boston Globe,* March 27. https://bit.ly/3g2QQoQ
37. Zakaria, F. (2020). The U.S. is still exceptional – but now for its incompetence. Fareedzakaria.com. https://bit.ly/31bng51
38. Liptak, K., Vazquez, M., Valencia, N., & Acosta, J. (2020). Trump says he wants the country "opened up by Easter," despite health experts' warnings. *CNN,* March 24. www.youtube.com/watch?v=B-DrS_PvOdo&t=5086s
39. Mangan, D. (2020). Trump dismissed coronavirus pandemic worry in January – now claims he long warned about it. *CNBC,* March 17. https://cnb .cx/3g5MENV
40. BBC News. (2020). Coronavirus: Prime Minister Boris Johnson tests positive. *BBC,* March 27. www.bbc.com/news/uk-52060791
41. Grigorenko, E. L., & Sternberg, R. J. (1998). Dynamic testing. *Psychological Bulletin,* 124, 75–111; Sternberg, R. J., & Grigorenko, E. L. (2002). *Dynamic testing.* New York: Cambridge University Press.
42. Gigerenzer, G. (2000). *Adaptive thinking: Rationality in the real world.* Oxford: Oxford University Press; Gigerenzer, G., Todd, P. M., & the ABC Research Group. (2000). *Simple heuristics that make us smart.* Oxford: Oxford University Press; Stanovich, K. (2010). *Rationality and the reflective mind.* Oxford: Oxford University Press; Kahneman, D. (2011). *Thinking, fast and slow.* New York: Farrar, Straus, & Giroux; Gigerenzer, G., Hertwig, R., & Pachur, T. (2015). *Heuristics: The foundations of adaptive behavior.*Oxford: Oxford University Press .
43. Siegel, E. (2020). Why "exponential growth" is so scary for the COVID-19 coronavirus. *Forbes,* March 17. https://bit.ly/3iQiUq4
44. Frensch, P. A., & Sternberg, R. J. (1989). Expertise and intelligent thinking: When is it worse to know better? In R. J. Sternberg (Ed.), *Advances in the psychology of human intelligence* (Vol. 5, pp. 157–88). Hillsdale, NJ: Lawrence Erlbaum Associates.

Index

AAIDD (American Association on Intellectual and Developmental Disabilities), 106
academic success, 16, *See also* teaching for adaptive intelligence
accommodation, 45
accountability, standardized tests and, 217–218
achievement versus ability tests, 225
ACT. *See* standardized tests
adaptation
  biological adaptation, 82, 91, 105
  broad versus narrow, 82
  context and, 168
  defined, 82
  standardized tests not measuring, 173
  triarchic theory and, 170–174
adaptive behavior, intellectual disability and, 106
adaptive intelligence; climate change; COVID-19 pandemic; history of adaptive intelligence theory; paradox of general intelligence and species-maladaptive destructiveness; teaching for adaptive intelligence
  as collective, 114, 249
  as modifiable, 249–250
  as new concept, 113
  as prescriptive theory, 109–110
  as too philosophical, 109
  as ultimate criteria, 12
  attitude toward life and, 248–249
  broadness of intelligence definition in, 108–109
  common good as key to, 15, 102, 240, 247–248
  conundrum of intelligence used to decrease, 82
  defined, 81, 102, 183, 245
  education not preparing for, 253
  ethical values and, 110–111
  evolution of, 183–195
  general intelligence compared, 81, 113, 116, 251
  implications for action about, 117–118
  IQ and, 3–4, 90, 247–248
  knowledge application versus acquisition, 142
  low level of, 215
  measurement of, 111–113, 191–217, 254–256

metaphors of mind and, 63–64
National Association for Gifted Children and, 107
need for, 2, 105
overview, 2–4, 74
practical intelligence and, 178
problem recognition and definition, 251–253
quantification and, 253–254
Rashomon and, 78
real-world adaptation and, 245, 255
relevance of knowledge tested and, 141
research base for lacking, 113
species extinction and, 89
survival perpetuated by, 4–6
uselessness of talking about, 116
wisdom-based skills and, 115–116
admissions. *See* college and university admissions
admissions officers, 223, 224, 226
adversity index, 220
African perspectives on intelligence, 56
aging, 41, 98, 137
air pollution, 88–89
amateurs versus experts, 135
American Association on Intellectual and Developmental Disabilities (AAIDD), 106
analogies
  componential analysis and, 154–156
  encoding and, 129–130
  People Pieces analogies, 154–160
  Spearman and, 48, 49, 154
  what is tested by, 154
analytical skills
  adaptive intelligence and, 192
  defined, 102
  importance of, 103
  information retrieval and evaluation, 16, 39, 136
  STEM careers and, 236–241
  teaching to encourage, 205–207, 218
anthropological metaphor of intelligence, 54–57
antibiotic resistance, 90

IQ and intelligence tests (cont.)
    discrimination based on, 20
    entrenchment and, 134, 219–220
    functioning versus, 93, 255
    hard science envy and, 20
    harm from, 152
    individual differences, focus on, 17–20
    individual scores and, 176
    limits of, 4, 93, 259
    predictive validity and, 17, 81
    purpose of, 4
    success in life and, 177
    validation of, 94
    xenophobia and, 21

Jacobs, A. J., 139, 140
Jensen, Arthur, 62, 160
Johnson, Wendy, 38
judgment-based approach to intelligence,
    33–34
Jung, Rex, 54
justification, 155

Kaleidoscope project, 226–227, 236
Kenyan perspectives on intelligence, 56
kinesthetic ability, 37
Knapp, John, 36
knowledge
    ability to use, 140–141
    acquisition versus storage of, 141–142
    application versus acquisition, 142, 248
    creativity and, 205
    cultural aspects of, 142
    news media and, 205

languages, intelligence testing and, 21
latency versus error rate, 151
law school attendance, 136
laziness, entrenchment and, 223, 257
lead toxicity, 164
leadership, 207–209
learning disabilities, 131, 167
lemmings, 76–77
lies and manipulations
    ability to evaluate as intelligence, 16
    analytical skills and, 206
    impacts of, 3
    importance of recognizing, 2
    increase of, 1
linear syllogisms, 161–162
linguistic intelligence, 58
local versus global planning skills, 130
logical-mathematical intelligence, 58
long-term versus short-term gains, 6–8, 13–14
luck, 228–229

luoro, 56
Luria, Alexander, 52

MA (mental age) in IQ, 39–43, 98
maladaptive habits, 214–215
map of the mind, 34–53
mapping, 155
marketing of colleges and universities,
    234–235
mass migration, 83
mass suicide. *See* climate change; COVID-19
    pandemic; Great Adaptive Intelligence
    Test; self-destruction
matrix problems, 161
maturation, 47
maximal-performance tests, 257–258
measles, 90
measurement of adaptive intelligence, 111–113,
    191–217, 254–256
media, 205, 234
mental age (MA) in IQ, 39–43, 98
mental energy, 48
mental representations, 151, 161, 166
mental set, 134
merit, 8
metacognition, 28
metacomponents, 163–167, 176
metaphors of mind
    adaptive intelligence as beyond, 63–64
    biological metaphor, 51–54
    computational metaphor, 47–51
    cultural metaphor, 54–57
    developmental metaphor, 44–47
    geographic metaphor, 34–53
    overview, 34
    systems metaphor, 57–63
migration due to climate change, 83
minority status, IQ and, 43
mistakes, repeating of, 142
modularity of mind, 60
moral disengagement, 185
Morrison, Scott, 140
MSNBC, 205
multiple intelligences theory, 58–62
multiple-choice questions
    adaptive intelligence tests and, 191
    as unrealistic, 76
    creativity and, 204, 221
    encoding and, 161
    Great Adaptive Intelligence Test lacking, 253
    problem solving transfer and, 84, 87, 173
    pseudo-objectivity of standardized tests and,
        221–222
multiple-regression modeling, 157
musical intelligence, 58

Lightning Source UK Ltd.
Milton Keynes UK
UKHW020819190221
378853UK00011B/214